PRAISE FOR

gluten-free MAKEOVERS

"Beth Hillson, a herald in the gluten-free industry, has successfully 'made over' our fondest and favorite recipes. Using her endless culinary talents and attention to the necessary details, *Gluten-Free Makeovers* provides us with the secret to creating exciting, delicious, and inspiring gluten-free recipes. It's a must-have in any wheat- and gluten-free kitchen."

— Robert M. Landolphi, The Gluten Free Chef, author of
Gluten Free Everyday Cookbook and *Quick-Fix Gluten Free*

"*Gluten-Free Makeovers* is so needed and an absolute addition to the cookbook collection of every person with celiac disease and gluten intolerance. Thanks to the time and talents of Chef Beth Hillson, we can now enjoy cooking fresh, creative, and healthy gluten-free versions of dishes that have been off-limits. Beth has succeeded in overcoming the culinary challenges of being gluten intolerant. There is something to appeal to every palate. Here's wishing you good food, food fun, and food friends! GF—gluten-free!"

— Elaine Monarch, Founder, Celiac Disease Foundation

"Thanks to Beth Hillson individuals with celiac disease and gluten intolerance can leave frustration at the kitchen door and learn how to modify and adapt recipes, even family favorites, to be tastefully gluten-free. This approach and the wonderful recipes makes *Gluten-Free Makeovers* a must-have for gluten-free cooks."

— Andrea Levario, JD, Executive Director,
American Celiac Disease Alliance

gluten-free
MAKEOVERS

gluten-free
MAKEOVERS

Over 175 Recipes—from Family Favorites to
Gourmet Goodies—Made Deliciously Wheat-Free

BETH HILLSON

Da Capo
LIFE
LONG

A Member of the Perseus Books Group

Copyright © 2011 by Beth Hillson
Photographs by Oksana Charla

Designed by Trish Wilkinson
Set in 11.5 point Goudy Old Style by the Perseus Books Group

Library of Congress Cataloging-in-Publication Data

Hillson, Beth.
    Gluten-free makeovers : over 175 recipes—from family favorites to gourmet goodies—made deliciously wheat-free / Beth Hillson.
        p.   cm.
    Includes index.
    ISBN 978-0-7382-1461-0 (pbk. : alk. paper)—
ISBN 978-0-7382-1536-5 (e-book) 1. Gluten-free diet—Recipes. 2. Wheat-free diet—Recipes. I. Title.
RM237.86.H55 2011
641.3—dc23   2011020867

First Da Capo Press edition 2011

Published by Da Capo Press
A Member of the Perseus Books Group
www.dacapopress.com

Da Capo Press books are available at special discounts for bulk purchases in the U.S. by corporations, institutions, and other organizations. For more information, please contact the Special Markets Department at the Perseus Books Group, 2300 Chestnut Street, Suite 200, Philadelphia, PA, 19103, or call (800) 810-4145, ext. 5000, or e-mail special.markets@perseusbooks.com.

10 9 8 7 6 5 4 3 2 1

Substitute Boldly and Eat Well

Dedicated
to the great cooks who inspired me,
to my sister, Jennifer, my son, Jeremy,
and all the other gluten-free guests who
open these pages—may you enjoy every bite!
To Joel, always

Contents

The Recipes

SAVORY FARE 81

SWEET TREATS 171

Foreword

By Jax Peters Lowell,
Author of the *Gluten-Free Bible*

Don't tell Beth Hillson she can't do something—unless, of course, you want her to do it.

From becoming a classically trained chef to founding the wildly successful *Gluten-Free Pantry* to food editor of *Living Without Magazine*, and activist for celiac disease awareness, this queen of the gluten-free makeover has set the standard for many of the recipes we count on to navigate lives that are mouth-wateringly full, and rich and uncompromised by the need for gluten-free alternatives.

It took chutzpah to take on the Holy Grail of Sunday brunch, that soft, yeasty vehicle for cream cheese and nova off-limits to millions of us. Her gluten-free bagel mix made its debut on *Good Morning America* decades ago when celiac disease was a distant blip on the horizon and you could Spackle® a wall with the bread that was available. Beth Hillson is the trailblazer whose determination changed the game for all of us.

Beth's genius is for making over the dishes we've eaten all our lives, the ones we long for when we become gluten-free. From brioche to biscuits, pierogi to pot stickers and chicken Wellington, there is virtually no recipe she can't convert with all the authenticity and taste we remember. In this treasury of makeovers, 175 in all, she gives us back the birthday carrot cake, grandma's Babka, vanilla blueberry Bundt cake, shortbread, chicken Marsala, even toaster tarts and, in so doing, returns our memories and traditions, even our daily routines, intact. She can do this because, as a professional chef, she knows the ratios of wet to dry, fat to flour, something she calls Recipe DNA, an apt term because the skeins of family and friends are forever entwined with food and table.

Don't take it from me.

Several years ago, Beth was in Philadelphia for the culinary professionals trade show and invited me to bring along a stack of books and sit with her. A rather large and inscrutable woman chugged by, picked up one of Beth's decadent chocolate brownies and chewed.

"That's Julia Child's taster," Beth whispered.

I wondered what must it be like to have one's very own taster.

A few minutes later, La Julia, in all her glory, swooped in, greeted Beth and plucked a brownie from the tray.

"Are these fat-free?" she asked Beth (I'm sure she was suspicious of anything that did not contain a pound of butter).

"No, but they're gluten-free."

"*Magnifique*," trilled the legend, raising her eyes heavenward.

And with that, Julia Child eyed the wastebasket, spat out the brownie, and was gone.

"Did the woman who taught us how to bone a chicken and spied for the free world, just spit out her food?" I asked.

"If she ate everything," Beth said, sputtering with laughter, "she'd be the size of a house, wouldn't she?"

The point is, Julia Child didn't know from gluten-free. But she knew excellence when she tasted it.

Beth and I met at a conference in Baltimore in 1995. My first book, *Against the Grain*, had just been published and the fates allowed tables next to one another. We told each other our stories and laughed about our responses to celiac disease. We nibbled her goodies until we thought we'd burst, and embarked upon a friendship that continues today, born of a determination to see what we can have versus what we can't, and a commitment to putting celiac disease on the map.

I still turn to Beth's gnocchi for a special dinner; its textural secret just the right mix of rice flour and potato starch. I crave her quick breads warm from the oven and her amazing General Tso's chicken with jasmine rice to soak up the heavenly ginger and garlic sauce. Ditto for her Pad Thai, soul satisfying, spicy and sweet, a savory sauté of rice noodles with shrimp and bean sprouts studded with peanuts. And I love that she uses nutritionally dense whole grain flours like sorghum, amaranth, chickpea, and teff, and with her trademark magic makes everything moist, light, and full of flavor.

Gluten-Free Makeovers is a major event from a major chef whose talent and ease in the kitchen has nurtured many of us for a long, long time. Be prepared to discover how easy it is to make over every dish you thought you could no longer have in your new gluten-free life. This is much more than a cookbook; it's a blueprint for your own kitchen adventures, one you will turn to again and again. It's the next best thing to having my amazing friend Beth looking over your shoulder, letting you know there is no such thing as can't.

—*Jax Peters Lowell*

Jax Peters Lowell is the author of the celiac classics, *Against the Grain* and *The Gluten-Free Bible*, and an illustrated children's book, *No More Cupcakes & Tummy Aches*. Her memoir, *An Early Winter*, is forthcoming.

Acknowledgments

Thank you to my testers: Janet Alquist, Beverly Chevalier, Pablo Douros, Sally Ekus, Daniel Hudner, Jennifer Hudner, Andrea Levario, Betsy Mantis, Brooke Mommsen, Debbie Stein, and Lisa Turcotte.

A very special thanks to Beverly Chevalier and her granddaughter, Brooke, who tested my recipes endlessly and asked for more. Beverly, Brooke, and the entire New Haven Celiac Group have a warm spot in my heart. I can't thank them enough for their support and for consuming all those calories on behalf of this project.

And to Oksana, Tom, Mikey, and Katie Charla whose enthusiasm and expert tasting bolstered me throughout. Heartfelt thanks to Oksana Charla who went way above and beyond in styling and photographing the food within these pages. I am fortunate to count the entire Charla family as part of my extended family. Where would I be without my agent Sally Ekus at the Lisa Ekus Group who believed in me, my project, and the wonders of great gluten-free food. I think Sally can relate when I say that "gluten-y is its own reward."

A big thank you to my editor Renée Sedliar who loved the concept from the first moment on and to the entire team at Da Capo who made this book so much better in every way. They are the frosting on my cake.

A special note of gratitude to my dear friend Jax Peters Lowell, author of *Against the Grain* and *The Gluten-Free Bible*. The moment Jax confided in me that she carried a caviar spoon in her purse when she went to parties, I knew I had met a kindred spirit. Whether it's caviar, sweet rolls, or birthday cake, the glass is always half full when I'm with Jax.

Grateful acknowledgment is also given to:

Glutino, GlutenFree.com, and Laura Kuykendall. A version of the following recipes first appeared at glutenfree.com: Apple Clafoutis, Auntie's Apple Cake, Grandma's Sour Cream Coffee Cake, Grilled Scallion Bread (Asian Pizza), Key

Lime Bars, Mexican Pizza, Healthy Oat Bars, Peanut Butter Bars, and Vanilla Blueberry Bundt Cake.

Kevin Harron and Denise Baron Herrera of Burton's Grill, Bob and Sue Spector at Nature's Grocer, and Alfred Chong at Lilli and Loo, for the scrumptious treats they offer the gluten-free world and the recipes they contributed to this book.

Susan Petragallo for the Baked Pasta recipe that graces the cover of this book.

Lisa Turcotte who introduced me to pierogi through her recipe for Cheese and Potato Pierogi.

Denise Appel, chef extraordinaire at Zinc restaurant for Charred Vietnamese Chicken and Lemon Sauce.

Living Without—Robert Englander, Philip Penny, Tom Canfield, Oksana Charla, Timothy Cole, and Alicia Woodward who supported me all the way and gladly allowed the epithet, *Food Editor*, to spill over into my cookbook. I am honored to have that affiliation.

To Andrea Levario, Executive Director of the American Celiac Disease Alliance, and Stefano Guandalini, MD, Professor and Chief, Section of Pediatric Gastroenterology, Founder and Medical Director, Celiac Disease Center, University of Chicago, for their help in verifying information in the section about gluten, celiac disease, and frequently asked questions.

And to the great bakers and cooks who inspired me. Thanks to P.J. Hamel and the crew at the *King Arthur Flour's Baker's Catalogue* for inspiring delicious recipe ideas and techniques including Pumpkin Whoopie Pies and Apple Caramel Monkey Bread. P.J. is the one who instructed cooks to spray the inside of cupcake liners so the cupcakes and muffins would not cling to the paper. Although others might have suggested it, I have to thank her for bringing tricks like this one to my attention. Technique is as essential to good baking as is a good recipe.

No one cooks alone and I have the entire culinary world to thank for inspiring my ideas, formulas, recipes, and simply enriching my cooking life. This includes but is not limited to: Lora Brody, Julia Child, Craig Claiborne, Marion Cunningham, Dorie Greenspan, Maida Heatter, Neil Kleinberg (Clinton St. Baking Company), Priscilla Martel, and Susan Purdy, who are among my culinary heroes. I would be remiss if I did not mention colleagues and gluten-free cookbook authors, Rebecca Reilly, Carol Fenster, and Robert Landolphi who inspire me with their words, recipes, and passion.

Like their authors, cookbooks are precious jewels to me and I could never part with any of them. Among the general baking books that I consult regularly are *Pillsbury: The Complete Book of Baking*, *Great Baking Begins with White Lily Flour*, and *The New Joy of Cooking*. And lastly, I must thank food writers and editors at the following magazines: *Eating Well*, *Bon Appétit*, *Gourmet*, and *Good Housekeeping*, for I cannot pick up a food magazine without being inspired to cook.

Introduction

I began cooking in earnest in the early seventies inspired by Julia Child's *Mastering the Art of French Cooking*, a gift that arrived just before I was diagnosed with celiac disease.

At the time, I was living in Frankfurt, Germany, a new and foreign city to me, and figured I could meet all my neighbors, German and American, if I threw a cocktail party. I cooked my way through Julia's book and created a feast that people talked about for months afterward. I loved the rewards, both to my tummy and my social life.

But, oh, the tummy—it had been a problem for years. Several doctors made my acquaintance over that time and each sent me away with a vague instruction—avoid milk, see a psychiatrist, take antacids. Finally an astute physician took my case and ran every test imaginable, eventually giving me a flexible tube (the Crosby Capsule) to swallow. Several hours later, he took a biopsy of my small intestine and, on my next visit, announced triumphantly, "It's celiac disease." The doctor handed me a photo of my biopsy, blunted villi and all, and told me I would recover completely as long as I followed a gluten-free diet. Then he turned me loose with these words: "Just avoid gluten."

It was 1976 and I was alone, no cooks by my side, no support groups where I could have my questions answered and no products to purchase. I was feeling healthy but isolated. One week on the diet and I was a new woman, but with an appetite that I could not satiate. The prospect of eating naked burgers, plain steaks, and baked potatoes for the rest of my life was not appealing. Through Julia Child, I had seen a new world of food. My taste buds were enthusiastic; my fingers, eager stewards. What had been awakened and excited could not be put back on the shelf because of dietary restrictions. So I created a plan.

I would go to culinary school and learn to eat defensively. I would learn how dishes were made, how soups were thickened, which meats were dusted in flour.

I would learn how to ask the crucial questions when I ate in restaurants. I was determined that being gluten-free was not going to stop me from enjoying life and food.

Being a glass-half-full person, I quickly realized that the recipes from cooking school held other secrets. I was standing at the back door of the culinary world looking in at the elements of baking and of cooking. If I removed flour and other offending ingredients and replaced them with the ingredients that were safe, I could create a recipe that came close to the real thing, only gluten-free. I would simply learn to make the same recipes, but make them differently—without gluten. Voilà! I did not need to give up eating good food after all.

I could omit the flour if a stew called for a roux and thicken it with cornstarch. I could add rice flour and cornstarch to a soufflé or a génoise and the results were perfect. Success after success, tasty treat after tasty treat, I was making over regular recipes so they were safe for my gluten-free diet.

The next step was discovering that a blend of gluten-free flours worked better than using straight corn flour or rice flour. The grit and crumbly texture could be overcome when I used a blend, preferably one that contained a high protein flour (see chart, page 14).

At that moment, I did not realize my future was in these recipes and techniques. But when I began blending dry ingredients for breads, pancakes, and cakes, something much larger was developing. These principles became the foundation for the Gluten-Free Pantry, a gourmet baking mix company that I started in 1993.

Soon, I was making big batches of dry ingredients for myself and a few others and one of the first gluten-free companies in the United States began. Not only was I enjoying convenient, great tasting baked foods, but I was giving that pleasure to other people who needed a gluten-free diet. The gift of my experimentation was seeing that enjoyment on their faces and hearing it in their voices.

Making over mainstream recipes has been my passion, my personal challenge for thirty-five years. When I see something I want to try, I simply reinvent it so it is safe to eat. I delight in creating everything from coffee cake to croissants, breads to scones, and everything in between. And I'm the first in line when the sampling begins. Gluten-y is truly its own reward.

As mixes became the foundation of Gluten-Free Pantry, my new flour blends became the basis for *Gluten-Free Makeovers*, a book that not only offers delicious recipes, but also techniques that can become your foundation, your ticket to great gluten-free baking and cooking in your own kitchen. So put on your apron, plug in your mixer, and get ready to embark on a yummy gluten-free adventure, a Gluten-Free Makeover.

What Is Gluten, Celiac Disease, and Other Frequently Asked Questions

What is gluten?

Gluten is the protein in wheat (including durum, semolina, spelt, kamut, einkorn, triticale, and faro), rye, and barley. In addition to the obvious items to avoid such as bread, pasta, desserts, crackers, and pizza, there are many not so obvious, including breading, croutons, cereal products, imitation seafood, imitation bacon, marinades, sauces, gravies, cold cuts, soup bases, soy sauce, communion wafers, supplements, Play-Doh, and over-the-counter and prescription medications.

Who needs to avoid gluten?

People diagnosed with celiac disease, gluten sensitivity, or gluten or wheat allergies need a gluten-free diet. (See page 5 for more on wheat allergies.)

What is celiac disease?

Celiac Disease (CD), sometimes called celiac sprue or gluten sensitive enteropathy, is a lifelong digestive disorder found in children and adults. Damage to the small intestine is caused by an autoimmune response to eating gluten and prevents the proper absorption of food.

Celiac disease potentially affects 1 in 133 people in the United States or about 3 million people. It is a chronic, inherited disease, and if untreated can lead to malnutrition, infertility, osteoporosis, anemia, and neurological disorders, to name a few. Symptoms of celiac disease vary widely, which is why it is difficult to diagnose. Symptoms can include diarrhea, short stature, lactose intolerance, bloating, constipation, and indigestion, or no symptoms at all. Patients are sometimes diagnosed through secondary disorders or other autoimmune diseases such as thyroid disease or type 1 diabetes.

Approximately 1 in 10 first-degree relatives could have celiac disease and should undergo testing once a relative has tested positive for the disease.

Patients who remain on the gluten-free diet will begin to feel better almost immediately as the small intestine begins to heal. Complete recovery may take several months or years.

What is the difference between wheat-free and gluten-free?

If a product is gluten-free, it is, by definition, wheat-free. However, the reverse is not true as products labeled "Wheat-Free" can still contain rye or barley-based ingredients that are not GF. Although spelt is a form of wheat, products containing spelt are sometimes erroneously labeled wheat-free. According to the FDA, the Food Allergen Labeling and Consumer Protection Act (FALCPA) requires foods containing spelt to list "wheat" in the ingredient statement. Products containing spelt that do not list wheat as an ingredient may be subject to recall by the FDA.

What is the difference between celiac disease, wheat allergy, and gluten intolerance/sensitivity?

Celiac disease, wheat allergy, and gluten intolerance/sensitivity are treated similarly, in that wheat is removed from the diet. But there are important differences between the three medical problems.

Celiac disease is an autoimmune condition, where the body's immune system starts attacking normal tissue, such as intestinal tissue, in response to eating gluten. Because of this, people with celiac disease are at risk for malabsorption of food in the GI tract, causing nutritional deficiencies.

Celiac disease also involves the activation of a particular type of white blood cell, the T lymphocyte, as well as other parts of the immune system. Because of this, patients with celiac disease are at increased risk for developing some forms of cancers, particularly lymphomas. Since wheat allergy and gluten sensitivity are not autoimmune conditions, people who have food allergies and intolerances are not at increased risk for these cancers.

While celiac disease, wheat allergy, and gluten intolerance/sensitivity may be treated with similar diets, they are not the same conditions. It is very important for a person to know which condition they have, as the person with celiac disease needs to monitor himself or herself for nutritional deficiencies, other autoimmune diseases, and GI cancers.

What is a wheat allergy?

Wheat allergy is one of the top eight food allergies in the United States. Allergic reactions after eating wheat may include reactions in the skin, mouth, lungs, and even the GI tract. Symptoms of wheat allergy can include rash, wheezing, lip swelling, abdominal pain, and diarrhea. The branch of the immune system activated in allergic reactions is different from the branch thought to be responsible for the autoimmune reactions of celiac disease.

Testing for a wheat allergy usually involves skin tests or eliminating wheat from the diet.

What is gluten intolerance/sensitivity?

People can also experience "intolerance/sensitivity" to gluten even in the absence of celiac disease. Such form of intolerance is not thought to be immune mediated, and currently there are no tests available to diagnose it. GI symptoms with wheat or gluten sensitivity may include gassiness, abdominal pain, abdominal distension, and diarrhea. These symptoms are usually transient, and are thought not to cause permanent damage.

Can I self-diagnose celiac disease?

Sometimes people decide they have celiac disease and start a gluten-free diet on their own. This is not a good idea as the gluten-free diet is a lifelong commitment. In addition, starting the diet before testing can make it difficult to diagnose the disease as antibodies to gluten must be present to obtain an accurate diagnosis. The body can only make these antibodies when gluten is ingested.

A panel of blood tests can be used to screen for celiac disease. However, a physician will often confirm the diagnosis with a small intestinal biopsy, the gold standard for determining celiac disease. For more information on testing, visit one of these resources:

Celiac Disease Foundation, www.celiac.org

Gluten Intolerance Group, www.gluten.net

National Digestive Diseases Information Clearinghouse, http://digestive.niddk
.nih.gov/ddiseases/pubs/celiac/

University of Chicago Celiac Disease Center, http://celiacdisease.net

Can I lick the frosting off the birthday cake or pull the burger off a bun (and other matters of cross-contamination)?

The answer is a resounding, "No." When it comes to celiac disease and the gluten-free diet, cross-contamination can be as big a problem as ingesting the actual ingredient. If a person is celiac, they must be as close to 100 percent gluten free as humanly possible. People with gluten or wheat sensitivities without the presence of celiac disease may be able to ingest tiny amounts of the offending grains without having a reaction.

Cross-contamination lurks anyplace where gluten meets gluten-free. Pitfalls include: sharing the same peanut butter jar, jam jar, or butter; using the same toaster; sharing pasta water; eating foods fried in a deep fryer that's been used to fry breaded products; sharing flour sifters; and using utensils that are not clean. Airborne wheat flour can also present a problem. And anything that has come in contact with gluten, such as frosting on a cake and burgers on buns, is just like eating gluten.

What about prescription drugs and pharmaceuticals?

FALCPA covers dietary supplements and vitamins. It does not, however, cover prescription drugs or over-the-counter medications. Individuals need to verify the ingredients on these medications by contacting the drug manufacturer, or through the pharmacist.

Can I have distilled alcohol and vinegar?

Distilled alcoholic beverages and vinegars are gluten-free. Research indicates that the gluten peptide is too large to carry over in the distillation process. This leaves the resultant liquid gluten-free. Wines are gluten-free. Beers, ales, lagers, and malt vinegar are made from gluten-containing grains and are *not* distilled, therefore they are *not* gluten-free. In the past few years, several gluten-free beers have come onto the market. These are great with pizza and a joy for those of us who like to cook with beer occasionally. The Bureau of Alcohol and Tobacco Tax and Trade Bureau will begin labeling wines, distilled spirits, and malt beverages in 2011.

Can I take medicine so I won't have to follow a gluten-free diet?

Unfortunately, the only treatment for celiac disease is lifelong adherence to a gluten-free diet. Trials studying medical treatments to supplement or even replace the diet are being conducted at medical centers around the country, and research into the triggers for this autoimmune response to gluten are underway. However, the availability for any of these treatments is several years away. Until then, it's very important to stick to the diet.

What if I am overwhelmed by this diet?

Take a deep breath and smile. It's the best medicine. Being proactive about a special diet is important, and a glass-half-full attitude is the best defense. Learn everything you can about your diet, and make a list of ingredients you can tolerate. When you see a recipe that contains offending foods, examine the ways in which you can change it to meet your needs. When presented with a problem, imagine how many ways it can be solved. Make substitution your ally. We'll do a lot of that within the pages of this book.

A Good Blend

Not all flour blends are created equal. I look for a balance of starch, fiber, and protein when I create a blend. And then I look for the balance that is best for creating crumb and texture in a recipe—breads and piecrusts need the most protein for structure. Cookies need the least. Too much of any one flour can result in a gritty mouth feel, a pronounced aftertaste, or a pastry or bread that rises beautifully and collapses as soon as it comes out of the oven.

The blends I've created work well with the recipes here and should work in all your baking. If you are avoiding a specific kind of flour that is listed in my blends, replace it with one that you can have that appears in the same column on the Flour Power Chart on page 14. It will perform nearly the same function in your baking.

To help replace gluten properties in baking, it's important to use xanthan or guar gum. These are thickening agents that provide the "glue" that minimizes the crumble factor and adds the necessary structure to allow the final product to rise. Potato flour can also be used to improve structure.

These blends create texture and taste that is very close to wheat flour according to my non-celiac tasters. I rely on nutritionally rich, high-protein ingredients like amaranth flour and sorghum flour. I think we can all stand a little more fiber and nutrition in our carbohydrate-laden gluten-free baking.

However, many cooks grumble at the prospect of creating yet another blend for baking. I hear you and I don't want that to be the deterrent in trying my recipes. With the flour blends in the Flour Power section, I've provided shortcuts: ways to turn basic, commercial blends into self-rising, bread, or pastry flour (see pages 15–17). I would rather you try my recipes using these than miss out.

Better yet, mix up double or triple batches of my flour blends on page 15 and store them in the refrigerator so they'll be ready when you are. I provide quantities in weights as well as in cups to make it easy to make these blends.

Tending of Gluten-Free Flours

- Avoid buying flours that are displayed in bins. Besides the unknown source of these flours, the commingling of scoops can be a hazard.
- Be careful of contamination. Some companies produce both wheat and non-wheat products and often mill and process them in the same location. Particles can linger in the air and on equipment surfaces. Most companies clean the equipment between the processing of different flours but that doesn't guarantee against contamination.
- If possible, purchase prepackaged flour from a manufacturer that uses a dedicated wheat-free, gluten-free facility (see Pantry, page 271).
- Store flours in airtight plastic or glass containers with a wide mouth so you can measure over the container.

- Refrigerate all gluten-free flours for a longer shelf life. Flours with more fat and protein, such as almond, brown rice, sorghum, or amaranth flours, can spoil quickly at room temperature.
- Allow refrigerated flours to come to room temperature before you use them.
- Use a wire whisk to get rid of flour clumps before you measure.

Living With Instead of Without

So often people give me a list of foods they cannot eat. I sense their frustration, but a simple exercise will help to bring success back to your baking.

Create a table of the prohibited foods. Under each, list similar foods you can have. For instance, if you can't have peanuts or tree nuts, maybe you can eat sunflower or pumpkin seeds. If you are allergic to potato, perhaps you can eat rice or tapioca. Add to this list as you discover other substitutions that work for you. You will find many more possibilities looking at your diet through this lens.

I once thought that being gluten-free was a challenge all its own. But lately questions about multiple food allergies are more prevalent than even those about gluten. "I can't have corn. What can I use instead?" "My doctor told me to avoid rice but everything that's gluten-free contains rice. What can I eat?"

I can hear the hopelessness in people's voices, even on e-mails, when they are hit with a laundry list of foods they must avoid. And because each individual has his or her own set of allergies, it is difficult to create a recipe that meets everyone's needs.

I try to list as many alternatives as possible in my own recipes here. Corn, dairy, eggs, and nuts are the big ones that I address. But don't fret if one of your specific allergies is not mentioned. Just insert a food from your customized list that works for you. Life will look a lot more delicious when you look beyond what you can't have and enjoy the foods you can eat.

Great Grains

Gluten-free bakers are fortunate to have a wonderful cadre of gluten-free flours to draw upon, each one with specific properties and functions. I categorize these flours into high protein, high fiber, starches, and light flours (like rice flour). I build blends that will deliver memorable texture and taste, drawing from flours in these categories. (See chart, page 14, for a breakdown of these ingredients.)

The chart includes all of the flours with similar properties so that you can use them interchangeably. If you don't like, can't have, or are allergic to one flour, select another one from that group. (Those that are not interchangeable have been left out.) Here's a description of our gluten-free flours listed alphabetically.

Almond flour is made from finely ground almonds and imparts a sweet, nutty flavor to baked goods. High in protein, fiber, and fat, almond flour and almond meal should be refrigerated and used within a few months to keep from becoming rancid. Make your own almond flour by finely grinding blanched nuts in a clean coffee grinder. (Don't overgrind; almond flour can turn into almond butter very quickly.) Leaving the skin on the almonds will darken the final baked product.

Amaranth is an ancient food used by the Aztecs. The seeds from this broad-leafed plant are milled into flour or puffed into kernels. High in protein and nutrients, this mildly nutty-tasting flour adds structure to gluten-free baked goods and helps them brown. Use 20 to 25 percent amaranth flour in your baking.

Buckwheat, despite its name, is not a kind of wheat. It is a fruit that is related to rhubarb. Buckwheat has a strong, robust flavor that combines well with other gluten-free flours. It's a great source of protein and is high in fiber and B vitamins. Light buckwheat flour is preferred for baking. For breads and rolls and pancakes, use up to 1 cup per recipe to impart a taste and texture that comes close to whole wheat. Use less when baking delicate cookies or pies.

Chestnut flour has a nutty, earthy flavor. It is used widely by Italian bakers to make everything from pasta and breads to cakes, pancakes, and muffins. Low in fiber and protein, it is best used in combination with a high-protein flour, such as bean, amaranth or soy flour, for structure in gluten-free products. Use up to 25 percent of the total flour blend in baking recipes. Chestnut flour should not be confused with water chestnut flour, which is a very starchy white powder.

Coconut flour, a low-carb, high-fiber flour with the subtle, sweet fragrance of coconut, is an ideal flour for people with food allergies as it is usually well tolerated by people with multiple allergies. Coconut flour can be as much as 15 percent of the flour blend in recipes for baked goods. People on low-carb diets often bake with 100 percent coconut flour.

Corn flour, **cornmeal**, and **cornstarch** have diverse baking properties. Corn flour is finely ground and suitable for breads, cakes, pancakes, and such. Cornmeal is coarsely ground and used primarily for making corn bread, breading, or polenta. If a recipe calls for corn flour and all you have is cornmeal, simply grind the cornmeal in a clean coffee grinder. Cornstarch is a fine white powder. While it provides little flavor or nutritional value, it's a key ingredient in many gluten-free flour mixes because it gives baked goods a delicate taste and lighter texture. It's also a good thickener for soups and gravies, as it gives a lovely sheen to the finished dish.

Expandex, the brand name for modified tapioca starch/flour, increases the moisture content of baked goods. If using Expandex to replace tapioca starch/flour in a recipe, reduce the amount of Expandex by 1 to 2 tablespoons and reduce the xanthan or guar gum by ½ to 1 teaspoon.

Flax seed and flax seed meal: Whole flax seed is not digestible so buy flax seed meal (ground flax seed) or make your own by grinding the seeds in a clean coffee grinder. High in fiber and omega-3 fatty acids, add 2 to 3 tablespoons of flax seed meal to recipes for baked goods or sprinkle it on yogurt or cereal for a nutritional boost. A mixture of flax seed meal and warm water is used as an egg replacer in vegan and egg-free baking (see page 268). Store both seeds and meal in the refrigerator or freezer.

Legume (bean) flours are high in protein, fiber, and calcium. Chickpea (garbanzo) flour is the most popular choice for gluten-free baking, but navy, pinto, red, and soy flour are also available. Garfava flour is a blend of flours made from garbanzo, fava, and Romano beans. Bean flours, particularly garfava and chickpea, tend to impart an aftertaste that some people find unpleasant, so use no more than 25 percent of these flours in a blend. The taste can be offset by adding brown sugar, molasses, chocolate, or spices to a recipe. For those who don't like the fairly pronounced flavor, quinoa flour is a good substitute.

Mesquite flour, ground from the pods of the mesquite tree, is a pleasantly sweet flour that's rich in nutrients and high in fiber. Mesquite flour imparts a dark color and slight molasses flavor to baked goods. Add up to 25 percent mesquite flour to other gluten-free flours. This flour is great for pancakes, brownies, and gingerbread but is not recommended for most breads, rolls, and delicate pastries.

Millet is an ancient food, possibly the first cereal grain used for domestic purposes. Millet flour has a mildly sweet, nutlike flavor and is nutrient rich. This high-protein, high-fiber flour creates light baked goods with a distinctive flavor. For best results, use no more than 25 percent millet flour in any flour blend.

Montina is made from perennial Indian rice grass, a dietary staple of Native Americans before the introduction of maize. Recently rediscovered and now grown in the western United States, Montina is a powerhouse of protein and fiber. Use up to 30 percent Montina flour in a flour blend to produce bread with a whole wheat taste and texture like my high fiber bread on page 36.

Oat groats, oat flour, and **oat flakes** are high in fiber and protein. Oats add taste, texture, and structure to cookies, breads, and other baked goods. Be sure to select only certified gluten-free oats. (See discussion about safe gluten-free oats below and the Pantry, page 274, for sources of safe oats.)

Oat groats are minimally processed whole oats that can be used as hot cereal or cooked like rice.

Oat flour is made from grinding oats into a fine powder that can be used in baking bread, rolls, quick bread, and pancakes.

Oat flakes are sold in several cuts from steel-cut to quick-cooking oats.

- Quick-Cooking Oats are thinner, flat flakes that cook in 1½ to 3 minutes. They are the best for most recipes in this book.
- Steel-Cut Oats are cut into small pieces. They are chewier and require a longer cooking time than flat cut oats. They are not suitable for most recipes but make great breakfast cereal
- Instant Oats are great for a quick breakfast, but become too mushy when used in baking. They will not produce the chewy, nutty texture that is so desirable when baking with oats.

> For many years, oats were off-limits for a person with celiac disease. It turns out the oats are actually not a problem for most celiacs. However, they are usually rotated with wheat crops and processed on the same machinery. Once the issues of cross-contamination were eliminated, a handful of producers in Canada and the United States started processing oats that are safe for the gluten-free diet. For a list, see the Pantry section on page 274.

Potato flour and potato starch: Potato flour, made from dehydrated potatoes, is a fine yellow-white powder that's high in fiber and protein. It is often used to replace xanthan gum or guar gum in gluten-free baking as it adds great structure to baked products. Add 2 to 4 tablespoons per recipe (reduce or eliminate the gum ingredients accordingly) to lend a soft, chewy mouth-feel to baked goods, homemade pasta, breads, and pizza crust.

Potato starch, made from the starch of dehydrated potatoes, is a white powder often used as a one-to-one substitution for cornstarch in recipes, although it produces a bit heavier consistency. It has excellent baking qualities, particularly when combined with eggs. Gluten-free recipes often call for ½ to ¾ cup of potato starch. Since it contains no protein or fat, it must be added as part of a flour blend. Potato starch is the "flour" of choice for Passover baking. Potato starch tends to clump so it should be stirred first for accurate measuring.

Quinoa flour, milled from a grain that's native to the Andes Mountains in South America, has high levels of B vitamins and all eight amino acids, making it a complete protein. It also is a good source of other important nutrients and fiber. This flour is easy to digest and has a delicate, nutty flavor similar to wild rice. Mix it with other flours to increase the nutritional value and structure of your recipes. Using large quantities (more than 30 percent of the total flour blend) can overpower the flavor in baked goods.

Rice flour is the gluten-free flour most people try first. Years ago, it was about the only alternative to wheat flour, so it was the key ingredient for many gluten-free baked goods. Relatively heavy and dense, rice flour works best in recipes when combined with other flours. It's available as brown rice (higher in fiber and nutrients), sweet rice (short grain with a higher starch content), and white rice. The texture varies, too, from fine to medium to coarse. The fine or medium grinds are more suitable for baked goods. Coarsely ground is best for cereal and coatings.

Sorghum flour (also called milo and jowar), available in red and white varieties, has a slightly sweet taste and is high in fiber and protein. It works best when blended with other flours. Use no more than 30 percent sorghum flour in any flour blend.

Teff flour, milled from one of the world's smallest grains, is a staple food and a key source of nutrition in Ethiopia. Teff flour is available in dark and light varieties. High in calcium, protein, and fiber, it has a mild nutty flavor that adds taste to quick breads, pancakes, and waffles. Combine teff flour with Montina in an all-purpose flour blend to produce high-fiber bread with a whole wheat taste. I prefer light teff flour but both will work.

Tuber and other root starches, made from tapioca, arrowroot, and sweet potato, are usually well tolerated by people with multiple allergies. These flours give baked goods a chewy texture. Arrowroot flour is pleasant-tasting and versatile, good for making breads and bagels. Sweet potato flour, which has a yellow-orange hue, imparts its color to baked goods and has a taste that works well in recipes that use chocolate, molasses, and spices. Tapioca starch/flour, made from the cassava (manioc) plant, is a good choice in breads, tortillas, and pasta. All three starches can be mixed with water to thicken sauces and stews. Expandex is a modified form of tapioca flour (see page 11).

Flour Power: Building a Blend

Use this chart as a guide to help select substitute flours for all your baking. Find the flour you wish to change and select another one from the same list. The properties, while not identical, will be similar and serve the same function in building the structure in a particular recipe.

Neutral (light) Flours	High Protein Flours	High Fiber Flours	Stabilizers— Add texture and moisture	Starches	Gums
Brown Rice Flour	Almond Flour	Almond Flour	Coconut Flour	Arrowroot Flour	Agar Powder
Corn Flour	Amaranth Flour	Amaranth Flour	Expandex	Cornstarch	Carrageenan
Sorghum Flour	Bean Flours	Bean Flours	Flax Seed Meal	Kudzu Root Starch or Kuzu	Gelatin Powder
Sweet Rice Flour	Buckwheat Flour	Buckwheat Flour	Oat Bran	Potato Starch	Guar Gum
White Rice Flour	Chickpea Flour	Chickpea Flour	Potato Flour	Sweet Potato Flour	Locust Bean Gum
	Millet Flour	Corn Flour	Rice Bran	Tapioca Starch	Xanthan Gum
	Montina Flour	Mesquite Flour			
	Oat Flour	Montina Flour			
	Quinoa Flour	Soy Flour			
	Sorghum Flour				
	Soy Flour				
	Teff Flour				

My Blends: The Essentials of Good Baking

Bread flours, which need to expand to allow the yeast to rise, require the most elasticity and therefore at least one third of the blend should come from a high protein flour. In addition, a bread blend requires 1 teaspoon of gum (xanthan or guar) per 1 cup of flour to ensure the end result will be a satisfying loaf with a chewy texture. Bread Flour #1 gets its protein from sorghum flour and amaranth flour while the protein in Bread Flour #2 comes from chickpea flour. Some people don't care for chickpea flour so I've included both formulas.

BREAD FLOUR #1
(Great for All Breads)

1¼ cups white rice flour (6.5 ounces) or brown rice flour (5.5 ounces)

1¼ cups sweet white sorghum flour (5.25 ounces)

½ cup amaranth flour (2 ounces)

¾ cup cornstarch (3.5 ounces) or tapioca starch (3.2 ounces)

3 teaspoons xanthan gum

1 teaspoon salt

BREAD FLOUR #2
(High Protein Blend with Chickpea Flour)

2¼ cups chickpea flour (9.5 ounces), quinoa flour (9.1 ounces), or another bean flour

2 cups cornstarch (9.6 ounces) or potato starch (11.2 ounces)

2 cups plus 2 tablespoons tapioca starch/flour (9.3 ounces)

2 cups brown rice flour (8.5 ounces)

½ cup packed light brown sugar (2.8 ounces)

2 tablespoons plus 2 teaspoons xanthan gum

3 teaspoon salt

Self-Rising Flour is used for muffins, quick breads, scones, and biscuits. The baking powder is included as it is called for in nearly all recipes in this category. Baking soda, however, is not a constant, and left to the baker to add as needed. The addition of amaranth and sorghum flour makes for a nutritionally dense, high fiber blend, but don't let that put you off. This mix produces light, delicate baked goods. The fact that they are a little healthier will be our secret.

SELF-RISING FLOUR

1¼ cups white rice flour (6.5 ounces)

1 cup sweet white sorghum flour (4 ounces)

¾ cup amaranth flour (3 ounces)

¾ cup cornstarch (3.5 ounces) or potato starch (4 ounces)

¼ cup tapioca starch/flour (1.1 ounces)

2 tablespoons baking powder

2 teaspoons xanthan gum

1½ teaspoons salt

Cake and Pastry Flour's job is to produce cakes and cupcakes that rise nicely but have a delicate crumb when cut. Less protein and gum are necessary to perform this task. Sorghum flour and cornstarch help promote the light, airy texture.

CAKE AND PASTRY FLOUR

1 cup sweet white sorghum flour (4 ounces)

1 cup white rice flour (5.4 ounces)

¾ cup cornstarch* (3.5 ounces)

1½ teaspoons xanthan gum (or guar gum)

½ teaspoon salt

---

*Allergic to corn? Replace with ½ cup potato starch (not flour) or tapioca starch/flour and increase the sorghum flour or rice flour to 1¼ cups to avoid a gummy texture.

The **Basic Blend** is for many cookie recipes and for those times when an all-purpose blend is called for. This can be replaced by using another all-purpose "white" blend with excellent results. You will need to add gum and salt unless they are already included in the blend.

BASIC BLEND

2¾ cups rice flour (15.4 ounces)

1¼ cups corn or potato starch (8 ounces)

⅓ cup tapioca starch/flour (1.5 ounces)

Batching It: Double Batches and Beyond

You can never have too much of a good thing when it comes to having these blends on hand anytime you want to bake. Make up multiple batches. Here's an easy way:

- To prepare a single batch: weigh out each dry ingredient using a kitchen scale. Weights are provided for a single recipe here.
- The amount of gum, salt, baking powder, and baking soda per single recipe are too small to weigh out. Instead, measure these in teaspoons and tablespoons and add to your blend.
- For larger batches: on a worksheet, multiply each ingredient by the number of recipes you would like to create. (I find that 5 or 10 work well.) Measure out the same multiple for the smaller ingredients like the gum, salt, baking powder, and baking soda, in teaspoons and tablespoons. Weigh this quantity in grams and write down the amount for future use.
- Now you are ready to make a large batch of a blend anytime you wish. Simply weigh ingredients in the multiple you've chosen and place the ingredients in a large bowl or plastic container. Mix very well.

Shortcuts

To make **Bread Flour #1** from a Commercial Blend: Add 1 cup amaranth or sorghum flour per 3 cups of commercial all-purpose blend. Add 1 teaspoon xanthan gum and ½ teaspoon salt per 1 cup of flour if not already included in the blend. If included, add only 1 teaspoon of additional xanthan gum for 3 cups of flour.

To make **Self-Rising Flour** from a Commercial Blend: Add 2 teaspoons baking powder per 1 cup of commercial blend. Add ¾ teaspoon xanthan gum and ¼ teaspoon salt per 1 cup of flour if not already included in the blend. If included, no other alterations are necessary.

To make **Cake and Pastry Flour** from a Commercial Blend: Add ¼ cup cornstarch per 1 cup of commercial blend. Add ¾ teaspoon xanthan gum and ¼ teaspoon salt per 1 cup of flour if not already included in the blend. If already included, it is not necessary to add additional salt or xanthan gum.

Makeovers Made Easy: Unlocking Recipe Secrets

When I was diagnosed with celiac disease, I attended culinary classes, knowing full well I might not be able to eat anything, but certain I could re-create it at home. When I held a recipe, I held its soul. I had the inside track into understanding how it worked, why it worked, and the relationship of wet to dry ingredients.

I pieced together ratios and methods, often examining two or more recipes for the same item to see which parts of it I preferred and cobbling together the parts that suited my taste buds and the specific personality of gluten-free flours. This premise started feeding me.

I studied cookbooks much like others read mystery novels. I uncovered the techniques that make them work—how did the creator give lift to the end product; was the fat added as a solid or a liquid? Then I looked at the end result—was it airy, dense, crumbly, flaky?

This helped determine the best blend of flours and the amount of xanthan or guar gum needed to achieve a gluten-free version.

I looked at the gluten containing ingredients—the quantity of flour needed, for instance helped me determine the extent of the makeover. If the recipe called for a dusting of flour or a tablespoon or two as in a cheesecake or a flourless cake, the substitution was easy—one kind of flour would work.

If the recipe was more complex, a fancy cake or a yeast bread, then the makeover required a bit more imagination. Doughs that needed elasticity such as piecrust or bread required a blend with a high protein flour and a teaspoon of gum per cup of flour. In a delicate cookie, I did not need something chewy, but rather something that would hold together, but impart a fine crumb. A light mild-tasting flour blend such as one containing white rice and corn or tapioca starch, and a tiny bit of gum would do.

Recipe DNA

Every recipe has its own personality that comes from the relationship of wet ingredients to dry, the amount of fat and whether it is a solid or a liquid, the quantity of sugar, eggs, and flavoring. These characteristics give a recipe its integrity, complexity, and name. In essence, its DNA.

When I do a recipe makeover, I do not alter those sacrosanct relationships and neither should you. If you change one ingredient, it will be necessary to change the others. To understand this delicate balance you need only imagine the last time you cut a recipe in half. When you did so, you cut every ingredient by the same amount. If you look at recipe makeovers in the same way, you will always have success.

A Simple Makeover

Here's a recipe we can try together:

Irish Tea Bread—A Makeover

My friend Beverly asked me to help her make over a family recipe for Irish Tea Bread. On the surface it looked like a simple task and I was happy to give her a hand. Ironically, what looked so easy took several attempts. It's a great recipe to help you understand how to convert a mainstream recipe into one that is gluten-free.

First, here's Beverly's family recipe. Notice the warning that the dough will be heavy and sticky. Also note the technique: the butter is cut into the dry ingredients until crumbly and the buttermilk and eggs are added later. This tea bread is probably a cross between an Irish Soda Bread and a scone (more scone than soda bread owing to the small amount of baking soda).

Irish Tea Bread

▶ Mix together in a large bowl the first five in-gredients. Cut in the butter until the mixture is crumbly. Add the raisins. Mix the beaten eggs and buttermilk together in a separate bowl. Make a well in the center of the flour mixture and pour in the wet ingredients. Mix with a wooden spoon until the mixture is moist. This is a very heavy and sticky dough.

▶ Grease and flour a 9-inch pan or a loaf pan. Spoon the batter into the prepared pan and pat lightly into the shape of the pan. Bake at 350°F for 1 hour, or until browned.

NOTE: It is essential to put raisins into the dry ingredients, otherwise they will sink to the bottom of the tea bread.

3 cups flour

½ cup sugar

2 teaspoons baking powder

½ teaspoon baking soda

½ teaspoon salt

5 tablespoons butter

1 cup raisins

2 eggs, slightly beaten

1 cup low-fat buttermilk

Here's how I approached making over the original recipe:

- My first concern was selecting a blend that was light and already contained some "lift." The self-rising blend fit the bill; it's also the one I use to make scones. I replaced 3 cups of flour with an equal amount of this blend.
- The original recipe called for 2 teaspoons of baking powder. I needed to find out if 3 cups of my blend would yield 2 teaspoons or more of baking powder. The ratio in my blend is 4 cups of flour for 2 tablespoons of baking powder or 1½ teaspoons per cup—no need to add additional baking powder to my makeover but a bit extra won't hurt in this dense batter.
- My self-rising blend does not contain baking soda because it is not always an ingredient in quick breads and muffins. I added baking soda to this recipe, but remembering that the dough would be dense, I added a bit more than the original recipe called for.
- The first time I made this recipe, I had made my own buttermilk, combin-ing vinegar and milk. I used commercial buttermilk the next time and the recipe did not work. I tried again and again before realizing the combina-

tion of baking soda and cider vinegar was critical in producing a delicate sconelike texture in this recipe. I went back to using a mixture of milk and cider vinegar. (I use that combo in several recipes in this book.)

- Adding raisins with the dry ingredients didn't seem like a good idea. I feared they would turn to mush when I cut in the butter or blended the liquids with a wooden spoon. Dusting the raisins with the flour blend and folding them in at the end prevented them from sinking to the bottom during baking.

- For a dairy-free version, I substituted soy milk for cow's milk and in place of butter, I used non-dairy spread. The spread is softer than butter, so I cut it into pieces and froze them briefly before cutting them into the flour. This created the same texture that cold butter produces as it begins to bake.

- I made no other changes to ingredients or amounts.

Here's the gluten-free version:

Beverly's Irish Tea Bread

SERVES 8

▶ Preheat the oven to 350°F. Lightly oil or grease a 9-inch springform pan.

▶ Combine the milk and vinegar and set aside to thicken.

▶ Combine the flour blend, sugar, and baking soda in a bowl. Cut in the cold butter until the mixture is crumbly. Combine the eggs and milk in a separate bowl. Make a well in center of the dry ingredients and add the milk mixture. Mix with a wooden spoon until the dry ingredients are moist. Toss the raisins with the reserved 2 tablespoons of flour blend until coated. Fold into the mixture.

▶ Spoon the dough into the prepared pan and smooth the top until even and the batter

1 cup milk, soy milk, or rice milk minus 2 teaspoons

2 teaspoons cider vinegar

3 cups self-rising flour blend, reserve 2 tablespoons to coat raisins

½ cup sugar

¾ teaspoon baking soda

5 tablespoons unsalted butter, cold, cut into small pieces

2 large eggs, slightly beaten

1 cup dark raisins

continues

continued

touches the sides of the pan. Bake for 55 to 60 minutes, until lightly browned and a toothpick inserted in the center comes out clean.

▶ Let cool for 15 minutes before removing the rim of the springform pan. Serve warm with soft butter and jam or remove the bottom of the pan and let cool before serving. This freezes well and can be sliced and reheated or toasted.

This is a great example of the approach I took to create all the recipes in this book. Apply this technique in your own kitchen and you'll have great results every time. Start with one of your favorite recipes and one of my blends and build from there. Before you know it, you'll be baking like a gluten-free pro and reaping the delicious rewards, too.

Baking Tips

1. If you make a recipe over and over, make a big batch of the corresponding flour blend. It will save time when you want to prepare the recipe.

2. Consider using cornstarch as your starch of choice. Over my years of gluten-free baking, I've found it produces the lightest cakes, muffins, and quick breads. It stands to reason since cake flour contains cornstarch. Even Julia Child once said that a gluten-free person could replace regular flour one-for-one with cornstarch in any recipe and have good results. I'm not sure I would go that far. Too much of a good thing is not a good thing when it comes to gluten-free baking and too much of any starch will produce a gummy texture. Some people have an allergy to corn or an aversion to cornstarch, so another starch may be substituted (see chart, page 14).

3. Most of my recipes can be made dairy-free by using substitutions for butter and milk that I list in the Simple Substitutions section on page 265. Many can also be made egg-free and nut-free and I offer substitutions when they can be used.

4. Measuring flours. For best results, spoon the flour into the measuring cup and level with the back of a knife. Using the measuring cup as a scoop can pack up to 20 percent more flour into the recipe.

5. Timing. Set the timer for the shortest time listed on the recipe and test for doneness at two minute intervals after that point to ensure that the recipe is not overbaked.

Get the Scoop: Tools of the Trade

Scoops range from 1 to 4 tablespoons. I use them in varying sizes to scoop out muffin batter, perfectly formed cookies, or for just about any baking task. As gluten-free dough tends to be sticky and difficult to handle, this makes easy work of transferring dough and forming it into the right sizes. If the dough is sticky, spray the inside of the scoop with vegetable spray before scooping it out.

Plastic Wrap and Vegetable Spray: Form or roll the dough on sheets of plastic wrap that are sprayed with PAM or other vegetable spray (be sure to check the ingredients). Smooth the surfaces of bread or rolls using these tools as a way to create a smooth, finished look on baked goods.

Heavy Duty Mixer: Gluten-free dough tends to be thick and heavy and may burn out lightweight mixers. Select a workhorse with at least 240 watts of power. (KitchenAid, Cuisinart, and Black & Decker all make them.) Or treat yourself to a stand mixer like a 5-quart KitchenAid if you do a lot of baking. You'll thank yourself.

Bread Machine: If you make bread, make friends with a programmable bread machine or one with a gluten-free cycle. Many of the breads in this book work well in a bread machine. For my money, I like the Zojirushi machine. I've had one for ten years and it's still working.

Oven Thermometer: Purchase a simple oven thermometer to double check the oven temperature before baking. Nothing is more frustrating than to spend time preparing a dish and find it is not properly baked because of oven temperature.

Instant-Read Thermometer: This is a great tool for checking the internal temperature of breads or for preparing candies and sauces.

Rubber Spatulas: Have an assortment of sizes of rubber spatulas on hand to help scrape dough and ingredients from the crevices of large and small containers.

Storing and Handling: The Care and Feeding of Gluten-Free Baked Goods

Gluten-free baked goods tend to dry out quickly when kept in the refrigerator. I prefer to wrap cooled baked goods and leave them on the counter to enjoy for one to two days. Anything remaining is sliced, wrapped well, and stored in the freezer. Be sure to date the package. The exception is items with perishable ingredients like meats or cheese. These and fruit desserts as well as cakes frosted with butter-cream, should be stored in the refrigerator. See more tips in each section.

The Secret Ingredient

Most important, I encourage you to be curious and experiment to see which flours, recipes, and ingredients suit your kitchen and taste buds. Use your imagination, have fun, and be prepared to substitute boldly.

Besides all of these tips, make sure you bring a generous portion of humor to your diet and your baking. A sense of humor goes a long way. To my mind, it's the secret ingredient in coping with a special diet.

A Good Place to Start

I often judge a cookbook after trying just one recipe. If that's you, here are a few suggestions that are sure to win you over: Antipasto Squares (page 95), Banana Bread with Streusel Crumb Topping (page 70), Challah Bread (page 40), Chocolate Shortbread (page 196), Corn Bread Extraordinaire (page 72), Grandma's Babka (page 45), Killer Brownies (page 180), Lemon Walnut Squares (page 183), Potato and Cheese Pierogi (page 138), Pumpkin Orange Brandy Layer Cake (page 224), Raspberry Dazzle Bars (page 185), The Best Carrot Cake (page 227), or Vanilla Blueberry Bundt Cake (page 228).

Bon appétit and happy gluten-free baking!

THE
Recipes

YEAST BREADS AND QUICK BREADS

Bread Machine or Oven?

People swear by both. Personally, I love my bread machine for convenience, especially if I am using a bread mix or have my ingredients measured out ahead of time. Once I add everything and feel confident that the balance of dry to wet ingredients is right, I can leave to do other things and return to find a freshly baked loaf of bread. It's as if someone has delivered me an embarrassment of riches when I take a bite, forgetting that I put the ingredients in the machine a few hours earlier.

However, there is less flexibility in using a bread machine. Baking times are set and it's difficult to add a few extra minutes if you think the bread is underbaked. I also think oven-baked bread tastes a bit better. And not every bread mix and recipe can be made with equal success using either method.

Whether you use a bread machine or bake your bread in the oven, here are a few tips to help ensure that every loaf is delicious.

Tricks and Tips:

- Warm liquids to 100°F before mixing or blending.
- Use flour and eggs at room temperature. Set cold eggs in a bowl of warm water for 5 minutes to warm.
- Good gluten-free bread depends on a delicate balance of wet to dry ingredients. Look for a shiny appearance and a texture like mashed potatoes when the dough is mixed.
- Too much liquid produces a floppy, gummy loaf with large holes and a flat or sunken top. If the bread rises beautifully but sinks when it is removed from the oven (or bread machine), that's also an indication of too much liquid.
- Too little liquid produces a lumpy, crumbly loaf that falls apart when sliced.
- Use butter and milk or non-dairy versions, rather than oil and water to add moisture and create a chewy crust. Egg substitute may be used in place of eggs but the bread will not rise as much.
- The internal temperature of a fully baked loaf of gluten-free bread should be between 190°F and 200°F.

Rising to the Occasion: Putting Yeast to Work

- Gluten-free bread dough rises best in a warm, draft-free room. (See Building a Proofing Box, page 32.)

continues

Bread Machine or Oven? *continued*

- Adding a sweetener helps activate the yeast. Molasses and honey also help produce a silky texture in gluten-free yeast dough. Be sure to count the molasses or honey as part of the liquid ingredients.
- Add 1 teaspoon cider vinegar to the liquids to tenderize the dough.
- If the bread doesn't rise at all, the yeast may be old or the liquids too hot. (Over 120°F will kill the yeast.) Too much salt can affect the performance of yeast as well.
- Don't worry if your bread has not risen to the top of the pan when it begins to bake. It will rise more during baking.

To Store:

- Allow the loaf to cool completely. Store in a plastic zip-top bag or wrap well in plastic wrap.
- If you are not using the entire loaf of bread in the next 24 to 48 hours, slice and freeze the remainder and take out slices as needed.
- To thaw, wrap bread slices in a paper towel and microwave for 30 to 60 seconds. Toast, if desired, or just enjoy!

Tips for Using Bread Machines

- Select a bread machine that has a gluten-free cycle or one with programmable features that allows you to use one knead and one rise cycle and has a 60-minute baking cycle. Or select the shortest yeast bread cycle. If the bread machine is also used to make wheat bread, clean down carefully or purchase a second pan and blade.

- Some bread machines knead gluten-free dough more effectively than others and some recipes work better in a particular brand of machine than in other models. Select a machine with some or all of these features: makes a 1½ to 2 pound loaf; includes programmable cycles and/or a gluten-free bread cycle; uses a horizontal shaped pan and two paddles. You'll find many of these features available on models made by Breadman, Cuisinart, and Zojirushi.

- Add ingredients in the order recommended by the manufacturer of your machine.

- It's not necessary to mix ingredients in a bowl before adding to the bread machine baking pan.

- A few minutes into the first knead cycle, lift the lid and use a rubber spatula to help mix the dough until it is smooth and moist in appearance (almost shiny). Don't be afraid to reach into the bottom of the pan. If the kneading blade hits the spatula, it will not harm the machine.

- If dry flour is sitting on the top or in the corners after mixing, the bread needs more liquid and/or better mixing. Add 1 teaspoon of warm water at a time, mixing after each addition, until the dough is smooth and "swirls" in the bread pan.

- For soupy batter, add 1 tablespoon of rice flour (or gluten-free blend of flours) at a time, stirring after each incorporation, until the dough is thick, "swirls," and pulls away from the sides.

- Once the kneading cycle has ended, use a rubber spatula to smooth the top so the bread will bake evenly.

- Don't touch the bread with your fingers, as it is very likely to be sticky.

- Avoid using the automatic cool down cycle. Cool on a wire rack to prevent the bread from becoming gummy. To revive, heat the uncut loaf in 350° oven for 5 minutes.

A Few Notes About Proofing and Yeast

Building a proofing box: To speed the rising process, place a bowl of water in the microwave and heat on high for 10 minutes. Set the rolls or bread on top of the bowl or next to it. Close the door. The warm, moist air is an excellent environment for getting heavy, gluten-free dough to rise more quickly.

About Yeast: When a recipe calls for yeast, choose instant active dry yeast or active dry yeast (SAF, Red Star or Fleischman brand). Both types work well in gluten-free bread baking including breads made in bread machines. No proofing is necessary unless you suspect the yeast is very old and might not activate. I do not recommend RapidRise yeast for gluten-free bread baking. Yeast should be stored in the refrigerator and can be frozen to extend the use-by date. For the latter, be sure to write the date of purchase on the package and use within six to nine months. The recipes in my book were tested with Lesaffre SAF-Instant Red Dry Yeast.

Apple Caramel Monkey Bread

MAKES 12 SERVINGS

This pull-apart bread, also called bubble bread, was inspired by a photo of Apple Cinnamon Monkey Bread in the *King Arthur Flour's Baker's Catalogue*. This bread looks just like the KAF version (see page 4 of the photo insert) and tastes outrageous—not too sweet with a pleasing amount of caramel.

1 recipe Delicious Slicing Bread dough (page 42)

1 teaspoon vanilla extract

2½ tablespoons granulated sugar

1½ teaspoons ground cinnamon

1 medium Granny Smith or McIntosh apple, peeled, sliced, and coarsely chopped

4 tablespoons (½ stick) butter or margarine

½ cup packed brown sugar

½ cup chopped pecans, optional

▸ Prepare the Delicious Slicing Bread, adding the vanilla extract to the dough. Set aside.

▸ Lightly grease a 10-cup Bundt pan or fluted pan.

▸ Combine the sugar and cinnamon in a small bowl. Toss 1 tablespoon of the sugar mixture over apples in a medium bowl and stir to coat. Set aside.

▸ In a microwave-proof bowl, melt the butter in the microwave on medium high for 30 to 40 seconds, until melted. Stir in the brown sugar until dissolved. Pour into the bottom of the prepared pan and sprinkle half the pecans, if using, over the brown sugar mixture.

▸ Spray a ¼-cup scoop with vegetable spray. Scoop out balls of the bread dough and arrange in one layer over the pecan and brown sugar mixture. (This will yield about eight scoops or half the dough.) Sprinkle half of the remaining cinnamon sugar over the balls of dough. Spread the apples over the dough and top with a second layer of balls of dough, using all the remaining dough. Sprinkle with the remaining cinnamon sugar and the remaining pecans over the top. Cover loosely with plastic wrap and set in a warm, draft free area to rise about 45 minutes.

continues

continued

▶ Preheat the oven to 375°F. Remove the plastic wrap from the dough and bake for 30 to 35 minutes, until the top is brown. Remove to a wire rack and cool for 10 minutes. Invert onto a serving plate. Let cool an additional 10 minutes. Pull apart or slice with a bread knife. The monkey bread is best served warm, and can be reheated in a 350°F oven for 5 to 7 minutes.

Shortcuts:

▶ Use a commercial bread mix in place of the Delicious Slicing Bread.

▶ Place pecan halves in a plastic zip-top bag and seal. Crush with a rolling pin until coarsely chopped.

Tip: Can't have nuts? Use ¼ cup raisins and spread evenly over the bottom of the pan.

Bagel Sticks

MAKES 30 BREADSTICKS

I tasted—OK, devoured—these awesome sticks at a local gluten-free dinner. They were made by Bob Spector who, with his wife Sue, owns Nature's Grocer in Vernon, Connecticut. In addition to the best selection of gluten-free and dairy-free products in the area, the store has a full bakery and café. The recipe is reprinted with Bob's permission.

- ► Line a baking sheet with parchment paper or bread stick pans with lightly oiled aluminum foil.
- ► In the bowl of a stand mixer fitted with the paddle attachment or handheld mixer with beaters, combine the flour blend, chickpea flour, yeast, xanthan gum, sugar, and Egg Replacer. In a separate bowl, combine the warm water, canola oil, honey, and vinegar. Add to the dry ingredients. Beat on low speed until the dry ingredients are moistened, then increase the speed to medium and beat for 3 minutes.
- ► Shape the dough by tablespoonfuls (about 2 tablespoons each) into 8- to 10-inch long sticks. Place 1 inch apart on the prepared baking sheet. Cover with plastic wrap that has been sprayed lightly with vegetable spray. Let rise 20 minutes.
- ► Preheat the oven to 375°F. Remove the plastic wrap and brush the sticks with egg wash or milk. Sprinkle with your favorite toppings.
- ► Bake for 18 to 20 minutes, until golden brown. Remove from the oven and let cool for a few minutes. Serve immediately or cool completely and store in a zip-top bag. Use within two days or freeze for later use.

2½ cups Bread Flour #1 (page 15)

½ cup chickpea flour

1 tablespoon instant active or active dry yeast

1 teaspoon xanthan gum

1 tablespoon sugar

1½ teaspoons Ener-G Foods Egg Replacer (see Simple Substitutions, page 268) or 1½ teaspoons baking powder

1¼ cups warm water (105° to 110°F)

2 tablespoons canola or other vegetable oil

2 tablespoons honey

1 teaspoon cider vinegar

1 egg, lightly beaten with 1 tablespoon water, or 3 tablespoons milk if eggs are not tolerated

Favorite toppings: roasted dehydrated garlic, poppy seeds, sesame seeds, coarse salt

Tip: *For ease of handling, roll the sticks on lightly oiled plastic wrap.*

Beth and Jen's High Fiber Bread

Dairy-free

MAKES ONE 2-POUND LOAF OR 16 SLICES

The taste and appearance of this bread are reminiscent of a whole wheat bread and the mix is full of healthy fiber and nutrients. The flours here can be replaced with equal amounts of other nutritious flours from the same column in my Flour Power Chart (page 14). Don't be put off by the lengthy list of ingredients. This bread is worth the effort. I make the recipe in my bread machine with great success. If this becomes a staple in your house as it is in mine, you might want to make up a big batch of dry ingredients. I've included weight measures to help. (See A Good Blend, page 7.)

- ▶ Lightly oil an 8½ x 4½-inch loaf pan.
- ▶ In the bowl of a stand mixer fitted with the paddle attachment, combine the millet flour, Montina flour, teff flour, chickpea flour, cornstarch, tapioca starch/flour, xanthan gum, yeast, salt, and cream of tartar. Sprinkle the brown sugar over the flour mixture and blend to remove any lumps.
- ▶ In a medium mixing bowl, combine the eggs, water, and olive oil. Add to the dry ingredients. Beat on low speed to moisten. Increase the speed to medium and beat for 3 to 5 minutes, until smooth and slightly shiny.
- ▶ Scrape the dough into the prepared pan. Cover with oiled plastic wrap and set in a warm, draft-free place to rise for about 40 minutes, or just until the dough has risen nearly to the top of the pan.
- ▶ Preheat the oven to 350°F. Remove the plastic wrap from the dough in the pan and bake on the center rack for 40 to 50 minutes. Remove to a wire rack to cool completely.

½ cup millet flour (54 grams)

½ cup Montina flour (65 grams)

⅓ cup teff flour (48 grams)

¾ cup chickpea flour (80 grams)

½ cup cornstarch (65 grams)

½ cup plus 1 tablespoon tapioca starch/flour (70 grams)

3½ teaspoons xanthan gum (9 grams)

2¼ teaspoons instant active or active dry yeast

1 teaspoon salt (6 grams)

¼ teaspoon cream of tartar

3 tablespoons brown sugar (38 grams)

3 large eggs, lightly beaten

1⅛ cups warm water (105° to 110°F)

3 tablespoons olive oil or vegetable oil

continues

continued

Bread Machine Method (for a large capacity machine):

▶ Combine all the dry ingredients *except for the yeast* in a large bowl. Crumble the brown sugar using your fingertips. Blend the liquids together in a bowl. Pour the wet ingredients into the machine's bread pan. Sprinkle the dry ingredients over the wet, and then sprinkle the yeast over the top. Or add the ingredients in the order recommended according to your bread machine manual. Set the machine to quick cycle, white bread, or programmable cycle. If the machine can be programmed, omit all but one knead and rise cycle. During the knead cycle, use a rubber spatula to scrape down the sides and help blend the dough. Smooth the top. Remove the bread when the bake cycle ends and transfer to a wire rack. Cool completely before slicing.

Brioche

MAKES 18 SMALL BRIOCHE ROLLS

These elegant little rolls were inspired by the gluten-free bread served at Cyrus Restaurant in Healdsburg, California. The smell of sweet dough and the delightful texture, sent me dashing to the kitchen. My thanks to Douglas Keane and his crew for providing the inspiration for this recipe. The dough should be prepared a few hours before it is needed. Leftover brioche make wonderful French toast.

- ▶ Combine the Basic Blend, sugar, yeast, xanthan gum, and salt in the bowl of a stand mixer fitted with the paddle attachment or use a medium mixing bowl and a heavy duty handheld mixer. In a separate bowl, combine the 4 eggs and milk and add to the flour mixture. Beat on low speed to blend. With the mixer on low speed, add the butter in pieces. Increase the speed slightly and beat until there are no lumps. Transfer to a large bowl, cover, and refrigerate the mixture for several hours or overnight. The mixture will rise as it sits so be sure to use a large enough container.
- ▶ Spray eighteen individual brioche pans or medium muffin cups. Set the pans on baking sheets for ease of handling. Fill ¾ of the way with the dough and let the dough soften at room temperature.
- ▶ Preheat the oven to 350°F. Brush the tops of the brioche with egg wash and bake for 12 to 15 minutes. Remove from the oven and set on a wire rack. As soon as the pans are cool enough to handle, turn the brioche onto the wire rack and cool slightly. These are best served slightly warm and reheat nicely.

4⅓ cups Basic Blend (page 17)

¼ cup sugar

1 tablespoon instant active or active dry yeast

2 teaspoons xanthan gum

1½ teaspoons salt

4 large eggs, at room temperature

⅞ cup warm milk, soy milk, or rice milk

¾ pound (3 sticks) unsalted butter or non-dairy buttery spread, softened and cut into pieces

1 large egg, lightly beaten with 1 tablespoon water for egg wash

Apple-Raisin Brioche

▶ In a medium saucepan, cook the apples, butter, cinnamon, sugar, and currants until the apples are soft. Prepare the dough as directed. Oil a large brioche pan and place half of the dough into the pan. Cover with the apple mixture, top with the remaining dough, and smooth. Allow the dough to rise in a warm environment until it reaches the top of the pan.

▶ Preheat the oven to 375°F. Brush with the egg wash. Bake 30 to 35 minutes, until a toothpick inserted in the center comes out clean.

1 large apple, peeled and chopped

1 tablespoon butter

2 teaspoons ground cinnamon

2 tablespoons sugar

½ cup currants or golden raisins

½ recipe Brioche dough (page 38)

1 large egg, lightly beaten with 1 tablespoon water for egg wash

Challah Bread

Dairy-free

MAKES ONE 9-INCH ROUND LOAF

This beautiful round bread is traditionally used to celebrate the Jewish holidays. However, you can enjoy this delicious loaf anytime of the year. It makes great toast and sandwich bread as well as French toast. The texture is so wonderful that I often have to check to make sure someone hasn't brought a gluten-filled bread into my house.

▶ Lightly oil a 9-inch springform pan.

▶ Combine the flour blend and yeast in the bowl of a stand mixer. In a separate bowl, combine the 4 eggs and 1 yolk, the olive oil, and water. Add to the dry ingredients. Using the paddle or beater attachment, beat on low speed for 1 minute to blend. Beat on medium-high speed for 3 minutes, or until the mixture is smooth and slightly shiny.

▶ Scrape the dough into the prepared pan. Cover with a sheet of plastic wrap that has been sprayed with PAM. Let rise in a warm place until the dough has reached the top of the pan.

▶ Preheat the oven to 375°F. Set the pan on a cookie sheet. Brush with the egg wash and sprinkle with sesame seeds if using. Bake for 40 to 45 minutes, until the top is golden and a cake tester inserted nearly to the bottom of the bread comes out without sticky crumbs. If the top browns before the center is cooked, cover loosely with aluminum foil for remainder of the baking time.

▶ Remove from the oven and set on a wire rack to cool completely without removing the side of the pan. When cool, remove the side, slice the bread, and serve.

▶ Leftover challah may be frozen.

5¾ cups Bread Flour #2 (page 15)

4 teaspoons instant active or active dry yeast

4 large eggs plus 1 yolk

5 tablespoons olive oil

1¾ cups warm water (105° to 110°F)

1 large egg, lightly beaten with 1 tablespoon water for egg wash

Sesame seeds or poppy seeds, optional

Shortcut:

▶ Make several batches of Bread Flour #2 and parcel 5¾ cups of the blend into individual zip-top bags. Label the contents and note the additional ingredients needed to make this recipe. It puts you that much closer to freshly baked challah when you want it.

Croissants

MAKES 18 TO 24 CROISSANTS

These delectable crescents transport me back to my gluten-filled days of sitting in cafés in Paris. The flaky outer layers coupled with soft yeasty interior brings back memories of those croissants of yesteryear. While this is not a true puff pastry with all the traditional "turns," it is very close. Next stop—Paris!

▶ Combine the flour blend and xanthan gum in a large bowl. Scoop 1 cup of the flour mixture into a medium mixing bowl. Add the yeast and sugar and blend thoroughly. Combine the milk and eggs in a separate bowl and add to the dry ingredients. Add the melted butter and beat until smooth. Set aside.

▶ Using a mixer or food processor, cut the cold butter into the remaining flour mixture until the butter pieces are the size of large peas. Pour the liquid batter into the flour mixture and stir or beat until moistened throughout. Scrape the dough into a bowl large enough to allow for doubling in size. Cover and refrigerate for 4 hours or overnight.

▶ Remove the dough from the refrigerator and divide into three equal parts. Wrap two pieces in plastic wrap and refrigerate. Roll the third piece into a 12-inch circle. Cut into six or eight pie-shaped wedges. Brush with jam and sprinkle with chocolate chips and nuts, if using. Roll the wedge toward the point. Shape into a crescent by curving the edges away from you. Set on a baking sheet lined with parchment paper. Repeat with the remaining pieces of dough. Cover with plastic wrap and let rise at room temperature until doubled. (This may take 1 to 2 hours if the room is cool.)

▶ Preheat the oven to 400°F. Brush each croissant with egg wash. Place the croissants in the oven and immediately lower the temperature to 350°F. Bake for 15 to 20 minutes, until golden.

4 cups Bread Flour #1 (page 15)

1½ teaspoons xanthan gum

4 teaspoons instant active or active dry yeast

⅓ cup sugar

1 cup warm milk, soy milk, or water (105° to 110°F)

2 large eggs

4 tablespoons (½ stick) unsalted butter or non-dairy buttery spread, melted

12 tablespoons cold unsalted butter or vegetable shortening, cut into small pieces

1 large egg, lightly beaten with 1 tablespoon water for egg wash

Optional Filling

½ cup seedless raspberry jam, softened briefly in microwave

½ cup mini chocolate chips

½ cup chopped pecans or walnuts

Tips: If using a non-dairy butter spread, cut and freeze for 15 minutes before using.

Avoid pressing or kneading the dough with your hands as this will soften the butter. Cold butter produces a flakier, lighter crust.

Delicious Slicing Bread

MAKES 1 LOAF

This all-purpose bread makes great sandwiches and toast and is the basis for the Apple Caramel Monkey Bread on page 33. It was inspired out of necessity, for who among us doesn't need a great sandwich bread? This is a staple in my kitchen.

- ▶ Spray an 8½ x 4½-inch or 9 x 5-inch loaf pan with vegetable spray.
- ▶ In the bowl of a heavy-duty mixer, add the flour blend, milk powder, brown sugar, and yeast and mix to combine. Mix together the water, eggs, and vegetable oil in a separate bowl. Add to the dry ingredients. Beat on low for 1 minute. Beat on medium-high speed for 3 minutes or until the mixture is smooth, shiny, and has thickened.
- ▶ Scrape the dough into the prepared pan. Cover with lightly oiled plastic wrap and set in a warm, draft-free area until the dough rises to the top of the pan.
- ▶ Preheat the oven to 375°F. Remove the plastic wrap and bake on the middle rack for 40 to 45 minutes, until the top sounds hollow when tapped and the internal temperature reads 190° to 200°F.
- ▶ Remove and turn out onto a wire rack. Cool completely before slicing.

Bread Machine Preparation:

- ▶ Combine the eggs, water, and vegetable oil and pour into the bread pan. Combine the flour blend and milk powder. Spoon over the wet ingredients. Sprinkle the yeast over the top. Follow the instructions of the machine for proper setting or pick a setting that allows for one knead and rise cycle and a 50 minute bake time.

3⅓ cups Bread Flour #1 (page 15)

½ cup non-fat dry milk powder (see Pantry, page 275), or milk substitute

½ cup lightly packed light brown sugar

2¼ teaspoons instant active or active dry yeast

1½ cups plus 2 tablespoons water (105° to 110°F)

2 large eggs

¼ cup vegetable oil

Avoiding Dairy?
Use Vance's DariFree or powdered soy milk in place of powdered milk (see Simple Substitutions, page 265).

Flaxseed Bread

Dairy-free

MAKES 1 LOAF

A former restaurateur with a classical culinary background and a great deal of curiosity, my friend Priscilla Martel has a better understanding of gluten-free baking than most gluten-free people I know. As such, she made sure that the fine professional baking tome, *On Baking*, contained a representation of gluten-free recipes. This one is adapted, with permission, from her book.*

- ▶ Lightly oil a 9 x 5-inch loaf pan.
- ▶ Combine the rice flour, tapioca starch/flour, flaxseed meal, xanthan gum, sugar, and salt in the bowl of a mixer fitted with the paddle attachment. In a separate bowl, whisk the egg with the oil, milk, and yeast. Add the mixture to the dry ingredients and beat on low speed for 1 minute, or until blended. Add the vinegar and beat on medium speed for 4 minutes.
- ▶ Scrape the dough into the prepared pan. Coat a rubber spatula or a sheet of plastic wrap with vegetable spray and smooth the top. Cover with oiled plastic wrap and set in a warm, draft-free area to rise to the top of the pan.
- ▶ Preheat the oven to 375°F. Remove the plastic wrap and bake 60 to 70 minutes, until an instant-read thermometer inserted in the center reads 190°F to 200°F. Let cool in the pan for 15 minutes, then turn onto a wire rack to cool completely. Slice and freeze any portion not used within three days.

*Recipe credit: Adapted with permission from Sarah R. Labensky, Eddy Van Damme, and Priscilla Martel, *On Baking: A Textbook of Baking and Pastry Fundamentals,* second edition (Prentice Hall: 2008).

1½ cups rice flour

1½ cups tapioca starch/flour

½ cup plus 2 tablespoons flaxseed meal

3 teaspoons xanthan gum

2 tablespoons sugar

1½ teaspoons salt

1 large egg

3 tablespoons olive oil

1½ cups warm milk or water (105° to 110°F)

4½ teaspoons instant active or active dry yeast

1 teaspoon cider vinegar

French Baguettes

Dairy-free

MAKES 2 OR 3 BAGUETTES

This dense, chewy bread is nutritious thanks to the addition of potato and chickpea flour. It was the culmination of a brainstorming session with fellow chef, Rebecca Reilly, who said she needed baguettes. "Who doesn't?" I said. These are great for rolls and bread sticks, too. Enjoy as is or slice and use for bruschetta. For a simple, yummy appetizer, top slices with a mixture of chopped pepperoni and grated cheese and broil until the cheese melts.

- ► Combine the flours, xanthan gum, and yeast in the bowl of a mixer. In a separate bowl, combine the water, eggs, olive oil, and vinegar. Add to the dry ingredients. Using a stand mixer or heavy-duty handheld mixer, beat at medium-high speed for 5 minutes, or until the mixture is smooth and thick. Add additional water, 1 tablespoon at a time, if necessary to achieve this consistency.

- ► Line a double or triple baguette form with aluminum foil. Spray with vegetable spray or lightly oil and sprinkle cornmeal over the surface. Spread half or one-third of the dough over each form. Lightly oil a sheet of plastic wrap and smooth and form the baguettes. Cover with lightly oiled plastic wrap and let rise 20 to 30 minutes in a draft-free space.

- ► Preheat the oven to 400°F.

- ► Brush the risen dough with the beaten egg, if using. Using a sharp knife, cut shallow slits diagonally on the surface of each baguette. Bake 25 to 30 minutes. Turn onto a wire rack and cool before slicing.

- ► To make hamburger rolls or bread sticks, just scoop this dough into bun pans, muffin top forms, or bread stick pans. Smooth the surface with lightly oiled plastic wrap. Let rise and bake. For bread sticks, bake 15 to 20 minutes; for rolls bake 20 to 25 minutes.

2¾ cups Bread Flour #1 (page 15)

½ cup chickpea flour

¼ cup potato flour

1 teaspoon xanthan gum

2 packages instant active or active dry yeast (4½ teaspoons)

1½ cups warm water (105° to 110°F)

3 large eggs, at room temperature, or flax gel

3 tablespoons olive oil

1 teaspoon cider vinegar

1 large egg, beaten for egg wash, optional

Tip: For a crispier crust, remove the baked baguettes from the pan and set on a rack in the oven. Bake for an additional 5 minutes.

Grandma's Babka

MAKES 2 LOAVES

Grandma's Babka might be redundant as babka means grandmother in Polish, probably because the traditional shape of this slightly sweet Easter bread is reminiscent of an old woman's wide full skirt. As I made over this Ukrainian version, I was reminded that gluten-free flour does not absorb liquids the same way that gluten-filled flour does. The original formula called for 4½ cups of milk, which produced a very wet dough that sank the minute I took it out of the oven. I cut back to 1¾ cups milk and now it is every bit as good as the babka my grandma made.

- ▶ Lightly oil two 6-cup brioche pans or two 8-inch springform pans.
- ▶ Combine the flour blend, lemon zest, and yeast in a bowl and mix well with a wire whisk; set aside.
- ▶ Place the sugar, egg, and egg yolks in the bowl of a stand mixer or a large mixing bowl. Using the paddle attachment or a heavy-duty handheld mixer, mix until the mixture has thickened and becomes pale yellow. Add 2 cups of the flour mixture and half the milk and beat to incorporate. Add the remaining flour mixture and the remaining milk and beat briefly. Add the butter and brandy and mix on low to blend. Increase the speed to medium and beat for 2 to 3 minutes, until the dough is smooth and thick. Fold in the raisins.
- ▶ Spoon the dough into the prepared pans. Smooth the top with a spatula and cover with lightly oiled plastic wrap. Let rise in a warm, draft-free area until doubled in size (up to 1 hour).
- ▶ Preheat the oven to 200°F. Remove the plastic wrap. Set the pans in the oven for 10 minutes to finish rising. Remove and brush the tops with the egg wash.
- ▶ Increase the oven temperature to 325°F. Bake 50 to 55 minutes, until a toothpick inserted in the center comes out clean or an instant-read thermometer registers 190°F. Cool in the pans for 15 minutes, and then turn onto a wire rack and cool.

5¼ cups Bread Flour #2 (page 15)

2 tablespoons lemon zest or 1 tablespoon dried lemon peel

4 teaspoons instant active or active dry yeast

½ cup sugar

1 large egg

4 large egg yolks

1¾ cups very warm milk, soy milk, or rice milk (about 110°F)

8 tablespoons (1 stick) unsalted butter or non-dairy buttery spread, melted

2 tablespoons brandy or milk

¾ cup golden raisins

1 large egg, beaten for egg wash

Oatmeal Bread with Sunflower and Pumpkin Seeds

Dairy-free

MAKES 1 LARGE LOAF OR 16 TO 18 SLICES

I have a passion for chewy, crusty bread and it's not often I find such a creature in the gluten-free world. This bread meets all the requirements and it's delicious to boot. Leaving the bread to cool down in the oven creates a wonderfully crusty exterior. If you prefer a softer crust, remove the baked bread and turn onto a wire rack to cool on the counter. I don't recommend making this in a bread machine.

- ▸ Coat an 8½ x 4½-inch loaf pan with vegetable spray or oil.
- ▸ In the bowl of a stand mixer, combine the bread flour, oat flour, and cream of tartar. Whisk to combine. Add the yeast and blend. In a separate bowl, combine the water, eggs, oil, and molasses. Add the liquid ingredients to the dry ingredients and blend on medium speed for 1 minute. Scrape down the sides of the bowl and the beater. Beat on medium-high speed for 3 to 5 minutes or until the mixture is smooth. Fold the pumpkin and sunflower seeds into the batter.
- ▸ Scrape the dough into the prepared loaf pan. Coat a sheet of plastic wrap with vegetable spray. Smooth the top of the bread and cover with the plastic wrap. Set in a draft-free area and let rise until the dough comes up to the top of the pan.

2¾ cups Bread Flour #2 (page 15)

¾ cup gluten-free oat flour

½ teaspoon cream of tartar

1 tablespoon instant active or active dry yeast

1 cup plus 6 tablespoons warm water (105° to 110°F)

3 large eggs

3 tablespoons vegetable oil

3 tablespoons dark molasses

3 tablespoons raw pumpkin seeds

2 tablespoons raw sunflower seeds

continues

continued

▶ Preheat the oven to 350°F. Remove the plastic wrap and bake 50 to 55 minutes, until the internal temperature on an instant-read thermometer registers 190° to 200°F. Remove the bread from the pan and set on a rack in the middle of the oven. Turn off the oven and leave the bread in it until it cools completely. Remove and slice.

Tips: *This recipe makes terrific rolls, too. Just scoop the dough into muffin top pans or muffin cups. Let rise for 40 minutes and then bake for 25 to 30 minutes, until the internal temperature on an instant-read thermometer registers 190° to 200°F. For a professional look, brush with egg wash or milk of choice and sprinkle with oat flakes or pumpkin seeds before baking.*

The bread can also be made using a handheld mixer. Just be sure it's a heavy-duty mixer (200 to 250 watts). Krups and KitchenAid both make them.

Don't have oat flour? Process gluten-free oats in a spice mill until finely ground. Measure out ¾ cup.

Parker House Rolls

This was inspired by a bread recipe from gluten-free bloggers, Vic and Hallie Dolcourt, and a photo of Parker House rolls in a *King Arthur Flour's Baker's Catalogue*. I made a few changes to Vic and Hallie's recipe and came up with these beautiful pull-apart rolls, the kind my mother served warm with pats of butter melting over their majestic crowns.

▶ Lightly oil eighteen muffin cups.

▶ Mix the bread flour, powdered milk, Expandex, potato flour, sugar, xanthan gum, salt, baking powder, and yeast in a large bowl. Combine the water, egg whites, vinegar, and honey in the work bowl of a mixer fitted with the paddle attachment. Add the dry ingredients 1 cup at a time while mixing on low speed. Allow the dough to rest for 10 minutes in the bowl. Add the melted butter and egg yolks. Mix on medium-high speed until blended, about 3 to 4 minutes, scraping down the sides halfway through mixing.

▶ Scoop out bits of dough and roll into balls about 1-inch in diameter in oiled plastic wrap. Place three balls in each muffin cup. Cover and let rise.

▶ Preheat the oven to 375°F. Brush the tops of the rolls with egg wash and sprinkle with poppy seeds or sesame seeds, if desired. Bake for 15 to 20 minutes, until an instant-read thermometer inserted into a roll reads 190° to 200°F. Turn onto a cooling rack and let cool for 10 minutes before serving. (If the tops of the rolls become too dark while baking, reduce the oven temperature to 350° or cover loosely with aluminum foil.)

▶ Store at room temperature for one to two days or freeze. To reheat, wrap in aluminum foil and heat in a 350°F oven. Thaw frozen rolls before reheating.

3¾ cups Bread Flour #2 (page 15)

⅓ cup dry powdered milk or Vance's DariFree (see Simple Substitutions, page 265)

¼ cup Expandex or sweet rice flour

¼ cup potato flour

¼ cup sugar

3 teaspoons xanthan gum

1½ teaspoons kosher salt

1½ teaspoons baking powder

1 tablespoon instant active or active dry yeast

1 cup warm water (105° to 110°F)

4 large eggs, separated

1 teaspoon cider vinegar

3 tablespoons honey

⅓ cup unsalted butter or non-dairy buttery spread, melted in microwave for 30 seconds

1 large egg, beaten with 2 tablespoons water for egg wash

Poppy seeds or sesame seeds, optional

Tip: A heavy-duty, handheld mixer may be used to prepare these.

Pablo's Cinnabon-Style Cinnamon Rolls

MAKES 12 ROLLS

My friend Andrea and I tried several versions of this recipe before we found one that her son, Pablo, approved. It's easiest to prepare this using a heavy-duty mixer, preferably a stand mixer. But I've made them both ways. Make sure all of the ingredients are at room temperature, except for the milk which you will need to warm.

- ▶ Lightly coat a 9-inch round cake pan with cooking spray.
- ▶ Mix together 1⅞ cups of the flour blend, the potato flour, sugar, and yeast in a large mixing bowl. Combine the eggs, vinegar, and vanilla in a separate bowl. Add the softened butter to the dry ingredients and beat briefly. Add the milk and egg mixture to the flour and beat 30 seconds to incorporate. Beat on high speed for 3 minutes.
- ▶ Make the filling: Combine the brown sugar and cinnamon together in a small bowl; set aside.
- ▶ Sprinkle the remaining flour blend over a wooden board. Use a spatula to remove the dough to the wooden board and form into a ball. Roll the dough in the flour until it is lightly covered. Gently press and roll into a 14 x 8-inch rectangle, about ⅛ inch thick. Lightly brush the surface with melted butter. Sprinkle the filling evenly over the surface.
- ▶ Starting with one long side, carefully roll up the dough jelly-roll fashion. With the seam side down, use a small, sharp knife to cut the dough crosswise into 12 slices. (Don't worry if slices seem loosely rolled.) Arrange the slices cut side up in the prepared cake pan, leaving space between each one. Cover with plastic wrap and let rise in a warm place

1⅞ cups plus 1 to 2 tablespoons Bread Flour #1 (page 15)

2 tablespoons potato flour

¼ cup sugar

1 tablespoon instant active or active dry yeast

2 large eggs, at room temperature

1 teaspoon cider vinegar

1 teaspoon vanilla extract

6 tablespoons unsalted butter or non-dairy buttery spread, softened and cut into chunks

1 cup warm 2% or low-fat milk, soy milk, or water (105° to 110°F)

1 tablespoon unsalted butter or non-dairy buttery spread, melted

Filling

⅓ cup packed brown sugar

¾ teaspoon ground cinnamon

Glaze

¾ cup confectioners' sugar

1 to 2 tablespoons milk, soy milk, or water

½ teaspoon vanilla extract

continues

continued

until the rolls have doubled in size and have filled the pan. This may take up to 80 minutes. Use a home-made proofer (page 32) to speed up this process.

▶ Make the glaze: Combine the confectioner's sugar, milk, and vanilla in a small bowl and stir until smooth and creamy. Set aside.

▶ Preheat the oven to 375°F. Position the rack in the center of the oven. Remove the plastic wrap and bake about 20 minutes, or until light golden and cooked through. Let cool 5 minutes, then spoon the glaze over the top of the rolls and serve. The cinna-mon rolls can be frozen. Thaw and reheat briefly in the microwave or oven.

Peasant Pumpernickel with Raisins and Walnuts

MAKES ONE 2-POUND LOAF

This hearty bread is nearly a meal in itself. Full of raisins and caraway seeds, and walnuts, it begs for a smear of cream cheese and a dollop of orange marmalade. The smell is as enticing as the taste so be sure to leave time for breakfast before you heat up the toaster.

▶ Lightly oil a 9 x 5-inch pan.
▶ Combine the flour blend, powdered milk, brown sugar, cornmeal, caraway seeds, if using, and orange peel in a large mixing bowl. In a separate bowl, combine the water, eggs, oil, molasses, and vinegar. Add the wet ingredients and the yeast to the dry ingredients. Beat on medium speed for 5 minutes, or until the dough is smooth. Add the raisins and walnuts, if using, and beat another minute or until blended.
▶ Transfer the dough to the prepared pan and smooth the surface. Cover with oiled plastic and let the dough rise nearly to the top of the pan.
▶ Preheat the oven to 375°F. Bake for 45 to 55 minutes, until the bread sounds hollow when tapped.
▶ Turn onto a wire rack to cool.

Bread Machine Method:

▶ Add the dry ingredients, yeast, and liquids, according to the manufacturer's instructions. Set the machine for quick cycle, white bread, or programmable cycle. After the dough has reached a smooth consistency, about 5 minutes into knead cycle, add the raisins and walnuts. Remove the loaf when the bake cycle ends and cool on a wire rack.

3 cups plus 3 tablespoons Bread Flour #1 (page 15)

⅞ cup dry powdered milk (not milk buds) or Vance's DariFree (see Simple Substitutions, page 265)

¼ cup lightly packed brown sugar

3 tablespoons cornmeal

3 teaspoons caraway seed, optional

2 teaspoons grated orange peel

1½ cups warm water (105° to 110°F)

3 large eggs, lightly beaten

⅓ cup vegetable oil

2 tablespoons molasses or honey

1 teaspoon cider vinegar

2½ teaspoons instant active or active dry yeast

½ cup dark raisins

½ cup coarsely chopped walnuts, optional

Perfect Popovers

MAKES 6 POPOVERS

Crunchy on the outside and airy on the inside, preparation of these delicate treats is simple. The trick is in the baking. I have the best luck using popover pans. Fill the cups two-thirds full and place the pan in a very hot oven. Don't be tempted to open the oven while they bake or these finicky devils might collapse. They are worth a little patience.

▸ Butter six popover tins. Preheat the oven to 450°F.

▸ In a medium mixing bowl, blend the basic blend, chickpea flour, xanthan gum, and salt. Set aside. Heat the milk and 1 tablespoon butter in the microwave until the butter melts, about 60 to 90 seconds. Add the eggs to the milk, whisking to blend. If the milk is very hot, let cool before adding the eggs or they will begin to cook in the mixture. Add the milk mixture to the dry ingredients and whisk until smooth. Let sit at room temperature for 30 minutes.

▸ Fill each popover tin two-thirds of the way with batter. Bake for 15 minutes. Reduce the temperature to 350°F and bake an additional 20 minutes, or until nicely browned. Resist the temptation to open the oven door while these bake or they will collapse.

▸ Turn out onto a wire rack to cool. Pierce the side of each with a sharp knife to release steam. This keeps the inside moist and the outside crisp. Serve warm.

▸ These cannot be frozen, but leftovers can be stored in a plastic bag at room temperature for up to three days. Warm in a 350°F oven for 5 minutes.

VARIATION: Add 2 to 3 tablespoons grated Parmesan cheese or fold in 2 teaspoons grated orange peel and 2 tablespoons ground pecans.

¾ cup Basic Blend (page 17)

¼ cup chickpea flour or other high protein flour

½ teaspoon xanthan gum

½ teaspoon salt

1¼ cups milk, soy milk, or rice milk

1 tablespoon unsalted butter or non-dairy buttery spread

2 large eggs, beaten

Tip: Heavy metal non-stick popover pans work best. Large muffin tins can be used but shape will be squat. Do not use glass cups.

Plymouth Bread

(Orange, Corn, and Molasses Bread)

MAKES ONE 2-POUND LOAF

This bread is reminiscent of the Anadama (corn and molasses) bread I ate as a child. The texture is similar but the orange peel gives it a grown-up twist.

- Lightly oil a 9 x 5-inch pan.
- Combine the flour blend, powdered milk, cornmeal, brown sugar, and orange peel in a large mixing bowl. Combine the water, eggs, oil, molasses, and vinegar in a separate bowl. Add the liquids and the yeast to the dry ingredients. Beat for 5 minutes, or until the dough is smooth.
- Transfer the dough to the prepared pan and smooth the surface. Cover with oiled plastic and let the dough rise nearly to the top of the pan.
- Preheat oven to 375°F. Bake 45 to 55 minutes, until the bread sounds hollow when tapped. Turn onto a wire rack to cool.

Bread Machine Method:

- Add dry ingredients, yeast, and the liquids, according to the manufacturer's instructions. Set the machine for quick cycle, white bread, or programmable cycle. Use a lightly oiled spatula to smooth the top after the knead cycle has finished. Remove the loaf when the bake cycle ends and cool on a wire rack.

Avoiding Corn? Replace ⅔ cup cornmeal with ⅓ cup rice bran and ⅓ cup brown rice flour.

3 cups Bread Flour #1 (page 15)
⅞ cup dry powdered milk or Vance's DariFree (see Simple Substitutions, page 265)
⅔ cup cornmeal
¼ cup lightly packed brown sugar
2 teaspoons grated orange peel
1½ cups warm water (105° to 110°F)
3 large eggs, lightly beaten
5 tablespoons vegetable oil
2 tablespoons molasses or honey
1 teaspoon cider vinegar
2½ teaspoons instant active or active dry yeast

Quinoa Sesame "Wonder" Bread

Dairy-free

MAKES 1 LARGE LOAF

This is the lightest gluten-free bread I have ever eaten. The texture reminds me of Wonder Bread, while the sesame seeds add a bit of a gourmet flare. Using quinoa flour is a bonus; instead of that empty carb-load, this bread is packed with nutrients.

- ▶ Lightly oil a 9 x 5-inch loaf pan.
- ▶ Heat a skillet over medium heat. Add the sesame seeds and stir until they begin to brown. Remove from the heat and cool.
- ▶ In a large mixing bowl, combine the sesame seeds, quinoa flour, cornstarch, tapioca starch/flour, brown sugar, xanthan gum, and salt. In a separate bowl, combine the eggs, water, and oil. Add the liquids and the yeast to the dry ingredients and beat for 2 to 3 minutes on medium speed until the mixture is smooth. The dough will be thick.
- ▶ Scrape into the prepared pan, using a lightly oiled spatula to smooth the top. Cover with oiled plastic wrap and let rise to the top of the pan, about 40 to 60 minutes.
- ▶ Preheat the oven to 350°F. Bake for 40 to 45 minutes. Turn onto a wire rack and cool completely before slicing.
- ▶ Slice and freeze any remaining bread after two days.

1 to 2 tablespoon sesame seeds

1⅛ cups quinoa flour

1 cup cornstarch

1 cup plus 1 tablespoon tapioca starch/flour

3 tablespoons brown sugar

3½ teaspoons xanthan or guar gum

1½ teaspoons salt

3 large eggs, lightly beaten

1⅛ cups warm water (105° to 110°F)

3 tablespoons olive or vegetable oil

2¼ teaspoons instant active or active dry yeast

continues

continued

Bread Machine Method (1½ to 2 pound capacity):

▶ In a large bowl, combine the sesame seeds with the dry ingredients, except for the yeast. Combine the wet ingredients in separate bowl. In the baking pan, add the dry ingredients, wet ingredients, and yeast in the order recommended for your machine. Set the machine for quick cycle, white bread, or programmable cycle. If the machine can be programmed, omit one knead and one rise cycle. If necessary, use a rubber spatula to assist the mixing during the kneading cycle. Use a lightly oiled spatula to smooth top after the knead cycle has finished. Remove the loaf when the bake cycle ends. Turn onto a wire rack and cool completely before slicing.

Yeast-Free, Egg-Free Whole Grain Bread

MAKES ONE 8-INCH LOAF

This bread is full of fiber and nutrients. Egg-free and yeast-free make it a plus for those who want a chewy, wholesome bread, but can't usually have it. The addition of flax meal and applesauce helps avoid dryness and creates a nice crumb. This was compiled from several recipes that had been sent my way over the years. Although I can have eggs and yeast, I prefer this bread, too.

▶ Preheat the oven to 400°F. Lightly oil a 9-inch springform or round cake pan.

▶ In a large mixing bowl, whisk together the flour blend, millet flour, flax meal, brown sugar, and sunflower seeds. In a separate bowl, combine the milk, applesauce, oil, and vinegar. Stir in the baking soda and then add to the flour mixture. Mix the batter with a fork, just until blended; the dough will be stiff.

▶ Coat your fingers with oil and form the dough into a ball, kneading it in your hands. Place in the center of the prepared baking pan and pat into a smooth 8-inch round disk that is 1½ to 2 inches high at the edges and mounded slightly in the center. Brush with oil or milk and press additional sunflower seeds into the top. Use a sharp knife to cut a deep "X" in the top of the dough.

▶ Place in the oven. Immediately reduce the temperature to 350°F. Bake for 55 to 60 minutes. Insert a knife in the center of the loaf to test for doneness. Return to the oven to bake for another 5 to 10 minutes if necessary. The loaf can also be cut into wedges and returned to the oven to finish baking. Remove from the oven and turn onto a wire rack to cool.

▶ For best results, slice and freeze individual pieces. To serve, defrost in the microwave, then toast.

2¼ cups Self-Rising Flour (page 16)

¾ cup millet or buckwheat flour

¼ cup ground flax meal

¼ cup packed light brown sugar

3 tablespoons sunflower seeds, plus additional for the topping

⅞ cup warm milk, soy milk, or rice milk

⅓ cup unsweetened applesauce

¼ cup canola or other vegetable oil

2 teaspoons cider vinegar

1½ teaspoons baking soda

Brick Oven-Style Pizza

MAKES SIX 6- TO 8-INCH THIN PIZZAS OR TWO 12-INCH TRADITIONAL PIZZAS

For best results, slice the toppings very thin so that they will cook in a short amount of time. This can also be made as a traditional pizza using a 12-inch round pizza pan and adding pizza sauce and cheese. Use this pizza recipe to make Antipasto Squares on page 95.

- Preheat a flat griddle to medium-high heat (about 425°F) or preheat an oven to 425°F.
- Combine the flour blend, xanthan gum, salt, and yeast in a large bowl. Add the water, egg, oil, and vinegar and beat for 2 to 3 minutes, until the mixture is smooth and well combined.
- Tear off 12-inch squares of aluminum foil and brush the surface of each with olive oil. Scoop out about ½ cup of the mixture onto the center of each piece of foil. Spray a sheet of plastic wrap with vegetable spray and cover the dough. Press or roll each ball of dough into a very thin circle (less than ⅛ inch thick).
- Remove the plastic wrap. Brush the griddle with more olive oil. For each pizza, flip the dough over onto the griddle surface, leaving the aluminum foil on top of the dough. After 2 minutes, remove the foil and continue baking another 3 minutes. Flip the pizza and quickly top with a small amount of pizza sauce, if using, your favorite toppings, and cheese. Let cook until the cheese melts, about 3 to 4 minutes. Remove to a plate and enjoy.
- Alternatively, preheat a cookie sheet on the lowest rack of the oven. Brush with olive oil and flip the prepared dough onto the hot cookie sheet. Follow the same procedure as above.

3 cups Bread Flour #1 (page 15)

1½ teaspoons xanthan gum

½ teaspoon salt

4 teaspoons instant active or active dry yeast

1⅓ cups warm water (105° to 110°F)

1 large egg, beaten

2 tablespoons extra virgin olive oil

½ teaspoon cider vinegar

Your favorite pizza toppings

continues

continued

Gas Grill Method:

▶ Preheat the grill on high. Brush the grates with olive oil and flip the pizza dough onto the grill, leaving the aluminum foil on top of the dough. Close the grill and grill for 3 minutes. Carefully remove the aluminum foil, flip the pizza over, and add your toppings. Cover the grill and grill for 3 to 5 minutes. Remove with a long-handled spatula and serve hot.

Tips: Use a small amount of pizza sauce, if any. (I prefer white pizza with cheese and thin slices of prosciutto and tomato.) All of the toppings should be cut very thin so they will cook in a short time.

Have all the toppings ready to go before baking the pizza so that you can work quickly.

Aluminum foil will easily peel off from the baking pizza when the dough has "set." If it does not come off easily, wait another minute and try again.

Freezing the dough: Roll the dough into personal pizza-size rounds, freeze them (unbaked) on a cookie sheet, and then store in a zip-top bag in the freezer. Remove one at a time and set on a sheet of oiled aluminum foil. Top with sauce and cheese and bake 12 to 15 minutes in a 425°F oven.

Fabulous Focaccia

MAKES 8 SERVINGS

This yummy focaccia recipe comes from Elise Wiggins, Executive Chef at Panzano in downtown Denver where she serves this to fellow wheat- and gluten-free people. The basic recipe is hers. The variation is mine. Either way, you are in for a treat.

- Lightly brush a 9 x 13-inch pan with olive oil.
- In the bowl of a stand mixer, combine the flours, xanthan gum, salt, and yeast. Using the paddle attachment or using a heavy-duty, handheld mixer, beat briefly to blend. Combine the water, eggs, and oil and add to the dry ingredients. Beat on medium speed for 10 minutes.
- Press the dough into the prepared pan. Let rise in a warm, draft-free area for 30 minutes.
- Preheat the oven to 425°F. Brush the top of the dough with olive oil and sprinkle with the Parmesan cheese. Bake for 20 to 25 minutes. Cut the focaccia into strips and serve warm.
- For the herb oil, combine ¼ cup olive oil with a blend of fresh or dried herbs (oregano, rosemary, thyme) and crushed garlic to taste.

2½ cups Basic Blend (page 17)

½ cup potato flour

1 tablespoon xanthan gum

1½ teaspoons salt

4½ teaspoons instant active or active dry yeast

1¼ cups warm water (105° to 110°F)

4 large eggs

¼ cup herb oil (see below) or olive oil

¼ cup Parmesan cheese

VARIATION:

Pizza Sticks

- After beating the focaccia dough for 10 minutes, fold in the mozzarella cheese, pepperoni, and herb blend, if using.
- Bake and cut into strips as above.

½ cup grated mozzarella cheese

½ cup chopped pepperoni or turkey pepperoni

2 teaspoons Italian herb blend, unless herb oil has already been added

Grilled Scallion Bread

(Asian Pizza)

Dairy-free

MAKES 6 SERVINGS

These Asian flatbreads are great with salad or part of a stir-fry menu. After devouring half of these alone, my friend Mikey (age 11) noted that they would make great individual pizzas. He's right. Simply omit the scallions, salt, and sesame oil. Brush with olive oil, bake, then add toppings, or store in the freezer and use as needed.

▶ Line three baking sheets with parchment paper; set aside.

▶ Combine the flours, cornstarch, xanthan gum, sugar, and yeast in the bowl of a food processor fitted with a steel knife. With the motor running, add 1 cup plus 3 tablespoons of the water in a slow stream. Add the eggs one at a time. Add the remaining 1 to 2 tablespoons of water, a little at a time, until the dough forms a smooth ball. Turn onto a surface lightly dusted with rice flour and knead 2 to 3 minutes. If the dough is too sticky, knead on a sheet of plastic wrap that has been sprayed with vegetable spray. Pat into a ball and flatten slightly. Cut into six equal pieces.

▶ Lightly oil a sheet of plastic wrap. Place one piece of the dough into the center of the plastic wrap. Roll into a 6-inch round. Turn onto one of the prepared baking sheets. Combine the oil, scallions, and salt in a small bowl and press some of the mixture into the surface of the dough. Cover with another sheet of oiled plastic and roll to smooth the surface. Repeat with the remaining dough rounds. Let the dough rise for 1 hour in a very warm place.

▶ Preheat oven to 350°F. Brush the bread with sesame oil and sprinkle with sesame seeds. Bake 25 to 30 minutes, until golden brown.

▶ These freeze nicely. Reheat in a single layer in a 350°F oven for 5 minutes.

2½ cups white rice flour, more for kneading dough

½ cup tapioca starch/flour

½ cup cornstarch or potato starch

3½ teaspoons xanthan or guar gum

¼ cup sugar

3 teaspoons instant active or active dry yeast

1 cup plus 5 tablespoons warm water

2 large eggs

3 tablespoons olive oil

½ cup finely chopped scallions

1 teaspoon coarse salt

¼ cup sesame oil for brushing

2 tablespoons sesame seeds

Wraps-ody in Gluten-Free Harmony

Dairy-free

MAKES 12 SERVINGS

A version of this recipe first appeared in my "Perils in the Pantry" column in the magazine *Living Without* several years ago. It makes delicious, pliable wraps that can also be used for roll-ups and flatbreads. The wraps will keep for two days in a plastic bag and remain soft and pliable. They may be eaten at room temperature or warmed slightly. These wraps are reminiscent of the wheat-filled Indian flatbread, roti and chapati. They freeze well.

3 cups Bread Flour #1 (page 15)

½ cup chickpea or other high protein flour

2¼ teaspoons instant active or active dry yeast

1 cup plus 3 tablespoons warm water

3 large eggs, or flax gel (see Simple Substitutions, page 268)

¼ cup vegetable oil or olive oil

3 tablespoons honey

▶ Mix together the flour blend, chickpea flour, and yeast in a large mixing bowl. Combine the water, eggs, oil, and honey in a separate bowl and add to the dry ingredients. Beat until smooth.

▶ Coat the surface of a piece of aluminum foil with vegetable spray. Scoop about ¼ cup of dough onto the center of the foil. Cover with a piece of oiled plastic wrap and press into a thin circle of dough without creating holes in the dough.

▶ Lightly oil the surface of a griddle or skillet and pre-heat on medium heat for 2 minutes. Remove the plastic from the dough and flip onto the center of the griddle. Press gently so that all of the dough is touching the hot pan. Remove the foil after 1 to 2 minutes of cooking. Continue to cook another 2 minutes or until lightly browned, then flip and cook 2 minutes longer. Remove to a platter and repeat with the remaining dough.

Muffins, Quick Breads, and Scones

Start with a good blend such as the Self-Rising Flour on page 16 and make over any mainstream recipe for muffins, scones, or quick breads by replacing the flour plus baking powder with an equal amount of this blend.

Some Tips:

- Ingredients should be at room temperature.
- Blend the dry ingredients carefully so that the baking powder and baking soda are evenly dispersed.
- Stir the liquid ingredients into the dry ingredients only until the flour is moistened. Overbeating can cause muffins to rise unevenly.
- Have the pans ready and the oven preheated before starting.
- Use a ¼-cup scoop to scoop the batter into muffin papers or oiled muffin tins. It's the perfect amount for a 2½- to 3-inch muffin cup.
- Once the ingredients are combined, bake immediately as the baking powder starts working when the liquids are added.
- To test for a muffin's doneness, insert a wooden pick into the center of a muffin that is in the center of the pan as they bake slower than the outer ones. If the toothpick comes out with a few moist crumbs (not clean) clinging to it, the muffins are done; if underbaked, they can fall flat when cooling.
- To make the muffins dome, preheat the oven to 425°F. As soon as the muffins go into the oven, reduce the heat to whatever the recipe says.

A Basic (Not-So-Ordinary) Muffin Formula

MAKES 12 MUFFINS

Imprint your own personality into this no-fail formula by adding dried or fresh fruit, nuts, or chips. These can also be frozen before baking, putting a fresh muffin within reach anytime (see Batter's Up below).

▶ Preheat the oven to 425°F. Grease a twelve-cup medium muffin tin or line with muffin papers and spray the insides with vegetable spray.

▶ In a mixing bowl, combine the flour, both sugars, and baking soda and blend well. In a separate bowl, mix the eggs, oil, buttermilk, and vanilla. Add to the dry ingredients and stir with a fork or wooden spoon, just until the dry ingredients are moistened. Fold in the raisins or blueberries.

▶ Scoop the batter into the muffin tins. Sprinkle the tops with additional sugar, if desired. Place on the middle rack of the oven and immediately lower the temperature to 375°F. Bake for 18 to 20 minutes or until a toothpick inserted in the center of a muffin comes away almost clean.

VARIATIONS:

• Add ⅓ cup chopped candied ginger to blueberry muffins.

• Use orange juice and add 1 tablespoon grated orange rind in place of the buttermilk. Omit the vanilla.

• In place of the blueberries or raisins, fold in ½ cup chocolate chips and ⅓ cup chopped dried cherries.

---

2 cups Self-Rising Flour (page 16)

½ cup granulated sugar

¼ cup packed light brown sugar

½ teaspoon baking soda

2 large eggs or 4 egg whites

5 tablespoons vegetable oil

¾ cup buttermilk, applesauce, or milk of choice

2 teaspoons vanilla extract

¾ cup raisins or 1 cup blueberries, fresh or frozen (unthawed)

Additional granulated sugar for dusting, optional

Batter's Up: *Muffin batter can be frozen before baking. Scoop into muffin tins that have been lined with muffin papers. Freeze in the muffin tins. Remove the filled muffin papers from the pan, place in a zip-top bag, and return to the freezer. When ready to serve, place one or more frozen muffins in a muffin tin and bake in a 400°F oven for 10 minutes. Lower the heat to 375°F and bake 15 minutes longer or until a cake tester inserted in the center comes out clean.*

Banana Chip Muffins

The tempting combo of bananas, chocolate, and coconut called to me from the pages of an old *Chocolatier* magazine and I could not resist. I originally used a muffin mix and added the trio of magic ingredients, but I prefer the delicate texture of this from-scratch rendition. It's pure ambrosia.

▶ Preheat the oven to 375°F. Lightly grease sixteen muffin cups or line with muffin papers and spray the insides with vegetable spray.

▶ In a large bowl, beat the butter and shortening together on high speed until light and fluffy. Add both sugars and beat an additional 2 minutes. Add the eggs one at a time, beating for 45 seconds after each addition. Add the vanilla and the bananas and beat about 1 minute longer. Reduce the speed to low. Add 1½ cups of the flour blend and beat just until incorporated. Beat in the buttermilk.

▶ Dust the chocolate chips with the remaining 1 tablespoon flour blend. Fold in the chocolate chips and coconut.

▶ Fill the muffin cups about three-fourths full with the batter and bake 18 to 20 minutes, until a toothpick inserted in the center of a muffin comes out clean. Let stand in the pans for 5 minutes before transferring to a cooling rack. Dust with confectioners' sugar, if desired.

7 tablespoons butter or non-dairy buttery spread, softened

1½ tablespoons organic shortening, such as Spectrum brand

½ cup packed light brown sugar

¼ cup granulated sugar

2 large eggs

2 teaspoons vanilla extract

⅞ cup mashed ripe banana (about 2 medium bananas)

1½ cups plus 1 tablespoon Self-Rising Flour (page 16)

¼ cup buttermilk or rice or soy milk mixed with ½ teaspoon cider vinegar

¾ cup semisweet chocolate chips

½ cup sweetened or unsweetened flaked coconut

Confectioners' sugar for dusting, optional

Date Oatmeal Muffins

MAKES 18 MUFFINS

Looking for a recipe for a simple, moist, delicious accompaniment to coffee, I consulted my *Silver Palate Cookbook*, the book I rely on for great recipes with a unique twist. I happened upon a muffin recipe that called for oats, dates, pecans and maple syrup. Having run out of pecans, I improvised the topping, creating my own unique twist—a rich crumb of oats, butter, and maple syrup. The results were stunning and friendly to those with a nut allergy.

▶ Preheat oven to 350°F. Spray the insides of eighteen muffin liners lightly with PAM. Line the muffin tins. Beat the eggs, buttermilk, and maple syrup together in a mixing bowl. In a second bowl, combine the flour, oats, cinnamon, and baking soda. Blend into the wet ingredients just until combined. Fold in the dates. Using a ¼-cup scoop, fill the muffin cups three quarters full.

▶ Make the topping: Combine the oats, butter, and syrup in a bowl and mix well. Sprinkle over the muffins.

▶ Bake for 20 minutes or until a toothpick inserted in the center comes out clean. Transfer to a wire rack and cool for 10 minutes. Turn the muffins out onto the rack and cool completely.

▶ These store well on the counter in a container for 2 to 3 days or may be frozen. Reheat frozen muffins by microwaving for 1 minute.

2 large eggs

1 cup low-fat buttermilk or vanilla soy milk

1 cup pure maple syrup

1½ cups Self-Rising Flour (page 16)

1½ cups gluten-free quick-cooking oats (see Pantry, page 274)

3 teaspoons ground cinnamon

1 teaspoon baking soda

1 cup chopped pitted dates

Topping

¾ cup gluten-free quick cooking oats

2 tablespoons butter or non-dairy buttery spread, softened

2 tablespoons pure maple syrup

Ginger Apricot Muffins

MAKES 20 TO 24 MUFFINS

Luscious ginger meets tangy apricot in these light muffins. If you prefer not-so-sweet muffins, cut the amount of sugar to ½ cup.

- 2½ cups Self-Rising Flour (page 16), divided
- ¼ cup candied ginger
- 1 cup dried apricots (about 6 ounces)
- ¾ cup sugar
- ½ teaspoon baking soda
- 1¼ cups low-fat buttermilk, or soy, hemp, or coconut milk
- 2 large eggs
- 2 teaspoons vanilla extract
- 8 tablespoons (1 stick) unsalted butter, melted, or 6 tablespoons vegetable oil

▶ Preheat the oven to 425°F. Lightly oil twenty to twenty-four medium muffin cups or line with muffin papers and spray the insides with vegetable spray.

▶ In the bowl of a food processor fitted with the knife blade, combine 1 cup of the flour blend and candied ginger. Process until the ginger is finely chopped. Transfer to a large mixing bowl. Combine the remaining 1½ cups flour with the dried apricots. Pulse until the apricots are coarsely chopped. Add to the flour mixture along with the sugar and baking soda. Whisk to blend.

▶ In a separate bowl, combine buttermilk, eggs, and vanilla and whisk lightly with a fork. Add to the dry ingredients, blending with a fork or wooden spoon just until the dry ingredients are moistened. Add the melted butter and stir to combine. Fill the muffin cups three-fourths full with the batter.

▶ Set the muffin tin in the middle of the oven and lower the temperature to 400°F. Bake for 20 minutes, or until a toothpick inserted in the center of a muffin comes out with a slight crumb. Set on a wire rack to cool for 10 minutes. Turn the muffins out onto a wire rack to cool completely. These freeze well.

Reducing Fat? *Replace half the butter with ¼ cup applesauce.*

Orange Blueberry Muffins

MAKES 16 MUFFINS

Gluten-free muffins benefit from the addition of a little acid to help the baking soda do its job. In this case, orange juice fuels that reaction and produces nicely domed muffins with great texture and crumb.

- ▶ Preheat the oven to 425°F. Oil sixteen muffin cups or line with papers and spray the insides with vegetable spray.
- ▶ Combine the flour, baking powder, baking soda, cinnamon, and xanthan gum in a large bowl and whisk together. In a second bowl, combine the brown sugar, orange juice, butter, eggs, and vanilla and blend. Add to the dry ingredients and whisk just to blend. Fold in the blueberries.
- ▶ Fill the prepared muffin tins two-thirds full with batter. Place in the oven and immediately lower the temperature to 400°F. Bake for 20 minutes or until the tops are light brown. Cool on a wire rack for 5 minutes, then turn the muffins out onto the rack to cool completely.

1¾ cups Self-Rising Flour (page 16)

½ teaspoon baking powder

½ teaspoon baking soda

½ teaspoon ground cinnamon

1 teaspoon xanthan gum

⅓ cup packed light brown sugar

1 cup orange juice

6 tablespoons unsalted butter, melted, or 5 tablespoons vegetable oil

2 large eggs

1 teaspoon vanilla extract

1 cup fresh blueberries, rinsed and drained, or frozen (unthawed) blueberries

Pumpkin Apricot Muffins

Dairy-free

MAKES 12 MUFFINS

This moist muffin is low in sugar and high in taste. It evolved when a neighbor was looking for a gluten-free recipe that was not sweet and used pumpkin (something she had on hand). Not only did she love the taste, but she particularly liked the fact that these were healthy enough to serve her family for breakfast.

▶ Preheat the oven to 400°F. Line a twelve-cup muffin pan with aluminum liners.

▶ Combine the flour blend, cornmeal, sugar, baking powder, baking soda, cinnamon, nutmeg, and cloves in a large bowl. In a separate bowl, mix together the pumpkin, juice, honey, oil, and eggs. Add to the dry ingredients and stir until blended. Fold in the apricots.

▶ Divide the batter among the muffin cups, filling each to the top. Bake for 20 minutes, or until a toothpick inserted in the middle of a muffin comes out clean.

1½ cups Self-Rising Flour (page 16)

¾ cup cornmeal

⅓ cup firmly packed brown sugar

1 teaspoon baking powder

1 teaspoon baking soda

2 teaspoons ground cinnamon

½ teaspoon freshly grated nutmeg

¼ teaspoon ground cloves

1 cup pumpkin purée

½ cup mango juice, orange juice, or other fruit juice

½ cup honey

¼ cup vegetable oil

2 large eggs, or flax gel

¾ cup dried apricots, chopped

Zucchini Nut Muffins

Dairy-free

MAKES 18 MUFFINS

One day, a gluten-filled version of these muffins appeared on the breakfast buffet at a vacation getaway. My husband devoured one and all I could do was drool. As the fragrance of cinnamon floated across the table, I asked him to describe the taste, the texture, the spices. For this reason, he has earned the nickname, "seeing eye pig," which, in this case, led me to cookbooks, zucchini breads, and then to these delightful muffins.

▶ Preheat the oven to 350°F. Line eighteen muffin cups with papers.

▶ Beat the eggs and sugar in a mixing bowl until fluffy, about 3 minutes. Add the oil and beat again until light. Add the zucchini, cinnamon, and nutmeg.

▶ In a separate bowl, whisk together the flour blend, baking powder, and baking soda. Fold into the egg mixture. Fold in the raisins and walnuts.

▶ Fill the muffin cups halfway with the batter. Bake for 20 to 22 minutes, until a toothpick inserted into the center comes away clean. Cool completely on a wire rack.

2 large eggs

1 cup sugar

½ cup vegetable oil

1 cup grated zucchini (about 1 small zucchini)

1½ teaspoons ground cinnamon

½ teaspoon freshly grated nutmeg

2 cups Cake and Pastry Flour (page 16)

3 teaspoons baking powder

2 teaspoons baking soda

½ cup dark raisins

½ cup chopped walnuts

Banana Bread with Streusel Crumb Topping

Dairy-free

MAKES 2 MEDIUM LOAVES

Ruth Moorhouse and her daughter Amanda have been involved in the celiac community in Springfield, Massachusetts, for many years. When I met Amanda, she handed me a dog-eared recipe for her favorite banana bread. "Can you make it over?" she asked. Here's what I came up with. It's also dairy-free. For even more decadence, I topped it with a pecan streusel topping on page 236.

- ▶ Preheat the oven to 350°F. Lightly oil two 8½ x 4½-inch loaf pans.
- ▶ Combine the flour blend, baking soda, cinnamon, and nutmeg in a bowl. In a separate bowl, whisk together the eggs, bananas, sugar, and oil. Add to the dry ingredients and whisk to combine. Fold in the pecans, if using.
- ▶ Divide the batter evenly between the two pans. Sprinkle ½ cup of the streusel topping over each loaf. Bake for 40 to 45 minutes, until a toothpick inserted in the center comes away clean. Set on a wire rack and let cool for 10 minutes. Turn the breads out onto the rack and let cool completely. Wrap with plastic and let sit overnight before slicing.

2 cups Self-Rising Flour (page 16)

½ teaspoon baking soda

¼ teaspoon ground cinnamon

⅛ teaspoon ground nutmeg

2 large eggs, at room temperature

1½ cups very ripe mashed banana (about 3 large bananas)

1 cup sugar

½ cup vegetable oil

¼ cup chopped pecans, optional

1 cup Streusel Crumb Topping (page 236); use non-dairy buttery spread

Beverly's Irish Tea Bread

My friend Beverly asked me to help her convert her family recipe for Irish Tea Bread. After several attempts, I realized the cider vinegar was the critical missing ingredient that re-created the light texture from the original gluten-filled version. Now that I've made it, I understand why she missed this sconelike treat so much. I feel like the luck of the Irish has smiled upon Beverly and me. And it will on you when you try this tea bread.

- ► Preheat the oven to 350°F. Lightly oil or grease a 9-inch springform pan.
- ► Combine the milk and vinegar and let sit to thicken.
- ► Combine the flour blend, sugar, and baking soda in a large bowl. Cut in the cold butter until the mixture is crumbly. In a separate bowl, combine the eggs and milk mixture. Make a well in the dry ingredients and add the milk mixture. Mix with a wooden spoon until the dry ingredients are moistened.
- ► Toss raisins with the remaining 2 tablespoons of the flour blend until coated. Fold into the mixture. Spoon the batter into the prepared pan and smooth the top until even and the batter touches the sides of the pan.
- ► Bake 55 to 60 minutes, until lightly browned and a toothpick inserted in the center comes away clean. Let cool for 15 minutes before removing the side of the pan.
- ► Serve warm with softened butter and jam, or remove the bottom of the pan and let cool and then serve. This freezes well and can be sliced and reheated or toasted.

1 cup minus 2 teaspoons milk, soy milk, or rice milk

2 teaspoons cider vinegar

3 cups Self-Rising Flour (page 16), reserve 2 tablespoons to coat raisins

½ cup sugar

¾ teaspoon baking soda

5 tablespoons cold unsalted butter, cut into small pieces

2 large eggs, slightly beaten

1 cup dark raisins

Tip: *If using Earth Balance or other dairy-free butter substitute, cut into small pieces and freeze for 15 minutes before cutting into the flour.*

Corn Bread Extraordinaire

MAKES 8 TO 10 SERVINGS

From the leather-bound gluten-free menu to an abundance of gluten-free choices, Burtons Grill goes all out to make food-allergic diners feel special. The CEO—who also has celiac disease—understands the thrill of being able to order a fried fish sandwich or drink a gluten-free beer. This rich corn bread from Burtons Grill is another dish that will thrill everyone who tries it. The original calls for two kinds of cheese and cans of corn puréed with heavy cream. I created shortcuts by using creamed corn and shredded Mexican blend cheese. I don't think these compromise the flavor one bit.

1 cup corn flour

1 cup cornmeal

4 teaspoons baking powder

1 teaspoon salt

½ pound (2 sticks butter), at room temperature

¾ cup sugar

4 large eggs

one 14.75-ounce can creamed corn (see Pantry, page 272)

1 cup shredded Mexican blend cheese such as Sargento 4 Cheese Mexican Cheese (about 4 ounces)

▶ Preheat the oven to 325°F. Lightly spray a cast iron or other 12-inch skillet with vegetable spray.

▶ Set the skillet in the oven to heat for 10 to 15 minutes. This will create caramelization on the bottom of the corn bread. Meanwhile prepare the corn bread.

▶ Mix together the corn flour, cornmeal, baking powder, and salt in a medium bowl and set aside. In a large bowl, lightly mix the butter and sugar with a wooden spoon just until small pieces of the butter are visible; set aside.

▶ In a separate bowl, lightly whisk the eggs. Mix in the creamed corn. Add to the flour mixture and mix just until moistened. Fold in the cheese. Scrape into the butter mixture and fold gently so as not to break the strands of cheese. Do not overwork the batter or it will make the texture more cakelike. Little pockets of dry mix should still be visible.

▶ Pour the batter into the hot skillet and bake 38 to 42 minutes, until golden brown or until the center feels firm and the cake tester inserted in the center comes out clean. Let cool for 10 minutes.

▶ This can be made ahead. Turn out onto a plate and cool. Wrap and reheat for 10 minutes before serving.

Cranberry Walnut Quick Bread

MAKES ONE LOAF OR 12 SLICES

A friend asked me to come up with a versatile, easy, and festive quick bread for a holiday brunch. This recipe hit the mark. Now that I have the formula, I can change the add-ins to fit other occasions, and you can, too.

▶ Preheat the oven to 350°F. Lightly oil an 8½ x 4½-inch loaf pan.

▶ Toast ½ cup walnuts, if using, for about 8 minutes. Let cool. In a medium mixing bowl, combine the flour blend, sugar, and baking soda. Blend with a fork.

▶ In a separate bowl, whisk together the buttermilk, oil, eggs, and vanilla. Add to the dry ingredients. Blend with a fork just until moistened. Fold in the cranberries and the toasted walnuts.

▶ Spoon into the prepared pan. Smooth the top using a lightly oiled rubber spatula or sheet of plastic wrap. Sprinkle 2 tablespoons of walnuts, if using, over the top. Press lightly into the batter. Bake 45 to 50 minutes, until a toothpick inserted in the center comes out clean. Cool 10 minutes in the pan. Turn out onto a wire rack and cool completely.

VARIATION: Use ¾ cup orange juice and 1 tablespoon freshly grated orange peel in place of buttermilk.

NOTE: Use ½ cup dried unsweetened cranberries, blueberries, or cherries. If sweetened, reduce the sugar to ⅔ cup.

½ cup coarsely chopped walnuts, optional

2 cups plus 1 tablespoon Self-Rising Flour (page 16)

¾ cup sugar

½ teaspoon baking soda

¾ cup low-fat buttermilk, milk, soy milk, or rice milk (if using milk, add 1 teaspoon cider vinegar to liquids)

4 tablespoons vegetable oil

2 large eggs

1 teaspoon vanilla extract

¾ cup fresh or frozen cranberries, coarsely chopped (see note below)

2 tablespoons chopped walnuts for topping, optional

Orange Blueberry Quick Bread

MAKES 12 SERVINGS

The first time I tested this, it failed badly. The sunken top and undercooked center told me something was very wrong with the balance of wet and dry ingredients. I retreated to another recipe in which the formula produced beautiful muffins and I brought the balance of ingredients into the bread recipe. The results were splendid. If you look at Ginger Apricot Muffins recipe in this book (page 66), you'll see a similarity.

- Preheat the oven to 425°F. Lightly oil a 3 x 7-inch loaf pan. In a medium mixing bowl, combine 1¼ cups of the flour, the sugar, and baking soda. In another bowl, combine the orange juice, orange peel, and egg. Beat with a fork to combine. Mix into the dry ingredients just to moisten. Add the butter and combine.
- In a small bowl, whisk the remaining 1 tablespoon of flour with the blueberries to coat. Fold into the batter.
- Pour the batter into the prepared pan and set in the middle of the oven. Lower the oven temperature to 400°F. Bake for 30 to 35 minutes, until a toothpick inserted in the center comes away clean. Remove to a wire rack and cool 10 minutes. Turn out onto a rack and cool completely before slicing.
- The bread may be frozen.

1¼ cups plus 1 tablespoon Self-Rising Flour (page 16)

⅓ cup sugar

¼ teaspoon baking soda

½ cup plus 1 tablespoon orange juice

1 teaspoon dried orange peel or 1 tablespoon fresh orange rind

1 large egg

4 tablespoons (½ stick) unsalted butter or non-dairy spread, melted

1 cup fresh blueberries, rinsed and drained, or frozen (unthawed) blueberries

Cherry White Chocolate Scones

MAKES 10 SCONES

Cherries and white chocolate—could anything be more decadent? Enjoy these for breakfast, snacking, and beyond. Slightly sweet, these scones are wonderful at tea time, which is anytime in my house.

6 tablespoons butter, cold

2 cups Self-Rising Flour (page 16)

⅓ cup sugar

½ teaspoon baking soda

¾ cup dried cherries

⅓ cup white chocolate chips

2 large eggs

½ cup low-fat buttermilk or milk of choice

1½ teaspoons vanilla extract

Additional sugar for sprinkling

- ▶ Preheat the oven to 375°F. Line two cookie sheets with parchment paper.
- ▶ Cut the butter into small pieces and freeze briefly (5 to 10 minutes).
- ▶ In the bowl of a food processor fitted with the steel blade, combine the flour, sugar, and baking soda. Process briefly to blend. Add the dried cherries and pulse until chopped. Add the butter pieces and pulse until the mixture is very crumbly. Add the chocolate chips and pulse briefly to combine.
- ▶ Lightly beat 1 egg in a bowl. Add the buttermilk and vanilla and mix together. Pour into the dry ingredients and pulse to combine. Be careful not to overmix. Turn out onto a sheet of parchment paper and gently knead to blend.
- ▶ Using a ¼-cup scoop, scoop the dough out onto the prepared cookie sheets and shape into circles. Leave 2 inches between the scones as they spread. Beat the remaining egg to use as an egg wash. Brush the tops of the scones with the egg wash and sprinkle with sugar.
- ▶ Bake for 18 to 20 minutes, until golden and a toothpick inserted in the center of a scone comes out clean. Transfer to a wire rack to cool.
- ▶ The scones may be frozen.

Corn Toasties
(Toaster Corn Cakes)

MAKES 9 TOASTIES

I lived on these slightly sweet toastable corn cakes as a child. Life could not get any better than popping a *Toastie* in the toaster then smearing it with honey and butter. I set out to re-create that recipe, replacing flour, baking powder, and salt with the Self-Rising Flour. I hope you enjoy these as much as I did as a kid—and, now, as an adult!

1¼ cups Self-Rising Flour (page 16)

1 cup cornmeal (see Pantry, page 273)

6 tablespoons sugar

2 large eggs

1 cup milk, buttermilk, or milk of choice

4 tablespoons (½ stick) unsalted butter, melted

- ▶ Preheat the oven to 350°F. Lightly oil nine muffin top cups.
- ▶ Combine the flour blend, cornmeal, and sugar in a large bowl. In a separate bowl, combine the eggs and milk. Whisk into the dry ingredients. Add the melted butter and whisk just to moisten and combine.
- ▶ Divide the batter among the muffin top cups and smooth the tops with a rubber spatula that has been sprayed with vegetable spray so that they are even.
- ▶ Bake for 20 minutes, or until the bottoms are golden brown. (The tops will brown in the toaster.) Turn out onto a wire rack and cool. Toast lightly before eating.
- ▶ If these are not used within a couple of days, they can be frozen for future use.

Cranberry Scones

MAKES 10 SCONES

Scones and I were never properly introduced. By the time they made it into the American culinary world, I was not able to eat them. However, if I could eat a gluten-filled scone, I imagine it would taste just like these—light and tender to bite, but substantial enough to satisfy.

▶ Preheat the oven to 425°F. Line a baking sheet with parchment paper. Sprinkle 1 tablespoon rice flour onto the paper.

▶ In a large mixing bowl, combine the flour blend, baking powder, and baking soda; mix well. Cut the butter into the flour mixture until it resembles coarse meal. (This can be done in a food processor, by using two forks, or with a pastry blender.)

▶ In a separate bowl, combine the buttermilk, brown sugar, 1 egg, cranberries, and orange peel. Make a well in the center of the dry ingredients and add the wet ingredients. Blend well until the dough begins to clump into a ball.

▶ Turn the dough out onto the prepared pan. Turn the dough a couple of time, pressing it and kneading it together. Press into an 8- or 9-inch circle and cut into ten wedges. Lightly beat the remaining egg and brush the top with the egg wash. Use a spatula to slightly separate the wedges.

▶ Bake 14 to 18 minutes. Remove from the oven and place the pan on a wire rack to cool for at least 10 minutes.

▶ The scones may be served warm or at room temperature. Do not serve directly from the oven. Serve with softened butter or jam. For a romantic tea party, serve with a pot of lemon curd (check ingredients as some brands may contain wheat) or clotted cream.

Rice flour for dusting

2¾ cups Self-Rising Flour (page 16)

2 teaspoons baking powder

½ teaspoon baking soda

6 tablespoons cold unsalted butter or non-dairy buttery spread, cut into small pieces

¾ cup buttermilk

¼ to ⅓ cup packed brown sugar (see tip below about sweetness)

2 large eggs

¾ cup dried cranberries

1 tablespoon grated fresh orange peel

Tip: In my mind, scones are meant to be more like a biscuit and therefore not too sweet. If you prefer a sweeter pastry, add more brown sugar.

Flaky Egg-Free Biscuits

MAKES EIGHT 3-INCH OR TWELVE 2-INCH BISCUITS

To create these delicate biscuits I borrowed elements from two outstanding mainstream biscuit sources—the classic Bakewell Cream biscuits and Neil Kleinberg's Buttermilk Biscuit recipe in the *Clinton St. Baking Company Cookbook*, then added a few of my own touches. These are easy to make and delightful to serve and eat. Softened butter and good quality preserves or marmalade are great accompaniments.

¾ cup milk, soy milk, or other milk

2 teaspoons cider vinegar

2 cups Self-Rising Flour (page 16)

1 teaspoon baking powder

1 teaspoon baking soda

4 teaspoons sugar

3 tablespoons cold unsalted butter or non-dairy buttery spread, cut into small pieces

3 tablespoons organic shortening cut into small pieces

Cream or milk of choice for brushing

▶ Preheat the oven to 400°F. Line a baking sheet with parchment paper.

▶ Mix the milk with the cider vinegar. Set aside.

▶ Combine the flour blend, baking powder, baking soda, and sugar in the bowl of a food processor fitted with the knife attachment. Pulse two or three times to blend. Place the butter and shortening pieces over the top of the flour. Pulse until the mixture is crumbly. Add the milk and pulse until the dough pulls away from the bowl.

▶ Turn the dough out onto a sheet of plastic wrap or parchment paper. (Be careful to keep fingers away from the knife blade. It's very sharp.) Knead the dough and pat into a circle about ¾ inch thick. Use a 2- or 3-inch biscuit cutter to cut out biscuits. Try not to twist the biscuit cutter as you remove it from the dough. Place the biscuits on the prepared baking sheet. Gather the remaining dough and roll out again, cutting out as many biscuits as you can. Repeat until all the dough is used. Brush the tops with cream.

▶ Place in the center of the oven. Lower the temperature to 375°F and bake 18 to 22 minutes or until the tops are slightly browned.

▶ Serve warm with jam and/or butter.

Tip: Adding cider vinegar to a baking powder–soda dough gives extra lift to gluten-free baked products.

Sweet Sorghum Banana Date Breakfast Cookies

MAKES 16 TO 18

I made these for breakfast one day when I had out-of-town visitors and found myself short on time and ingredients. These sconelike cookies called for something crunchy and all I had was gluten-free granola flavored with bananas and dates. It inspired this recipe, which I've since converted, to use two favorite ingredients of mine—banana and dates. Now I always keep them on hand just to make this recipe.

▶ Preheat the oven to 375°F. Line two cookie sheets with parchment paper.

▶ Combine the sorghum flour, brown rice flour, tapioca starch/flour, brown sugar, baking powder, baking soda, xanthan gum, cinnamon, and salt in a large bowl. Mix until the brown sugar is blended into the ingredients. Cut in the butter until the mixture resembles coarse meal.

▶ In a separate bowl using a mixer, beat the eggs until light yellow and thick, about 3 minutes. Add the dry ingredients and beat about 1 minute. Beat in the buttermilk and vanilla until smooth. Fold in the dried banana and dates.

▶ Using a medium scoop, scoop the dough onto the prepared cookie sheets, leaving about 1 inch between each scone. Use a sheet of plastic wrap to gently press and smooth the scones into 1-inch-thick disks. Brush with buttermilk, sprinkle with brown sugar, and bake for 18 to 20 minutes. Serve warm.

▶ The cookies may be reheated. These freeze well.

¾ cup sweet white sorghum flour

¾ cup brown rice flour

½ cup tapioca starch/flour

⅓ cup packed light brown sugar

1 tablespoon baking powder

½ teaspoon baking soda

1 teaspoon xanthan gum

1 teaspoon ground cinnamon

½ teaspoon salt

5 tablespoons cold unsalted butter or buttery non-dairy spread, cut into small pieces

2 large eggs

½ cup buttermilk (or soy milk combined with 2 teaspoons cider vinegar)

2 teaspoons vanilla extract

¾ cup coarsely chopped dried banana slices

¾ cup chopped dates

Additional buttermilk or soy milk for brushing

Additional brown sugar for sprinkling

Savory Fare

Entrées, 146

Buckwheat Blueberry Pancakes or Waffles

MAKES FOURTEEN TO SIXTEEN 3-INCH PANCAKES

I can't tell you the number of times I have suffered from Pancake Envy as I watched plates of thick, luscious pancakes going to other tables at restaurant brunches. So I set my sights on coming up with a recipe that not only looked like the beautiful stacks I'd seen but also satisfied my craving. I referred to books of the past, such as Marion Cunningham's *The Breakfast Book* and I went to contemporary bakers like Neil Kleinberg who co-authored *Clinton St. Baking Company Cookbook* with his wife, Dede Lahman. These *are* the best pancakes I've ever eaten. I think my tutors would be proud.

▶ Combine the flour blend, buckwheat flour, baking powder, and sugar in a bowl. In a separate bowl, whisk the egg yolks, milk, vanilla, and butter together to combine. Add the dry ingredients to the wet ingredients and whisk to blend.

▶ In a mixing bowl, beat the whites on high until soft peaks form (when lines begin to form and stay on the surface as you beat the whites). Do not overbeat. Fold half the egg whites into the batter and blend, then fold in the remaining half. Do not blend completely. (You will still see bits of white foam.)

1¾ cups Self-Rising Flour (page 16)

¾ cup buckwheat flour

1 teaspoon baking powder

¼ cup sugar

3 large eggs, separated

1½ cups 2% milk, soy milk, or milk of choice

1 teaspoon vanilla extract

6 tablespoons unsalted butter or non-dairy buttery spread, melted

1 cup fresh blueberries (frozen will not work as well) or bananas, cut into chunks

Maple syrup or blueberry compote for serving, optional

continues

continued

▶ Preheat a non-stick griddle or flat pan to medium-high (350°F to 375°F). Lightly oil the surface. Using a ¼-cup scoop, drop the batter onto the griddle. After the batter has begun to set, sprinkle blueberries or banana pieces over the surface. When the bottom is golden brown, flip the pancakes and cook an addition 3 to 5 minutes or until browned on the other side. Serve with maple syrup, blueberry compote, or enjoy as is.

VARIATION: The batter without fruit makes great waffles. Lightly oil and preheat a waffle iron. Add about ¼ cup batter (just enough to cover the center of the baking surface without spreading to the edges) and cook according to the manufacturer's instructions.

Tip: Make sure the griddle is fully preheated before using.

Crêpes with Two Fillings

MAKES FIFTEEN TO TWENTY 6-INCH CRÊPES

The trick is to make these very thin so they are pliable and easy to roll. This recipe, with the cheese filling below, is a dead ringer for the blintzes my grandmother made. However, it comes from a basic formula I prepared in French culinary school—made over the gluten-free way!

▶ Whisk together the eggs in a large bowl. In a separate bowl, combine rice flour, tapioca starch, salt, xanthan gum, and sugar, if using. Whisk into the eggs just until moistened. The mixture will be very thick and gloppy.

▶ Add the milk, a little at a time, stirring vigorously until the mixture is smooth and the consistency of heavy cream. Cover and chill for at least 1 hour and up to 24 hours.

▶ Lightly oil one or two 6-inch crêpe pans or heavy frying pans and set over medium heat. Pour about 2 tablespoons of the batter into each pan and swirl until the pan is coated. Pour any excess batter back into the bowl. Cook the crêpe until the edges look very dry, about 1 minute. With a sharp knife, loosen the edges of the crêpe. Use your fingers to grab the edges and flip the crêpe. Cook another 30 seconds and remove each crêpe to a platter. Continue until the remaining batter is used, lightly oiling the pans with a paper towel dabbed in oil as necessary.

▶ Serve with a dollop of jam, fruit, or Ricotta Raisin Filling (on page 87). For a hearty meal, try the Deviled Chicken Crêpes recipe on page 88.

2 large eggs

¾ cup rice flour

¼ cup tapioca starch/flour

½ teaspoon salt

¼ teaspoon xanthan gum

1 tablespoon sugar (if used for dessert)

1¼ cups milk, soy milk, or rice milk

Ricotta Raisin Filling

- Preheat the oven to 375°F. Butter a 9 x 13-inch baking dish.
- Whisk together the ricotta, sugar, eggs, raisins, lemon juice, and lemon rind in a bowl. Place 2 to 3 tablespoons of the filling in the center of each crêpe and roll up the crêpes. Set seam side down snugly into the baking dish.
- Cover the pan with buttered foil and bake for 20 minutes. Serve warm, dusted with confectioners' sugar.

one 15-ounce container reduced-fat ricotta cheese

⅓ cup sugar

2 large eggs

1 cup golden raisins

1 tablespoon lemon juice

2 teaspoons grated lemon rind

1 recipe Crêpes (page 86)

Confectioners' sugar for dusting

Deviled Chicken Crêpes

This makes a lovely brunch or luncheon dish, or a great contribution to a potluck gathering. These can be assembled ahead, but do not bake them in advance or the crêpes might tend to break apart.

▶ Preheat the oven to 350°F. Lightly oil a 9 x 13-inch baking dish.

▶ Melt the butter in a large skillet. Add the onion and bell pepper and sauté until soft. Add the chicken, capers, mustard, and lemon juice and stir to combine. Remove from the heat.

▶ In a small saucepan, bring the chicken broth to a boil. Add the cornstarch mixture and stir until the broth thickens. Reduce the heat and simmer for 1 minute. Remove from the heat and add the cream.

▶ Spoon ½ cup of the broth mixture into the chicken mixture and mix well. Spoon ¼ cup of the filling into the center of each crêpe and roll the crêpes. Set seam side down snugly into the baking dish. Pour the remaining sauce over the crêpes and sprinkle with the cheese. Cover with a sheet of buttered aluminum foil and bake for about 20 minutes, or until bubbly.

1 tablespoon unsalted butter or non-dairy buttery spread

1 medium onion, chopped

1 green bell pepper, chopped

3 cups chopped cooked chicken

1 tablespoon capers

1 teaspoon Dijon mustard

Juice of 1 lemon

2 cups gluten-free chicken broth

2 tablespoons cornstarch mixed with 2 tablespoons water

½ cup heavy cream, milk, or milk substitute

1 recipe Crêpes, omitting the sugar (page 86)

½ cup grated Parmesan cheese or dairy-free cheese, optional

Featherlight Multigrain Flapjacks

MAKES SIXTEEN TO EIGHTEEN 4½-INCH PANCAKES

To me the ultimate comfort food is light, hearty pancakes topped with warm maple syrup. In the realm of gluten-free baking you might think *light* and *hearty* are mutually exclusive, but these flapjacks will prove that anything is possible.

▶ Preheat a griddle to medium (350°F).

▶ Whisk together the flours, cornmeal, brown sugar, baking powder, xanthan gum, salt, and cinnamon in a large bowl. In a separate bowl, combine the milk, butter, honey, and eggs. Add the liquid ingredients to the dry ingredients and mix gently with a fork just to combine.

▶ Spray the griddle with vegetable spray or lightly oil the surface. Spoon ¼ cup of the batter onto the griddle and cook until bubbles begin to form on the surface and the edges start to dry, about 2 to 3 minutes. Flip and cook another 2 minutes, or until lightly browned on the bottom. Serve warm or keep warm in an oven set on low heat.

VARIATION: Sauté coarsely chopped apples and fold into the batter.

¾ cup millet flour

½ cup amaranth flour

½ cup sorghum flour

⅓ cup cornmeal

2 tablespoons light brown sugar

2 teaspoons baking powder

1 teaspoon xanthan gum

¾ teaspoon salt

½ teaspoon ground cinnamon

1¾ cups milk, soy, or rice milk

4 tablespoons (½ stick) unsalted butter or non-dairy buttery spread, melted

¼ cup honey

3 large eggs, or flax gel

Granola Breakfast Bars

Egg-free

MAKES 16 BARS

These bars rival any in the gluten-filled world. They are perfect for snacking or tucking into school lunch boxes and backpacks and can be made with any gluten-free granola. However, the secret to their success is to start with a granola that you really like. My choice is Jen's Deluxe Granola on page 91 or Maple Cranberry Granola from Bakery on Main.

▶ Preheat the oven to 350°F. Lightly grease a 9-inch square baking pan.

▶ Pour the granola into a zip-top bag and seal. Coarsely crush the granola using a rolling pin. Set aside.

▶ In a medium mixing bowl, combine the sorghum and chickpea flours, tapioca starch, xanthan gum, cinnamon, and salt. Add the crushed granola and mix well.

▶ Spoon the peanut butter into a medium microwaveable bowl. Microwave on high for 30 seconds. Add the maple syrup, honey, milk, oil, and vanilla and almond extracts and mix well. Add to the dry ingredients and mix until evenly moistened. Stir in the chocolate and coconut. Press the mixture into the prepared baking pan. Use lightly greased hands or plastic wrap to smooth and spread evenly.

▶ Bake for 22 to 25 minutes, until the top is golden brown. Cool and cut into bars.

2½ cups Jen's Deluxe Granola (page 91) or commercial brand (see Pantry, page 274)

¾ cup sorghum flour

½ cup chickpea, quinoa, or soy flour

¼ cup tapioca starch/flour

1½ teaspoons xanthan or guar gum

1½ teaspoons ground cinnamon

½ teaspoon salt

½ cup chunky or smooth peanut butter, almond butter, soy butter, or sunflower butter

⅓ cup maple syrup

¼ cup honey

¼ cup milk, soy milk, or rice milk

2 tablespoons vegetable oil

2 teaspoons vanilla extract

1 teaspoon almond extract

½ cup mini semi-sweet chocolate morsels

¼ cup sweetened shredded coconut

Jen's Deluxe Granola

Dairy-free and Egg-free

MAKES 8 CUPS

When gluten-free oats became available and I could add them to my diet, I felt like I had reached another milestone in gluten-free living. This recipe from my sister, Jennifer, is the ultimate granola and one of the additions to the gluten-free diet that I celebrate with each handful. To shorten preparation time, chop the fruit in a food processor.

▶ Preheat the oven to 350 °F.

▶ Toss the oats, coconut, and almonds together in a large bowl. Whisk together the oil, honey, and vanilla in a small bowl and pour over the oat mixture. Stir with a wooden spoon until well coated. Pour onto a 13 x 18 x 1-inch baking sheet.

▶ Bake until the granola turns a golden brown, stirring frequently, about 45 minutes. Remove from the oven and let cool, stirring occasionally.

▶ Add the dried fruit and sunflower seeds and mix well. Store in an airtight container. This mixture will keep for several weeks at room temperature. It is great for snacking, and as a topping for cereal, yogurt, or ice cream.

4 cups gluten-free quick-cooking oats (see Pantry, page 274)

2 cups sweetened shredded coconut

2 cups sliced almonds

¾ cup vegetable oil

½ cup honey

1 tablespoon vanilla extract

1½ cups small diced dried apricots

1 cup small diced dried figs

1 cup chopped dates

1 cup dried cherries

1 cup dried cranberries

1 cup unsalted sunflower seeds, toasted

Avoiding Oats? Replace with 4 cups quinoa flakes, gluten-free corn flakes, or rice cereal.

Maple Cheddar Breakfast Casserole

MAKES 8 SERVINGS

When my friend Lisa described this recipe to me, I was salivating from the get-go. Inspired by McDonald's McGriddles—a breakfast sandwich consisting of sausage, egg, and cheese served between two pancakes with maple syrup, this casserole is an easy, hearty, make-ahead breakfast, or a dish for an elegant company brunch. Either way, you'll be drooling when you smell the fragrance of maple and cheese coming from the oven.

- ▶ Lightly oil a 9 x 13-inch baking dish.
- ▶ In a skillet, heat the oil over medium heat. Crumble the sausage and cook until brown, with no pink visible. Drain on paper towels.
- ▶ Mix together the milk, eggs, maple syrup, vanilla, and cinnamon in a large bowl. Add the browned sausage, bread cubes, and cheese. Pour into the prepared dish, cover, and refrigerate overnight.
- ▶ Preheat the oven to 350°F. Bake 35 to 40 minutes, until the center is set. Cut into squares and serve. This reheats well.

1 tablespoon vegetable oil

1 pound Jones Maple Sausage or other gluten-free sausage

2 cups milk, soy milk, or rice milk

8 eggs

¼ cup real maple syrup or sugar-free maple syrup

2 teaspoons vanilla extract

1 teaspoon ground cinnamon

8 cups cubed dense gluten-free sandwich bread

1 cup shredded sharp cheddar cheese or dairy-free cheese (about 4 ounces)

Oat Groats with Dried Fruit

Dairy-free and *Egg-free*

MAKES 3 TO 4 SERVINGS

After a little experimenting, I discovered this nutritious whole grain can be handled very much like brown rice. In fact, I often make it in my rice steamer as I did this hearty, warm breakfast dish. Make a big batch of oat groats ahead of time and refrigerate, reheating smaller portions for breakfast. Add extra fruit and brown sugar to taste.

1 cup gluten-free oat groats (see Pantry, page 274), rinsed and drained

2½ cups water

2 to 3 tablespoons brown sugar

⅓ cup golden raisins

½ teaspoon ground cinnamon

¼ teaspoon salt

▶ Combine the groats, water, brown sugar, raisins, cinnamon, and salt in a small rice cooker. Cook according to manufacturer's instructions. Serve warm or refrigerate and reheat individual portions in the microwave.

Tip: *Oat Groats are the whole oat kernel before processing. They also make wonderful pilaf. Add sautéed onion, celery, carrots, and spices to the groats and cook in chicken or vegetable broth.*

Sausage and Goat Cheese Strata

MAKES 8 SERVINGS

This is a perfect brunch dish that falls into the Make and Take category. If it becomes your contribution to a potluck meal, you can be sure you'll have plenty to eat and enough to share.

- ▶ Spray a 9 x 13-inch baking dish with vegetable spray.
- ▶ Heat the oil in a skillet over medium heat. Add the mushrooms and scallions and sauté for 1 to 2 minutes. Add the sausage and sauté another 2 minutes. Stir in the basil, oregano, and thyme. Continue to cook until the mushrooms are tender. Remove from heat. Add the roasted peppers and stir to combine.
- ▶ In a bowl, whisk together eggs and milk; set aside.
- ▶ Line the prepared dish with half the bread slices. Cover the bread with half the sausage mixture. Sprinkle with half the goat cheese. Pour half the egg mixture over the bread and sausage. Repeat the layers with the remaining bread, sausage mixture, goat cheese, and egg mixture. Sprinkle with the Parmesan cheese. Cover and refrigerate for several hours or overnight.
- ▶ Preheat the oven to 350°F. Bake, uncovered, for 40 minutes, or until set. Cut into squares and serve. This does not freeze well.

Tip: Many brands of fully-cooked gourmet sausages are gluten-free including Al Fresco, Aidell's, and Applegate Organics. Read ingredient labels as not everything from these companies is gluten-free.

2 tablespoons olive oil

8 ounces sliced mushrooms

1 cup chopped scallions, top third removed and discarded

16 ounces fully-cooked gluten-free chicken sausage (any flavor), chopped

½ teaspoon dried basil

½ teaspoon dried oregano

½ teaspoon dried thyme

one 12-ounce jar roasted red peppers, drained and chopped

4 large eggs

3 cups milk, soy milk, or rice milk

12 slices gluten-free bread, such as Delicious Slicing Bread (page 42), or commercial bread

4 ounces crumbled goat cheese or dairy-free cheese (see Simple Substitutions, page 267)

3 tablespoons grated Parmesan cheese

Antipasto Squares

MAKES 30 SQUARES

This recipe was sent to me by Clare Popowich several years ago. She didn't know its origin, but recalls that the original recipe called for tubes of crescent rolls. I substituted the Brick Oven–Style Pizza Dough on page 57 and made a few adjustments to add a gourmet flare. My thanks to Clare and anyone else who had a hand in bringing this amazing appetizer to me.

▶ Preheat the oven to 350°F. Lightly oil a 9 x 13-inch baking dish.

▶ Prepare the pizza dough. Between two sheets of plastic wrap, roll out half the dough to fit in the bottom of the dish. Remove the top layer of wrap and gently fit the dough into the bottom of the pan. Layer the sopressata, provolone, ham, mozzarella, and pepperoni over the dough. Top with the roasted peppers. Beat 2 of the eggs in a bowl and add the seasoning. Pour over the layers.

▶ Roll out the remaining dough and lay it over the top. Lightly beat the remaining egg and brush over the dough. Sprinkle with the Parmesan cheese. Cover with foil.

▶ Bake for 30 minutes. Remove the foil and bake an additional 30 minutes. Cut into squares. Serve warm or at room temperature.

▶ The antipasto squares can be made ahead. Keep refrigerated and reheat in the microwave for 3 minutes or in a 350°F oven for 10 minutes.

1 recipe Brick Oven–Style Pizza Crust (page 57)

⅓ pound sopressata, thinly sliced

¼ pound provolone cheese, thinly sliced

¼ pound rosemary ham or other ham, thinly sliced

1½ to 2 cups shredded mozzarella cheese (6 to 8 ounces)

⅓ pound pepperoni, thinly sliced

one 12-ounce jar roasted red peppers, drained

3 large eggs

½ teaspoon dried Italian seasoning

⅓ cup grated Parmesan cheese

Apricot Hazelnut Spread

MAKES 2½ CUPS

This quick, festive spread is the perfect accompaniment to sliced gluten-free baguettes on page 44 or gluten-free crackers. Omit the hazelnuts if they are a problem. I don't recommend substituting dairy-free ingredients, but folding apricots and hazelnuts into soy cream cheese would be a satisfying, dairy-free alternative.

▶ Heat the preserves in a microwave on high for 1 minute. Set aside to cool slightly.

▶ In a food processor, combine the cream cheese, goat cheese, and sour cream until smooth. Add the apricots and pulse just to mix.

▶ Spread the mixture evenly onto a small serving plate with a lip or in a small bowl (about 5 to 6 inches in diameter). Smooth the surface with a spatula and coat with the melted preserves. Sprinkle the hazelnuts evenly over the preserves and press gently into the top.

▶ Cover and chill for 1 hour. Serve with crackers or toasted bread.

2 tablespoons apricot preserves

one 8-ounce package light cream cheese, at room temperature

one 8-ounce package goat cheese

2 tablespoons light sour cream

½ to ¾ cup finely chopped dried apricots

⅓ cup chopped hazelnuts, toasted

Assorted crackers or slices of toasted French bread

Baked Brie with Fig Spread en Croûte

MAKES 8 SERVINGS

For many holiday seasons, I eyed the Brie in Puff Pastry in the deli section of my favorite market. I thought anything encased in pastry was out of reach to the gluten-free baker, until I created this pseudo-puff pastry. Light and pliable, this crust is flaky without being crumbly. Use this pastry for Chicken Wellington on page 150, too.

one 3- to 4-inch wheel Brie (French Brie is best)

2 to 3 tablespoons fig or apricot jam

1 recipe Nearly Puff Pastry Crust (on page 98)

1 large egg, beaten for egg wash

▶ Cut the Brie horizontally in half. Spread the jam over the cut side of one half and top with the other half. Wrap in plastic wrap and freeze for 1 hour.

▶ Meanwhile prepare the puff pastry crust.

▶ Preheat the oven to 375°F. Line a baking sheet with a lightly oiled piece of parchment paper or aluminum foil.

▶ Divide the puff pastry dough in half, reserving one half for a later use. Roll the remaining piece of pastry into a 12-inch round between sheets of plastic wrap. It should be thin but still have enough structure to lift off the plastic easily and without crumbling. (Breaks can be patched with leftover dough.)

▶ Remove the top piece of plastic wrap and set the frozen Brie in the center of the round. Fold the pastry around the frozen Brie. Overlap at the top, removing any excess dough as you pinch the edges to seal. Use the bottom sheet of plastic wrap to guide the dough. Seal the top and sides by patting gently with moistened fingers. Cut out decorative leaves from any leftover dough and place on top of the dough, if desired. Brush the top and sides with the egg wash.

continues

continued

▶ Bake for 25 to 30 minutes, until the top is golden brown. Remove from the oven and let cool 20 minutes before serving. Serve with crackers, if desired. The remaining pastry dough can be wrapped in plastic and refrigerated for several days or frozen for up to six weeks.

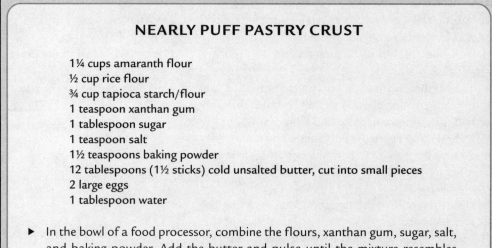

NEARLY PUFF PASTRY CRUST

1¼ cups amaranth flour
½ cup rice flour
¾ cup tapioca starch/flour
1 teaspoon xanthan gum
1 tablespoon sugar
1 teaspoon salt
1½ teaspoons baking powder
12 tablespoons (1½ sticks) cold unsalted butter, cut into small pieces
2 large eggs
1 tablespoon water

▶ In the bowl of a food processor, combine the flours, xanthan gum, sugar, salt, and baking powder. Add the butter and pulse until the mixture resembles coarse meal. Add the eggs and water and pulse to combine. Remove to a work surface and knead into a ball.

Cheese Bitz
(Goldfish-Style Crackers)

Egg-free

MAKES 60 TO 75 CRACKERS

I like to think of these as art imitating life. I don't know how many times I've been asked to come up with a recipe for gluten-free goldfish crackers. This recipe is both easy and satisfying and, while I have never eaten the real Goldfish, I am told these are very close.

1 cup plus 1 tablespoon Self-Rising Flour (page 16)

Salt and black pepper or pinch of cayenne pepper

4 tablespoons (½ stick) cold unsalted butter or non-dairy buttery spread, cut into small pieces

2 cups grated cheddar cheese or non-dairy cheese (about 8 ounces) (see Simple Substitutions, page 267)

3 to 4 tablespoons cold water

Olive oil

Coarse salt

▶ In a food processor fitted with the steel blade, combine the flour blend and salt and pepper to taste. Add the butter and cheese and pulse until the mixture is crumbly. Add the water a little at a time and process for 30 to 60 seconds, until the dough comes together. Turn onto a sheet of plastic wrap, knead, and form into a smooth ball. Wrap in plastic and chill 1 hour or overnight.

▶ Preheat the oven to 375°F.

▶ Roll out the dough onto parchment paper to ⅛ inch thick. Using a pizza cutter or sharp knife, cut the dough into 1-inch squares. (There is no need to separate the squares. They will break apart easily after baking.) Arrange the squares on a cookie sheet. Prick the squares with a fork, brush with olive oil, and sprinkle with coarse salt.

▶ Bake 15 to 20 minutes, until light brown. Watch carefully so they do not overbake.

▶ If you like crispy crackers, roll the dough out a bit thinner, cut into squares. Bake until golden brown.

Shortcut:

▶ Purchase one 8-ounce bag of grated cheddar cheese.

Cheese Puffs Gougères

MAKES 36 PUFFS

Based on the classic pâte à choux or cream puff pastry from my culinary school days, this elegant and easy appetizer can be made ahead. It can be prepared dairy-free, too, but egg substitutes won't work as the eggs are necessary to help create the structure of these bite-size treats.

▶ Preheat the oven to 400°F. Line two baking sheets with parchment paper.

▶ Combine the flour, cornstarch, xanthan gum, salt, and chile pepper in a medium mixing bowl.

▶ Combine the milk, water, and butter in a large saucepan over medium-high heat and bring to a boil. Remove from the heat. Add the dry ingredients and beat briskly with a wooden spoon until thoroughly incorporated. Return the saucepan to the stove and reduce the heat to low. The mixture will begin to pull away from the side of the pan. Stir for 3 to 4 minutes, letting any moisture evaporate.

▶ Remove from the heat and let stand at room temperature for about 5 minutes or until cooled slightly. Add the eggs one at a time, stirring briskly after each addition until the egg is thoroughly incorporated.

▶ Form the dough into 2-tablespoon size mounds and drop onto the baking sheets, leaving 1 to 2 inches between each puff. Top each with a generous tablespoon of cheese and sprinkle with salt and pepper to taste.

1¼ cups white rice flour

¼ cup cornstarch

¼ teaspoon xanthan gum

¾ teaspoon salt

½ teaspoon ground ancho chile pepper

1 cup milk or dairy-free milk

1 cup water

6 tablespoons unsalted butter or non-dairy buttery spread, cut into 1-inch pieces

4 large eggs, at room temperature

2 cups shredded Gruyère cheese or dairy-free cheese (about 8 ounces) (see Simple Substitutions, page 267)

Coarse salt and cracked black pepper

continues

continued

▶ Bake in the oven for 15 minutes. Reduce the temperature to 350°F and bake for 30 minutes longer, rotating the pans halfway through. Turn off the oven and prop open the oven door slightly. Let the puffs cool in the oven for an additional 30 minutes. Serve warm or at room temperature.

▶ These can be frozen for up to one month and reheated in a 350°F oven for about 8 minutes. (Do not thaw first.)

VARIATIONS:

• Add 2 tablespoons chopped chives and ½ cup grated Parmesan cheese to the dough for an interesting appetizer. Slice the puffs horizontally and fill with shrimp, tuna, or chicken salad.

• With minor alterations, this recipe can be made into yummy profiteroles, filled with ice cream and topped with chocolate or caramel sauce. Go to page 250 for the recipe.

Tip: *Don't use a commercial all-purpose gluten-free baking mix that already contains xanthan or guar gum as this will produce a gummy texture.*

Corn and Smoked Bacon Cakes

MAKES 32 TO 36 BITE-SIZE CAKES

These fabulous little cakes were inspired by two recipes—one in *Eating Well Magazine* and one that appeared in the *Hartford Courant*. I combined elements of both. They make wonderful appetizers but can also be served as part of a meal. Serve with yogurt and chives.

▶ Whisk together the flour blend, milk, oil, egg yolks, and pepper in a large bowl. Stir in the corn and bacon; set aside.

▶ In a separate bowl, beat the sugar and egg whites on medium-high speed until nearly stiff but not dry. Fold half the egg whites into the batter. Gently fold in the remaining whites. Some white streaks may still be visible.

▶ Heat a griddle to medium high (375°F). Wet a paper towel with oil and brush over the griddle surface. Drop the batter by the tablespoonful onto the griddle. Cook about 2 minutes, or until the edges are dry. Flip and cook until golden brown. Remove to a platter and repeat with the remaining batter.

▶ Serve with a dollop of yogurt and a sprinkling of chives.

¾ cup plus 2 tablespoons Self-Rising Flour (page 16)

¾ cup milk, soy milk, or rice milk

2 tablespoons canola oil

3 large eggs, separated

¼ teaspoon freshly ground pepper

2 to 3 cups fresh or frozen (thawed) corn

6 slices smoked bacon, crisp-cooked and crumbled

2 tablespoons sugar

one 6-ounce container plain Greek yogurt

2 tablespoons chopped fresh chives

Tip: *Stiffly beaten egg whites add lift to these delicate, airy pancakes.*

Mexican Pizza

MAKES 8 SERVINGS

Years ago Lora Brody created a gluten-filled version of this pizza for a presentation. It made me so hungry watching people devour it that I had to create a version I could enjoy. This makes a great appetizer and a festive Make and Take dish that will impress everyone, gluten-free or not.

▸ Preheat the oven to 425°F. Lightly oil a 14-inch deep-dish pizza pan.

▸ Combine the flour, cornstarch, tapioca starch, cornmeal, powdered milk, yeast, chili powder, xanthan gum, and salt in a large mixing bowl. Mix well with a fork. In a separate bowl, combine the refried beans, oil, honey, eggs, vinegar, and water. Add to the dry ingredients and beat using a mixer for 3 minutes, or until the dough is smooth.

▸ Spread the dough into the pan. Oil a sheet of plastic wrap and lay it, oiled side down, over the dough. Press the dough evenly into the pan and all the way up the sides. Remove the plastic and spread the cream cheese over the dough. Spoon the salsa over the cream cheese and sprinkle with the shredded cheese.

▸ Bake 25 to 30 minutes, until the edges of the crust are deep brown and the cheese is bubbling. Cool slightly. Top with olives, if desired. Slice and serve.

Dairy-free? Use soy cream cheese and dairy-free cheddar cheese or replace with additional refried beans.

Egg-free? Use flax gel (page 268) in place of eggs.

1½ cups white rice flour

1 cup plus 2 tablespoons cornstarch or potato starch

6 tablespoons tapioca starch/flour

½ cup cornmeal

3 tablespoons dry powdered milk or Vance's DariFree (see Simple Substitutions, page 265)

1 tablespoon instant active or active dry yeast

2 teaspoons chili powder

2 teaspoons xanthan gum

1½ teaspoons salt

1 cup low-fat vegetarian refried beans

¼ cup olive oil

2 tablespoons honey

2 large eggs

1 teaspoon cider vinegar

⅔ cup plus 2 tablespoons water

two 8-ounce packages low-fat gluten-free cream cheese, at room temperature

two 16-ounce jars gluten-free salsa, excess liquid drained off

2 cups shredded Monterey Jack or cheddar cheese (about 8 ounces)

two 2-ounce cans sliced black olives, well drained, optional

Mini Quiches

MAKES 30 PIECES

This versatile recipe is the perfect finger food for any party. For variety add chopped, cooked bacon, mushrooms or onions, or bake the shells and add roasted vegetables. See other variations on page 105.

▶ To make the crust, combine the flours, xanthan gum, and salt in a food processor fitted with the steel blade. Pulse to combine. Add the butter and pulse until the mixture resembles coarse crumbs. Add the egg and pulse until the dough forms a ball.

▶ Spray 30 metal or silicone mini muffin cups or mini tart pans. Press 2 teaspoons of dough evenly into the bottom and up the sides of each cup. Pierce the bottoms with a fork. Cover with plastic wrap and refrigerate for 1 hour or overnight.

▶ Preheat the oven to 350°F. Bake the shells for 10 minutes, or until the edges are golden brown. Remove to a wire rack and cool for 10 minutes.

▶ Meanwhile prepare the filling ingredients. Whisk together the half-and-half, eggs, and mustard in a bowl. Add the cheese and whisk until well combined.

▶ Set the mini muffin cups on baking sheets for easy handling. Spoon a scant tablespoon of filling into each shell, or enough to fill each shell without overflowing. Bake 15 to 20 minutes or until the filling is set. Cool on a wire rack. Serve slightly warm or at room temperature.

Crust

¾ cup sorghum flour

½ cup white rice flour

¼ cup tapioca starch/flour

1½ teaspoons xanthan or guar gum

¼ teaspoon salt

8 tablespoons (1 stick) cold unsalted butter or non-dairy buttery spread, cut into ½-inch pieces

1 large egg, lightly beaten, or flax gel (see Simple Substitutions, page 268)

Filling

1½ cups half-and-half

2 large eggs

1 teaspoon Dijon mustard

1½ cups shredded Swiss or cheddar cheese (about 6 ounces)

continues

continued

Shortcuts:

- ▶ Shells can be formed and refrigerated up to three days prior to baking.
- ▶ Baked shells may be cooled, frozen, and filled as needed.
- ▶ This recipe can be prepared to completion one day in advance and reheated just before serving.
- ▶ Bake the shells. Add a small piece of goat's milk cheese or grated cheese and top with a dollop of pepper jelly. Bake 5 minutes or just until cheese has melted.

Avoiding Dairy? Fill fully baked shells with roasted vegetables and serve.

Mock Matzo

Egg-free and *Dairy-free*

MAKES SIX 5-INCH MATZOS

Every Passover I make these for the three of us who are gluten-free, but everyone else prefers them to real matzo. Now I double or triple the recipe. However, no need to wait for Passover to make this recipe and no need to overlook it if you do not celebrate this holiday. This makes wonderful crackers, too.

- ▶ Preheat the oven to 425°F. Line two cookie sheets with aluminum foil or parchment paper.
- ▶ In a medium bowl, combine the potato starch, almond flour, sorghum flour, flaxseed meal, xanthan gum, and salt. Using your fingers, a fork, or mixer, cut in the non-dairy spread until the mixture resembles coarse meal. Add water, a little at a time, until the dough forms a ball and isn't too sticky. Knead until smooth.
- ▶ Press walnut-size pieces of the dough onto the cookie sheets with the palm of your hand until the dough forms a thin circle. Smooth out the edges, if desired. Prick the surface with a fork.
- ▶ Bake 10 to 12 minutes, until the edges are slightly brown. Watch carefully to make sure these do not overbake. Remove and set the cookie sheet on a wire rack to cool. Store cooled matzo in a plastic bag at room temperature. These will keep for several days.

⅓ cup potato starch

⅓ cup almond flour

2 tablespoons sorghum or brown rice flour

1 tablespoon flaxseed meal

¼ teaspoon xanthan gum

¼ teaspoon salt

2 tablespoons non-dairy buttery spread or solid coconut oil

2 to 3 tablespoons warm water

P.F. Chang-Style Chicken in Lettuce Wraps

Dairy-free and *Egg-free*

MAKES 4 SERVINGS

I brake for Chicken Lettuce Wraps from P.F. Chang's China Bistro. But when I don't have P.F. Chang's in my sights and I am hungry for this refreshing and filling appetizer, I feed my craving with my own rendition, created when I was attending Chinese cooking school many years ago. I think you'll agree that it comes close to the real deal.

▶ For the marinade: In a medium bowl combine the sherry, cornstarch, tamari, and black pepper. Add the ground chicken and mix well. Set aside while making the sauce.

▶ For the cooking sauce: Combine the Sriracha sauce, tamari, sherry, and sugar, together in a small bowl. Set the cooking sauce aside.

continues

Marinade

1 tablespoon dry sherry

2 teaspoons cornstarch

2 teaspoons wheat-free tamari or soy sauce (see Pantry, page 276)

Ground black pepper to taste

1 pound ground chicken

Cooking Sauce

2 teaspoons Sriracha chili sauce, or Chinese or Thai chili sauce (see Pantry, page 276)

1 tablespoon wheat-free tamari

2 teaspoons dry sherry

Pinch of sugar

continues

continued

▶ For the filling: Heat a wok or large skillet over high heat. Add 1 to 2 tablespoons oil. When heated, add the ground chicken and stir-fry until the chicken is golden, breaking the mixture into small pieces as you stir. Add the mushrooms and stir-fry for 1 minute. Add the garlic, ginger, green onions, water chestnuts, and bamboo shoots and sauté 2 minutes or just until the green onions are wilted. Add the cooking sauce and stir to coat. Stir in the sesame oil and remove from the heat.

▶ Heat 1 cup of oil in a small saucepan over medium-high heat. Add a handful of rice vermicelli and cook for 30 seconds, until they are puffed. Use a large slotted spoon and transfer to a plate lined with paper towels and drain. Repeat with the remaining vermicelli.

▶ Arrange a lettuce leaf on a serving plate and spoon about ½ cup of the stir-fry mixture onto each lettuce leaf. Top with a handful of the crisp noodles. Sprinkle with additional tamari sauce, if desired. Fold the ends and sides of the leaf and roll up.

Tip: To detach the lettuce leaves, cut around the stem and gently release the leaves from the stalk.

Shortcut:

▶ Use Dorot brand frozen minced garlic and ginger (see Pantry, page 277).

Filling

Vegetable oil or olive oil for cooking

1 cup finely chopped fresh shiitake mushrooms

2 garlic cloves, minced

1 teaspoon minced ginger

½ cup chopped green onions, white and light green parts (about 6 onions)

one 8-ounce can water chestnuts, drained and finely chopped

½ cup bamboo shoots (½ of one 8 ounce can), drained and finely chopped

1 teaspoon toasted (dark) sesame oil

1 cup broken rice vermicelli

8 to 10 iceberg lettuce leaves, rinsed and drained

Pot Stickers

Dairy-free and *Egg-free*

MAKES 24 TO 32 LARGE DUMPLINGS

When I met Alfred Chung, chef and owner of Lilli and Loo, an Asian restaurant chain in New York City, he gave me his tempura recipe (page 112) and I gave him this recipe, which he now serves as part of their gluten-free menu. Don't skimp on the ginger and other flavorings. They make the dish.

▶ For the filling: Combine the ground chicken, cabbage, ginger, green onions, sherry, soy sauce, salt, garlic, and sesame oil in a large bowl. Cover and refrigerate for 30 minutes.

▶ For the dipping sauce: Combine the soy sauce, vinegar, sesame oil, garlic, and red chili oil. Set aside.

▶ For the dough: Combine the tapioca starch, cornstarch, rice flour, and xanthan gum in the bowl of a food processor fitted with the steel blade. Process while slowly adding the boiling water in a thin stream just until the dough begins to clump and form a ball. Add the remaining 1 to 2 tablespoons water, a little at a time, until the dough is soft and pliable. Process 10 seconds more. Remove the dough and form into a ball. Knead gently for 2 to 3 minutes on a surface dusted with rice flour or between sheets of oiled plastic wrap.

▶ Divide the dough in half. Wrap one half tightly in plastic wrap. Using both hands, roll the other half into a log about 1 inch in diameter. Cut the log into four equal pieces. Then cut those four pieces into four equal slices (16 total). Repeat with the remaining half of the dough.

continues

Filling

½ pound ground chicken or pork

¼ cup finely chopped Chinese cabbage

1 tablespoon chopped fresh ginger

2 green onions, chopped

1½ teaspoons dry sherry

1½ teaspoons gluten-free soy sauce (see Pantry, page 276)

¼ teaspoon coarse salt

1 garlic clove, minced

1½ teaspoons toasted (dark) sesame oil

Dipping Sauce

1½ tablespoons gluten-free soy sauce

1 tablespoon rice vinegar

¼ teaspoon toasted (dark) sesame oil

1 teaspoon minced garlic

Dash of red chili oil or red pepper flakes

Dough

⅔ cup tapioca starch/flour

⅔ cup cornstarch

⅔ cup white rice flour

½ teaspoon xanthan gum

¾ cup boiling water, 1 to 2 tablespoons reserved

continues

continued

▶ Set a piece of dough on a smooth surface. Cover the remaining pieces with a moist paper towel. Using the palm of your hand, press the dough into a 3-inch round. Place 1 tablespoon of the filling off-center on the circle and fold the edges over the filling to form a half circle. Bring the edges together, pleating in accordion-fashion from the outside to the center. Repeat with the remaining dough and the remaining filling.

▶ Heat a large, heavy skillet over medium-high heat. Add enough oil to coat the bottom of the skillet. Add enough dumplings, seam side up, to cover the pan in one layer. (You may have to make two or more batches.) Fry until the bottoms are crisp and golden brown, but not scorched, about 5 minutes. Brown on the sides and then turn upright again. Add enough chicken stock to come ½ inch up the sides of the dumplings and cover tightly. Reduce the temperature to low and simmer 5 minutes, or until most of the liquid is absorbed. Remove the lid and let the remaining liquid evaporate. Lift a dumpling with a spatula and check the bottom. When it feels crispy to the touch, turn out onto a platter. Serve with lots of dipping sauce.

▶ Dumplings may be frozen for later use before cooking. Thaw and follow instructions for cooking. May be frozen after they are cooked. To reheat, sauté in a lightly-oiled skillet turning once or twice. Add 2 tablespoons of chicken broth or water and allow to simmer until evaporated.

Shortcut:

▶ Buy Dorot brand frozen minced cubes of ginger and garlic located in your supermarket freezer (see Pantry, page 277). It will save on preparation time. Each cube measures 1 teaspoon.

continued

Vegetable oil for cooking

1 cup gluten-free chicken stock (see Pantry, page 277) or water

Risotto Squares

Comfort food Italian style, this easy cheese, spinach, and rice dish can be done a day ahead and warmed just before serving. I cut these into small squares and serve them with cocktails, but this is perfect as a Make and Take dish for a potluck or buffet meal.

- ▶ Preheat the oven to 350°F. Lightly oil a 9 x 13-inch baking dish.
- ▶ In a medium saucepan, sauté the onion in oil over low heat just until translucent. Raise the heat to medium, add the rice, and toss to coat. Cook about 2 minutes. Add the wine and simmer until most of the liquid has evaporated. Add 1 cup of the chicken broth and simmer until most of the liquid has been absorbed. Gently shake the pan. If the rice is not moving, loosen with a spoon but do not stir. Add the remaining broth, 1 cup at a time, allowing the liquid to be absorbed before the next addition. Add salt and pepper to taste.
- ▶ Spread the spinach over a plate and microwave for 2 minutes. Squeeze the spinach dry to remove the extra moisture and set aside.
- ▶ Combine the ricotta and eggs in a mixing bowl and beat well. Stir in 1 cup of the Parmesan cheese and the nutmeg. Fold in the spinach and the rice mixture. Spread into the dish.
- ▶ Bake for 25 minutes. Top with the remaining Parmesan cheese and bake an additional 5 minutes. Let cool on the counter or in the refrigerator, until the mixture is set and firm. Cut into squares and serve.

1 medium onion, finely chopped

Olive oil

1¼ cups Arborio rice

¾ cup white wine

3 cups gluten-free chicken broth (see Pantry, page 277)

Salt and pepper

2 cups frozen, chopped spinach

one 16-ounce container part-skim ricotta cheese

3 large eggs

1¼ cups grated Parmesan cheese

Several grinds of fresh nutmeg or ¼ teaspoon ground nutmeg

VARIATION: Make Risotto Cakes *Arancini* by combining 3 cups Risotto Square mixture and 1 cup gluten-free dried bread crumbs. Spread another cup of bread crumbs over the surface of a large plate. Scoop out golf ball–size portions of the risotto square mixture and form into 12 to 16 patties. Dredge each patty in the bread crumbs. Fry in oil over medium heat until golden, about 3 to 5 minutes on each side. Transfer to a cookie sheet and bake in a 350°F oven for 10 minutes. Serve with good quality marinara sauce, if desired.

Rock Shrimp Tempura

Dairy-free

MAKES 30 PIECES

Asian food can be a quagmire for gluten-free diners and tempura is virtually always off-limits. This is the exception and it's deliciously addictive, light, and crispy. The recipe comes from Alfred Chong, chef and co-owner of Lilli and Loo's in Manhattan, and is offered as part of their extensive gluten-free menu.

2 cups mayonnaise

1 to 2 tablespoons orange juice

1 tablespoon sugar

Zest and juice of 1 lime

Zest and juice of 1 lemon

2½ tablespoons Sriracha chili sauce or other spicy chili sauce (see Pantry, page 276)

1 cup cornstarch

⅓ cup cold water

2 cups rock shrimp or other small shrimp, peeled

2 cups vegetable oil

▶ Combine the mayonnaise, orange juice to taste, and sugar in a large bowl. Mix well with a wire whisk. Add the lime and lemon zest and juice and the Sriracha sauce. Mix well. Taste and add more chili sauce according to your desired spiciness. Set aside.

▶ In a separate bowl, mix together 4 to 5 tablespoons of the cornstarch and the water to form a thin batter. The batter should be smooth and without lumps. Add the rock shrimp to the batter and mix to coat.

▶ Coat a flat plate with a thin, even layer of cornstarch. Remove the rock shrimp from the batter to the plate and roll to evenly coat. (The shrimp will look lumpy.)

▶ Heat the oil to 325°F in a heavy saucepan. Place the coated shrimp into the hot oil, a few at a time and fry until crispy, about 4 to 5 minutes. Drain on paper towels.

▶ Put crispy shrimp in a shallow bowl. Add 2 tablespoons, or more of the citrus mayonnaise and toss to coat well. Stack the rock shrimp tempura on a plate and garnish with a wedge of lime or a sprig of mint. Serve with the remaining sauce for dipping.

Avoiding Shellfish? *The shrimp may be replaced with 2 cups of boneless, skinless chicken breast cut into ½-inch cubes, or 2 cups of chunks of zucchini or mushrooms.*

Socca

(Chickpea Flatbread)

Dairy-free and *Egg-free*

MAKES 2 TO 3 FLATBREADS

This delightful flatbread makes a perfect appetizer to have with a glass of wine or gluten-free beer. Even people who don't like the taste of chickpea flour will enjoy this Provençal street food. The mixture needs to sit for several hours, so mix the ingredients in advance.

1 cup chickpea flour

¾ teaspoon coarse salt

¼ teaspoon ground chipotle pepper, optional

6 to 8 tablespoons good quality olive oil

1 cup lukewarm water

▶ Combine the chickpea flour, salt, chipotle pepper, 2 tablespoons olive oil, and the water. Whisk to remove any lumps. Cover and let stand at room temperature 2 to 4 hours, until the mixture thickens and resembles pancake batter.

▶ Place the oven rack in the lowest position. Preheat the oven to 500°F or the hottest setting. Pour 1 to 2 tablespoons oil in a cast-iron or other heavy-duty ovenproof skillet. Set in the oven to heat for 2 to 3 minutes. Remove, using a heavy oven mitt.

▶ Whisk the batter and pour one-third to one-half over the pan. Swirl to cover the bottom and bake on the lowest rack for 8 to 10 minutes, until the edges are brown and the center no longer looks opaque. Carefully remove the pan from the oven. Brush the socca with olive oil. Use a wide spatula to remove to serving tray. Top with a combination of toppings below or use your favorites. Repeat until all batter is used. Cut Socca into wedges and serve.

Tip: Instead of a cast-iron skillet, a pizza pan may be used, but it will not be as easy to handle. Use two mitts to balance and move the pan in and out of the oven.

Toppings:

▶ Thinly slice a medium onion and sauté with a sprinkle of sugar until caramelized. Spread over socca and top with pine nuts.

▶ Slice sundried tomatoes (in oil) into thin strips. Crumble goat cheese or grated Parmesan cheese over socca. Add tomato strips, and halved Nicoise olives.

▶ Top with hummus and roasted red peppers.

Antipasto Pasta Salad

MAKES 8 SERVINGS

Summer picnics are filled with potluck dishes that are orphaned by their owners. Other than a naked burger, I'm usually nervous about touching any of these delicious-looking dishes. This flavorful salad is my solution: it's a meal in itself and one that everyone enjoys. If I load up on this salad, I can enjoy the company and not worry about going hungry.

▶ Combine all the ingredients in a large bowl and toss. If making ahead, prepare all the ingredients but do not toss or dress until just before serving.

Tip: *The problem with doing a pasta salad ahead is that gluten-free pasta, particularly rice pasta absorbs all the dressing as it sits and the pasta starts to break down. For do-ahead: prepare all the ingredients the day before and mix everything a couple of hours before serving.*

8 ounces corn or corn and quinoa pasta (fusilli or elbow shape), cooked al dente, rinsed, and drained

1 head Romaine lettuce, washed, dried, and cut in ½-inch strips

one 12-ounce jar roasted red peppers, drained and sliced into strips

1 pint cherry tomatoes, washed and halved

2 cups canned chickpeas, rinsed and drained

¾ cup kalamata olives, halved

½ pound thick-sliced pepperoni, cut into 1-inch strips

½ pound thick-sliced ham, cut into 1-inch strips

½ pound mozzarella cheese, cubed

Handful pepperoncini peppers

1 cup good-quality bottled Caesar dressing, plus more if needed

Broccoli Cranberry Salad

Dairy-free

MAKES 6 SERVINGS

When I saw a version of this salad at every pool party and school function, I wondered if I could eat it. Although some were probably okay, I didn't try any of them. Was the bacon real, what was in the dressing? I couldn't know for certain. This updated, calorie-reduced version imparts the slightly sweet and tart flavors of cranberries, orange, and bacon that perk up the traditional picnic favorite.

▶ In a large bowl, combine the broccoli florets, onion, cranberries, pecans, and bacon.

▶ For the dressing: In a small bowl, combine the mayonnaise, orange juice, vinegar, sugar, and pepper.

▶ Toss the salad gently with the dressing and refrigerate for at least 4 hours or overnight.

1 large head broccoli, florets only, or one 16-ounce bag frozen florets, thawed

¾ cup chopped red onion

½ cup dried cranberries

½ cup chopped pecans or ⅓ cup sunflower seeds

5 to 6 slices turkey bacon, crisp-cooked and crumbled

Dressing

¾ cup low-fat mayonnaise

¼ cup orange juice

2 tablespoons cider vinegar

2 tablespoons sugar

Freshly ground black pepper

Chicken Salad with Grapes, Pecans, and Blue Cheese

MAKES 6 SERVINGS

This elegant, easy salad bursts with flavor thanks to the marriage of slightly bitter blue cheese and the crisp sweetness of red grapes. So simple now, this tasty dish would have been impossible a few years ago when most blue cheese was grown on bread mold. Today, most manufacturers inject gluten-free mold into the cheese to create the dark blue veins. Be sure to check labels, however. Some artisanal cheesemakers still use traditional techniques.

▶ In a large serving bowl, combine the chicken, grapes, blue cheese, and pecans and toss. Add the chives and parsley and stir to combine.

▶ For the dressing: Whisk together the mayonnaise, vinegar, and sugar in a bowl.

▶ Toss the dressing with the chicken salad. Refrigerate for at least 2 hours or overnight to allow the flavors to mingle.

1 gluten-free rotisserie chicken, meat cubed

2 cups halved seedless red grapes

½ cup blue cheese, crumbled (see Pantry, page 272)

1 cup pecan halves, toasted lightly and broken into pieces

3 tablespoons dried or chopped fresh chives

¼ cup dried parsley or ½ cup chopped fresh parsley

Dressing

¾ cup light mayonnaise

3 tablespoons sherry vinegar

2 teaspoons sugar

The scoop on blue cheese: Many leading scientists and food chemists believe that all blue cheese is safe as the mold, even if grown from bread, is many generations removed from the actual cheese and tests do not show any traces of gluten. Nevertheless, some artisanal cheesemakers still say "contains wheat" on their labels while other manufacturers state that their product is gluten-free. See the Pantry section on page 272 for gluten-free brands.

Quinoa Salad with Apples, Grapes, and Roasted Cashews

Dairy-free and *Egg-free*

MAKES 6

This refreshing salad can be served with almost any meal in any season. You can replace grapes with dried cranberries. If the cranberries are sweetened, reduce the amount of honey to 1 tablespoon.

▸ Combine the quinoa with the cold water and ½ teaspoon salt. Bring to a boil and simmer 12 to 15 minutes or until the quinoa is tender. Drain and cool.

▸ In a large serving bowl, mix the vinegar, honey, sherry, oil, the remaining ¼ teaspoon salt, dill, celery, grapes, and apple. Add the cooled quinoa and let sit in the refrigerator at least 1 hour. Add the cashews just before serving.

Tip: *To make quinoa, rinse several times in cold water before cooking to remove any lingering bitter aftertaste.*

⅔ cup white or red quinoa

1⅓ cups cold water

¾ teaspoon salt

2 tablespoons white or dark balsamic vinegar

2 tablespoons honey

2 tablespoons dry sherry

2 tablespoons olive oil

2 teaspoons chopped fresh dill or 1 teaspoon dried dillweed

1 celery stalk, sliced

½ cup red seedless grapes, sliced in half

½ cup chopped unpeeled apple

⅓ cup roasted cashews

Stir-Fry Asian Vegetables

Dairy-free and *Egg-free*

MAKES 2 TO 4 SERVINGS

This simple dish has a fresh, slightly exotic taste. It's great paired with Charred Vietnamese Chicken on page 148 or served as is. To add protein, cube one-half of a boneless, skinless chicken breast and sauté with fish sauce or soy sauce (see Pantry, page 276). Spoon around the vegetables just before serving and accompany with steamed white rice.

▶ In a hot sauté pan, heat the olive oil. Add the bok choy and Napa cabbage and sauté for 1 minute. Add the mushrooms and sauté an additional minute. Add the sugar and sherry and stir to coat the vegetables. Season with salt and pepper. Arrange on a serving dish.

1 tablespoon olive oil

1 cup large diced bok choy, green leaves discarded

2 cups large diced Chinese Napa cabbage, leafy portion discarded

1 cup sliced shiitake mushroom caps, stems discarded

1 teaspoon sugar

2 tablespoons dry sherry

Salt and pepper

Wrap-up Filling: Turkey and Veggie

MAKES ENOUGH FOR 1 WRAP

Double, triple, or quadruple these ingredients based on the number of servings needed.

▶ Combine the mayonnaise and salsa in a small bowl. Spread over the wrap. Arrange the turkey slices over the spread. Top with the corn, lettuce, tomato, and cheese. Roll up and enjoy.

Shortcut:

▶ Use commercial gluten-free wraps (see Pantry, 277) in place of the homemade wraps.

2 tablespoons mayonnaise

1 tablespoon good quality salsa

1 or more Wraps-ody in Gluten-Free Harmony (page 61)

3 slices smoked turkey breast

2 tablespoons frozen corn niblets, thawed

¼ cup shredded lettuce

1 small tomato, chopped

Shredded cheddar cheese, optional

Wrap-up Filling: Teriyaki Beef or Chicken with Asian Slaw

Dairy-free

MAKES 4 SERVINGS

- ▸ Marinate the steak or chicken in the teriyaki sauce for 1 hour.
- ▸ Combine the mayonnaise, rice vinegar, sugar, and sesame oil. Toss with the coleslaw mix and chill.
- ▸ Remove the meat from the marinade and broil on both sides until cooked through, about 10 minutes. Slice thinly.
- ▸ Spread several pieces of meat in the center of each wrap and top with ½ cup of the slaw mixture. Roll up the wraps and enjoy.

½ pound sirloin steak or 4 chicken fillets (about ½ pound)

¼ cup teriyaki sauce (see Pantry, page 276)

¼ cup low-fat mayonnaise

2 tablespoons rice vinegar

2 teaspoons sugar

2 teaspoons toasted (dark) sesame oil

2 cups (about 3 ounces) coleslaw mix

4 Wraps-ody in Gluten-Free Harmony (page 61)

Butternut Squash Bisque

MAKES 8 SERVINGS

When the air turns crisp and butternut squash and pumpkins replace corn and tomatoes at the farmers' market, this soup becomes a staple in my house. It's a great pick-me-up on chilly days and a delicious company dish. As part of a special meal, I like to add ¼ cup Calvados or substitute 1 cup of cider for 1 cup of broth.

- 2 tablespoons olive oil
- 1 medium onion, finely chopped
- 1 medium leek, white and pale green parts only, chopped
- 6 cups peeled and cubed butternut squash
- 2 teaspoons good-quality curry powder
- 2 large Granny Smith apples, peeled, cored, and chopped
- 4 cups chicken or vegetable broth, plus more as needed (see Pantry, page 272)
- 4 slices of gluten-free bread (page 42), crust removed, cut into quarters, and toasted
- Crème fraîche or plain Greek-style yogurt
- Toasted, slivered almonds, optional

▸ Heat the oil in a large saucepan. Add the onion and sauté over low heat until slightly opaque. Add the leek and sauté until the onion and leek are soft and translucent. Add the squash and toss to coat. Sauté for 2 minutes. Add the curry and apples and continue to cook over low heat an additional 3 to 4 minutes.

▸ Add 4 cups of the broth. Cover and simmer 25 to 30 minutes or until the squash and apples are soft. Cool slightly and purée in batches in a blender or food processor. If the soup is too thick, add a small amount of additional broth until you reach the desired consistency. Keep warm.

▸ Place 1 to 2 squares of toast in the bottom of each bowl. Ladle soup into bowls and top with a dollop of crème fraîche and a handful of almonds. Serve.

Shortcuts:

▸ Buy butternut squash that's already peeled and cubed. Use an immersion blender to purée the soup in the pot.

▸ Purchase prepared gluten-free bread.

Condensed Cream of Mushroom Soup

Egg-free

MAKES 2 TO 2½ CUPS

For years, people bemoaned the fact that going gluten-free meant giving up the condensed soups that led to many time-honored casseroles. My intention, when I created this recipe, was to bring back that medium. However, as the recipe evolved, I realized this was almost too delicious to add to a casserole. On the other hand, imagine what heights you'll reach when you use this easy recipe as the base of your next one-dish meal?

- 2 tablespoons olive oil
- 1 shallot, minced
- ½ pound mushrooms: shiitake, cremini, or button, stems discarded and caps chopped
- 1 tablespoon unsalted butter or non-dairy buttery spread
- 3 tablespoons rice flour
- 2 cups beef broth, plus more as needed (see Pantry, page 277)
- ½ cup milk, soy milk, or rice milk
- Salt and pepper

▸ Heat the oil in a medium saucepan over medium heat. Sauté the shallot and mushrooms until the mushrooms are tender and the liquid has evaporated, about 3 minutes.

▸ Add the butter and melt. Sprinkle the rice flour over the butter and mushroom mixture and stir so the flour does not burn. Add 1 cup of broth, a little at a time, until the mixture thickens. Add the milk and salt and pepper to taste. Bring to a simmer. Purée or serve as is.

▸ The soup will thicken as it cools. Thin with broth to the desired consistency.

▸ This can be stored in the refrigerator for several days or frozen for several weeks.

Connie's Un-Matzo Balls and Chicken Soup

Dairy-free

MAKES 8 TO 10 MATZO BALLS

MAKES 4 SERVINGS

I can't take credit for this wonderful discovery—only for knowing the ingenious cook, Connie Margolin, who gave me the formula for un-matzo balls several years ago. I'm told it's inspired by a recipe from *Jewish Holiday Kitchen* by Joan Nathan. I've made a few of my own changes and I make a double or triple batch as they disappear before the meal is over. Use this recipe for dumplings, too.

- ▶ Beat the eggs with the chicken fat in a large bowl. In a separate bowl, combine the potato flakes, potato starch, salt, baking soda, xanthan gum, and cinnamon and add to the egg mixture. Add ¼ cup of chicken broth and chill for 20 to 30 minutes.
- ▶ Using wet hands, shape the matzo mixture into 1-inch balls and steam on a steaming ring in a wok. Allow the balls to steam, covered, for about 20 minutes.
- ▶ Bring 4 cups of chicken broth to a simmer in a large saucepan fitted with a lid. Add the carrots and simmer until fork tender. Add the matzo balls and heat. Serve one or two matzo balls with some broth and a spoonful of carrots.

4 large eggs

3 tablespoons rendered chicken fat, softened,* or non-dairy buttery spread

1 cup instant potato flakes (not powdered instant potatoes)

2 tablespoons potato starch

½ teaspoon salt

¼ teaspoon baking soda

¼ teaspoon xanthan gum

¼ teaspoon ground cinnamon

¼ cup plus 4 cups chicken broth (see Pantry, page 277)

1 cup chopped carrots

*If starting with homemade chicken soup, scoop the fat from the top of the chilled soup.

Cream of Chicken Soup

Egg-free

MAKES 6 CUPS

This beautiful soup serves so many purposes in a gluten-free pantry. Add chunks of cooked chicken and enjoy as a soup or purée and use for casseroles and sauces.

- ▶ In a large saucepan, heat the oil over medium heat. Add the onion, celery, and carrots and cook until soft, about 15 minutes. Do not let the vegetables take on color. Sprinkle the flour over the vegetables and stir. Cook about 2 minutes, stirring continuously.
- ▶ Add 6 cups of the broth, stirring constantly. Bring to a boil, whisking to thicken evenly. Reduce the heat to a simmer and add the parsley, thyme, and bay leaf. Cover and simmer for 10 to 15 minutes. Remove from the heat.
- ▶ Use a slotted spoon to remove the bay leaf and parsley and discard. Scoop out some of the vegetables into a strainer being held over the soup pot and mash the vegetables through the strainer into the soup. Scrape the outside of the strainer to make sure all the vegetable essence goes back into the pot. Add the milk and sherry, if using. Check the consistency and add 1 to 2 cups of the remaining chicken broth as needed. If using as a sauce or gravy, purée the vegetables or strain them out of the mixture before using.

2 tablespoons olive oil

1 medium onion, chopped

1 celery stalk, chopped

2 carrots, peeled and chopped

⅓ cup rice flour

7 to 8 cups gluten-free chicken broth (see Pantry, page 277)

2 parsley sprigs

2 teaspoons thyme

1 bay leaf

½ cup milk, rice milk, or soy milk

1 to 2 tablespoons dry sherry, optional

Salt and pepper to taste

Roasted Turkey Gravy

Egg-free

This is my favorite Thanksgiving gravy recipe. For variation, replace wine and orange juice with ½ cup dry sherry.

▸ Spoon the pan juices from the roasted turkey and the roasting pan into a 3-cup measuring cup. Let cool and skim off the fat. Add enough giblet stock and chicken broth to make 2 to 3 cups; set aside.

▸ Sauté the mushrooms, if using, in 1 tablespoon olive oil in a small pan. Set aside.

▸ In a saucepan, melt 2 tablespoons of the butter over low heat. Add the onion and sauté until soft, about 3 minutes. Add the wine and orange juice. Simmer until reduced by half. Add the pan juices and broth mixture and simmer for 6 minutes to reduce. Stir in the cornstarch mixture and stir until thickened. Add the sautéed mushrooms, if using. Check the seasonings and add salt and pepper as needed. Serve warm.

one 14 to 16 pound roasted turkey, pan juices reserved

Giblet stock (page 126)

Chicken broth

¾ cup sliced mushrooms, optional

3 tablespoons unsalted butter or olive oil

1 medium onion, chopped

¼ cup white wine

⅓ cup orange juice

2 tablespoons cornstarch mixed with 3 tablespoons orange juice

Salt and pepper to taste

Tips: *Here's another way to thicken gravy: For each cup of gravy, mash together 1 tablespoon softened butter and 1 tablespoon brown rice flour to form a paste. Whisk into the thickened, simmering gravy. Add more butter and flour if necessary to achieve the desired consistency.*

To reduce saltiness, add the juice of ½ lemon.

Giblet Stock

Dairy-free and Egg-free

▶ In a medium saucepan, combine the giblets, carrot, onion, parsley, garlic, and salt and pepper. Cover with 2 to 3 cups of water. Simmer, covered, for 1 hour or until the giblets are tender. Remove the giblets; reserve if desired. Strain the stock and mash the vegetables through the strainer. Chop the giblets and return them to the stock, if using.

Turkey giblets, rinsed

1 large carrot, unpeeled and cut into chunks

1 small onion, peeled

Handful of fresh parsley sprigs

1 garlic clove, peeled and slightly crushed

Salt and pepper to taste

Baked Potato Gnocchi

Dairy-free

MAKES ABOUT 50 PIECES

This quick and delicious recipe was a happy accident. I was trying to convert a potato dumpling recipe but then I started rolling and cutting tiny pieces and dropping them into the boiling water. They cooked up in no time and were far more delicate than any gluten-free gnocchi I've ever tasted. I use my Basic Blend (page 17) but you can use any all-purpose flour blend you have on hand. This is a great way to use up leftover baked potatoes.

1 large Idaho baking potato

½ cup plus 1 tablespoon Basic Blend or other all-purpose gluten-free flour (page 17)

1 large egg

½ teaspoon salt

¼ teaspoon ground or freshly grated nutmeg

▶ Preheat the oven to 400°F.

▶ Pierce the potato in several places and wrap in aluminum foil. Bake for about 1 hour, or until soft. Let cool and then refrigerate for 2 to 24 hours. Peel and chop the potato.

▶ In a medium mixing bowl, mix the chopped potato with the flour blend, egg, salt, and nutmeg. Knead the mixture until it forms a paste. Don't worry if you feel tiny lumps of potato. Break up the bigger lumps between your fingers and work into the paste.

▶ Form the dough into a ball; divide the dough into three pieces. Roll each piece in a sheet of plastic wrap into ¾-inch-thick rope. Slice each rope into 1-inch pieces using a sharp knife and place on a baking sheet. Roll the tines of a fork over each piece, if desired.

▶ Bring a large low pot of salted water to a boil. Lower the heat to a gentle simmer. Drop one third of the gnocchi into the simmering water and cook for about 2 to 4 minutes or until they float. Using a slotted spoon, skim them out gently and transfer to a bowl. Toss with marinara sauce and serve.

▶ If not serving immediately, transfer the gnocchi to an ice water bath. When they are cool, remove with a slotted spoon and place on a baking sheet that has been coated with olive oil.

Baked Risotto

Egg-free

MAKES 8 SERVINGS

This easy and delicious meal, perfect for company, is adapted from a recipe given to me by Betty Lockwood of Chicago who first served this at a support group gathering I attended. It's easy and another one that's ideal to Make and Take.

▶ Preheat the oven to 325°F. Lightly oil a 9 x 13-inch ovenproof baking dish.

▶ In a large ovenproof pan, heat 2 tablespoons of the oil over medium heat. Crumble the sausage into the pan and sauté until no longer pink. Using a slotted spoon, remove to a plate and set aside.

▶ Add the remaining 1 tablespoon of oil and sauté the mushrooms and onion until soft. Add the rice and stir to coat. Return the sausage to the pan and stir. Add the sherry and bring to a boil. Allow the liquid to reduce some. Add the chicken broth. Check the seasonings and add salt and pepper if needed.* Bring to a simmer and transfer the risotto to the prepared pan. Bake uncovered for 20 minutes, adding more chicken broth if the risotto looks dry.

▶ Fold in 2 tablespoons of the cheese and return to the oven to bake another 15 minutes, or until the rice is tender but still retains a tiny bit of crunch. Top with the remaining cheese and serve.

▶ The risotto can be made a few hours ahead, if it is not fully baked. Overbaking will cause the rice to be mushy.

*The chicken broth, sausage, and cheese impart plenty of salt to this dish so I do not add salt when I make it. Unless you like a lot of salt in your food, you probably will not need more either.

---

3 tablespoons extra virgin olive oil

3 links chicken sausages (combination of hot and mild), casings removed

8 ounces cremini or other mushrooms, cleaned and chopped

1 medium onion, diced

1¼ cups Arborio rice

½ cup dry sherry

3 cups good-quality chicken broth, plus more as needed

Salt and pepper to taste

¼ cup grated Parmesan cheese

Tip: I prefer the taste of dry sherry in this recipe, but white wine will work, too.

Caesar Spaghetti

MAKES 4 TO 6 SERVINGS

I saw a version of this recipe in *Woman's Day Magazine* many years ago and several other versions have appeared in my life since. I am not sure if it's the anchovies or the sautéed Romaine lettuce that called to me, but the results are delicious. Anchovies are standard in this recipe. If you don't care for them, they can be omitted but add a little salt to punch up the flavor.

▶ Cook the spaghetti in a large pot of lightly salted boiling water until al dente.

▶ Heat 1 tablespoon olive oil in a large skillet over medium-high heat. Add the bread crumbs and stir to coat with oil. Continue stirring until the bread crumbs are toasted, about 2 to 3 minutes. Transfer to a bowl. Wipe out the skillet.

▶ Heat the remaining tablespoon of oil in a skillet. Add the garlic and sauté 1 minute or until fragrant. Add the broth and Romaine. Cover and cook about 3 minutes or until the lettuce is wilted. Add the anchovies and red pepper flakes and stir to combine. Add the cooked spaghetti and tomatoes and toss to coat. When the mixture is heated through, transfer to a serving platter. Combine the bread crumbs and cheese in a small bowl and sprinkle over the pasta.

12 ounces rice or corn spaghetti

2 tablespoons olive oil

½ cup dried plain bread crumbs (see Pantry, page 272)

1 tablespoon minced garlic

1 cup gluten-free chicken broth

1 head Romaine lettuce, washed, drained, and cut crosswise into strips (about 8 cups)

one 2-ounce can flat anchovies, drained and chopped, or 1 to 2 tablespoons anchovy paste

¼ teaspoon red pepper flakes

5 canned or fresh plum tomatoes, cut into 1-inch chunks

⅓ cup grated Parmesan cheese

Chicken Pasta with Mushroom Soup and Sun-Dried Tomatoes

MAKES 4

Many people wonder how to replace cream of mushroom soup in their favorite recipes. There are several alternatives including a recipe for mushroom soup on page 122. This was inspired by a recipe I saw in the *Hartford Courant* and the availability of gluten-free commercial brands of mushroom soup.

- ▶ Heat 2 tablespoons of the oil in a large skillet over medium heat. Brown the chicken for about 5 minutes on one side. Turn and brown on the other side about 3 additional minutes. Remove to a platter and set aside.
- ▶ Heat the remaining tablespoon of oil and sauté the onion until slightly brown and soft. Add the soup, wine, tomatoes, basil, and vinegar. Simmer 3 minutes or until the mixture begins to thicken. Add the chicken and simmer an additional 2 to 3 minutes.
- ▶ Spread the pasta over a serving platter. Remove the chicken from the sauce with a slotted spoon and place on top of the pasta. Pour the sauce over the chicken and sprinkle with the cheese, if using.

Shortcut:

- ▶ Several companies make a commercial mushroom soup that is gluten-free. My favorite is Creamy Portobello Mushroom by Imagine Soups. It is dairy-free, too. See page 277.

3 tablespoons olive oil

3 boneless skinless chicken breast halves (about 1⅓ pounds), sliced into ½-inch-thick strips

1 small onion, finely chopped

1½ cups mushroom soup

½ cup white wine

⅓ cup thinly sliced sun-dried tomatoes

2 tablespoons fresh chopped basil

1 tablespoon red wine vinegar

6 ounces fettuccine or other wide gluten-free noodle, cooked and drained

¼ to ⅓ cup grated Parmesan cheese, optional

Company Pasta

MAKES 12 SERVINGS

The ingredients in this recipe can be done ahead so that everything is ready just before company arrives. I've found that corn pasta holds up best and no one can tell that it's gluten-free. The recipe evolved out of necessity when I needed to create something to take to a party for housebound relatives. I had to prepare everything ahead so we could heat and serve it in their very small apartment. In addition, I had to make sure I made something my son and I could also enjoy. The "do-ahead" techniques saved the day.

▶ Cook the pasta in a large pot of boiling salted water for half the time specified on the package. Drain and rinse in cold water. Toss with 2 tablespoons of the olive oil. Set aside.

▶ Preheat the oven to 350°F.

▶ Place the broccoli rabe in a large microwave-proof bowl with a small amount of water. Cover and microwave on high for 3 minutes or until softened slightly. Drain.

▶ In a large skillet, heat the remaining 2 tablespoons of olive oil over medium heat. Crumble the sausage into the pan and sauté with the onion just until the onion is translucent. Add the mushrooms, garlic, and red peppers and sauté for 3 minutes or until the mushrooms begin to give off their juice and the peppers begin to soften. Add the red pepper flakes and salt and pepper.

▶ Add the wine and cook until the liquid is slightly reduced. Add the chicken stock and broccoli rabe and simmer about 5 minutes. Set aside to cool.

1· pound gluten-free pasta
(see Pantry, page 275)

¼ cup extra virgin olive oil

1 bunch broccoli rabe, trimmed and coarsely chopped

5 links spicy chicken sausage, casings removed

1 large onion, chopped

12 ounces cremini or other mushrooms, sliced

3 garlic cloves, minced

1½ red bell peppers, coarsely chopped

Dash of red pepper flakes

Salt and pepper to taste

½ cup white wine, optional

2 cups chicken stock

1½ cups marinara sauce

4 ounces grated smoked mozzarella cheese (plus more for garnish)

continues

continued

▶ The recipe can be prepared up to this point one day ahead. Transfer the pasta and the sausage mixture and store in separate containers in the refrigerator until ready to assemble.

▶ In a large aluminum pan that is at least 3 inches deep, combine the pasta and the sausage mixture. Mix gently and check the seasonings. Toss with the marinara sauce and cheese and cover tightly with aluminum foil. Bake for 15 to 20 minutes or until the cheese is melted and the pasta is soft. Top with additional cheese and serve.

Avoiding Dairy? Omit the cheese or substitute rice or soy cheese (see *Simple Substitutions,* page 267).

To make this a vegetarian meal, omit the sausage and add other vegetables, if desired. Olives and artichoke hearts would work well.

Corn Bread Stuffing

MAKES 8 TO 10 CUPS
(ENOUGH FOR A 12 TO 14 POUND TURKEY WITH SOME LEFT OVER TO BAKE SEPARATELY)

Here's the stuffing recipe that I use most often with the Roasted Turkey on page 163. If you can't have corn or don't like the taste, replace with 6 to 8 cups of your favorite gluten-free bread.

- ▶ Preheat the oven to 350°F.
- ▶ Cut the corn bread into small cubes. Spread over a large cookie sheet and toast for 15 minutes. Cool and set aside.
- ▶ Heat 2 tablespoons of the oil over medium heat in a large skillet. Sauté the celery and onion until soft. Add the apples and 1 to 2 tablespoons of oil and sauté just until the apples soften. Add the raisins, seasoned salt, mustard, nutmeg, and corn bread cubes and toss to coat. The stuffing can be made ahead of time up to this point and refrigerated.
- ▶ Add the orange juice and toss. Add additional juice, if needed, just until the corn bread cubes are moistened.
- ▶ Use as much stuffing as needed to lightly pack the turkey cavity and cook according to the weight of the bird. (See page 163.)
- ▶ Lightly oil a baking dish. Press the remaining stuffing into the dish. Cover and bake for 30 minutes. Remove the cover and bake until the stuffing browns slightly, about 10 minutes.

8-inch square or round gluten-free corn bread, from a gluten-free mix or from scratch

¼ cup extra virgin olive oil

¼ cup chopped celery

¾ cup chopped onion

3 large apples, peeled and chopped

½ cup raisins

2 teaspoons seasoned salt

¾ teaspoon dry mustard

½ teaspoon ground nutmeg

1 cup orange juice, more as needed

Debbie's Applesauce Noodle Pudding

Dairy-free

MAKES 10 SERVINGS

I love the way recipes are passed around and, with them, good friendships. This is one of those recipes that has made the rounds. Being gluten-free, Debbie re-created this dish with adjustments so that she could enjoy it. She brought this noodle pudding to my house when my father passed away. Noodle puddings have a way of showing up at those sorts of things. I have a warm spot for this easy recipe and you will, too, when you try it.

▶ Preheat the oven to 400°F. Grease a 9 x 13-inch baking pan.

▶ Cook the noodles according to the directions on the package. (For a sweeter pudding, add 1 to 2 table-spoons sugar to the water.) Drain well.

▶ Combine the eggs, oil, applesauce, raisins, sugar, cinnamon, and salt in a large bowl. Fold in the cooked noodles until well coated. Pour into the prepared baking pan.

▶ Combine the 2 teaspoons of cinnamon with the sugar in a small bowl and sprinkle over the top of the noodles. Bake uncovered for 45 minutes.

---

one 12-ounce package Thai medium wide rice noodles or 14-ounce Thai Kitchen Stir-Fry Noodles or ¾ package of Notta Pasta Brand Rice Linguine or Fettucine

6 large eggs or 3 whole eggs plus 6 egg whites

½ cup oil

2 cups applesauce

¼ cup golden raisins

¾ cup sugar

¼ teaspoon ground cinnamon

½ teaspoon salt

2 teaspoons ground cinnamon

1 tablespoon sugar

No-Fuss Stuffing

MAKES 10 TO 12 CUPS

Use your favorite prepared bread, bread mix, or recipe for sandwich-style bread, such as the Delicious Slicing Loaf on page 42 to make the bread cubes. A variation on this recipe appeared in my "Perils in the Pantry" column in *Living Without* magazine a few years ago. The best thing about this recipe is that you can add, omit, or substitute wildly and it will always be delicious.

- ▶ Preheat oven to 350°F.
- ▶ Spread the bread cubes in a single layer on cookie sheets and bake until the cubes are dry, about 15 minutes.
- ▶ In a large skillet, heat the oil and sauté the onions and celery until soft. Add the apples and sausage and sauté until the apples are soft, about 3 minutes. Remove from the heat.
- ▶ In a large mixing bowl, combine the bread cubes, the onion mixture, and the cranberries, broth, eggs, poultry seasoning, and chestnuts, if using. Mix until the bread is thoroughly moistened.
- ▶ Use as much stuffing as needed to lightly pack the turkey cavity and cook according to the weight of the bird.
- ▶ Press the remaining stuffing into a lightly oiled baking dish. Cover and bake at 350°F for 45 minutes. Remove the cover and continue baking to let the stuffing brown, about 10 minutes.

8 to 10 cups gluten-free bread cubes

3 tablespoons olive oil

2 cups chopped onions

4 celery stalks, chopped

4 medium apples, peeled and chopped

4 links fully-cooked chicken and apple sausage, chopped

1 cup dried cranberries

1½ cups chicken broth

4 large eggs

2 teaspoons poultry seasoning

¾ cup cooked and peeled chestnuts, chopped, optional

Avoiding Eggs? Omit the eggs *and replace with an additional ½ cup chicken or vegetable broth.*

Pad Thai

Dairy-free

MAKES 2 SERVINGS

Have a yearning for takeout? Well, you could have this wonderful Thai noodle dish on the table in less time than it takes to pick up an order, and you can be sure there's no hidden gluten when you make this recipe yourself. Let the noodles soak while you organize the remaining ingredients.

- ▶ Soak the rice noodles in cool water for 1 hour then drain.
- ▶ Heat the oil in a large frying pan or wok over high heat until the oil begins to smoke. Add the shrimp and sauté for 1 minute. Break the eggs over the shrimp and allow to sit for 1 minute, then scramble the mixture. Add the rice noodles and paprika; stir briefly. Add the fish sauce, sugar, vinegar, and peanuts, if using. Sauté for 30 seconds.
- ▶ Combine the green onions, bean sprouts, garlic, and red pepper flakes in a small bowl and add to the mixture. Toss to heat. Remove from the heat, spoon into a serving dish, and garnish with a lemon wedge.

3½ ounces medium rice noodles (about 1½ cups after soaking)

¼ cup vegetable oil

6 large shrimp, peeled and deveined

2 large eggs

½ teaspoon paprika

¼ cup fish sauce (see Pantry, page 276)

2 tablespoons sugar

¼ cup rice vinegar

¼ cup ground unsalted peanuts, optional

4 green onions, cut into 1-inch pieces

½ cup fresh bean sprouts, rinsed and drained

2 garlic cloves, minced

¼ to ½ teaspoon red pepper flakes

Lemon wedge

Penne with Pancetta and Asparagus in Vodka Sauce

MAKES 6 SERVINGS

This velvety tomato sauce is spiked with a hint of vodka and spice. Add more cream and grated cheese for richness, if desired. Serve with a Caesar salad and a glass of Pinot Noir and you'll be all set for an evening of fine dining. My tester, Daniel, used artichoke hearts in place of asparagus and omitted the pancetta and thought the results were wonderful.

- Bring a large pot of water to a boil. Cook the penne until just tender, according to the package directions. Drain.
- Heat a large saucepan over medium heat. Add the pancetta and sauté until the pieces begin to brown. Remove to a paper towel lined plate to drain. Discard all but 1 tablespoon of the drippings from the pan.
- Over medium-low heat, add the leek to the drippings and cook until soft, about 3 minutes. Add the garlic and cook an additional minute. Add the vodka and bring to a boil. Simmer until reduced by half, about 2 minutes. Stir in the tomatoes, half-and-half, Worcestershire sauce, and crushed red pepper to taste. Reduce the heat to a simmer. Cover and cook until thickened, about 10 minutes, stirring frequently. Stir in the basil, pepper, and asparagus. Heat briefly.
- Spoon the pasta into a large serving dish. Top with the sauce and sprinkle with cheese, if using.

9 ounces brown rice or corn penne (see Pantry, page 275)

6 ounces pancetta, finely diced

1 small leek (white and light green parts), rinsed thoroughly and chopped

3 garlic cloves, chopped

½ cup vodka

one 28-ounce can crushed tomatoes

¼ to ½ cup half-and-half or non-dairy creamer

2 teaspoons Worcestershire sauce

¼ to ½ teaspoon crushed red pepper

¼ cup chopped fresh basil

Freshly ground pepper to taste

2 cups (1-inch-long pieces) grilled or blanched asparagus

Grated Parmesan cheese, optional

Potato and Cheese Pierogi

MAKES 28 TO 32 PIEROGI

Every Christmas, Lisa Turcotte and her grandmother made pierogi from an old family recipe. The two were covered in flour and the kitchen was a disaster, but they had so much fun that it became a tradition of its own. First they experimented with different fillings and doughs until they found one that the family preferred. When Lisa was diagnosed with celiac disease, the two adapted the family recipe so she could continue to enjoy the pierogi. Her grandmother is gone, but Lisa needs only prepare a batch of these delicious Polish delicacies to return to those special times. Whether you come to pierogi by tradition or for the first time, you, too, will think a grandmother has visited your kitchen when you taste this gluten-free makeover.

▶ For the filling: Boil the potatoes in salted water until soft. Rinse and drain well.

▶ While still hot, mash the potatoes with the cream cheese, American cheese, and mozzarella cheese. Taste and add salt and pepper. Refrigerate until firm which will make it easier to fill the pierogi. Any extra filling can be served in place of regular mashed potatoes.

▶ For the dough: In a large bowl, combine the flour blend, chickpea flour, xanthan gum, and salt. Mound the flour mixture and make a well in the center. Drop the eggs into the well and cut into the flour with a knife to break the yolks. Add the water and knead until firm. The dough will be sticky, but do not add additional flour.

Filling

2½ pounds small white or red potatoes, peeled and cubed

4 ounces regular or low-fat cream cheese

4 to 6 ounces deli-sliced American cheese, broken up into pieces (individually wrapped slices are not recommended)

¾ cup shredded mozzarella cheese (about 3 ounces)

Salt and pepper to taste

Dough

1½ cups Basic Blend (page 17)

½ cup chickpea flour or other high protein flour

2 teaspoons xanthan gum

½ plus ¼ teaspoon salt

2 large eggs

½ cup water

Salt

Olive oil

continues

▶ Place the dough on a work surface and let rest for 10 minutes covered with plastic wrap. Divide the dough in half. Between sheets of plastic wrap that have been sprayed with vegetable oil spray, roll each half into a thin (1/16 of an inch) circle. Cut the circles with a 3- to 4-inch biscuit cutter. Roll out the excess dough and cut until all the dough has been used.

▶ Place a small spoonful of the filling a little to one side of each round of dough. Do not overfill or the pierogi will be difficult to seal. Fold over and pinch the edges together firmly, using oiled plastic wrap. Use the tines of a fork to form lines along the edges, if desired. If they are not sealing well, moisten the edges with water. Cover with plastic wrap.

▶ Bring a large skillet of water to a boil and reduce to a simmer. Add salt and olive oil. Drop the pierogi into the water. Do not crowd the pan or they will stick together. Cook for 3 to 5 minutes, stirring gently to make sure they do not stick to the bottom of the pan. They will rise to the top as they cook. Lift out of the water carefully with a slotted spoon. Arrange in a single layer on a large platter.

▶ Do not crowd or pile the pierogi. The uncooked will stick and the cooked will lose their shape and lightness.

▶ To serve: In a medium skillet, melt 1 tablespoon of the butter over medium heat and sauté the onion until nicely caramelized, about 10 minutes. Remove from the pan. Heat the remaining butter and sauté a few pierogi at a time. Serve pierogi with the caramelized onions, sour cream, and sauerkraut or a mixture of these.

▶ Boiled pierogi can be frozen. Cool completely and wrap in a single layer in wax paper and then place in a zip-top bag to freeze. Reheat by sautéing or boiling briefly.

For serving

2 tablespoons butter or non-dairy buttery spread

1 large onion, peeled, halved, and thinly sliced

Sour Cream

Sauerkraut

Potato Pancakes

(Grandma's Latkes)

Dairy-free

MAKES 18 TO 25 PANCAKES

It took hours for my grandmothers to make potato latkes, a traditional Hanukah soul food. The two grated potatoes by hand until the grater nicked their knuckles. Then they fried the pancakes in a thick layer of molten Crisco. Thanks to the food processor, you can whip up these gluten-free latkes in minutes, not hours. And, instead of Crisco, fry them in a small amount of olive oil. Serve with applesauce, apple jelly, or sour cream. They are wonderful anytime of the year.

3 large russet potatoes (about 2½ pounds)

1 small onion

3 large eggs

¼ cup potato starch

1½ teaspoons salt

Olive oil for frying

- ▶ Peel the potatoes, cut into small pieces, and submerge in a bowl of cold water to prevent discoloring.
- ▶ Peel the onion and cut into large pieces. Drain the potatoes and coarsely grate the potatoes and onion using the grater attachment of the food processor. Transfer to a large mixing bowl. Add the eggs, potato starch, and salt and stir to blend.
- ▶ Preheat the oven to 250°F. Line two cookie sheets with aluminum foil or parchment paper. Top each with a double thickness of paper towels.
- ▶ Coat the bottom of a large skillet with 1 to 2 tablespoons of olive oil and heat to medium high. Drop about 2 tablespoons of the potato mixture into the hot oil. Press gently to flatten and fry for 3 to 4 minutes, or until the underside is golden. Flip and brown on the other side. Drain the pancakes on the cookie sheets while frying the remaining mixture. Blot with paper towels and transfer to an ovenproof platter. Place in the oven to keep the latkes warm until ready to eat.

Shortcut Pasta

This dish is the shortest route from stove to table—a must for gluten-free families on the go. Start with a rich garlic and white wine sauce and add a range of options—whatever you have on hand. Chicken, tomatoes, and basil; shrimp with artichokes and Kalamata olives; butternut squash and sage are all combos that I rely on, but you may find others that suit your taste.

- Cook the pasta in boiling, salted water until chewy but not brittle (undercook by about 4 minutes). Drain, reserving ½ cup pasta water. Rinse the pasta in cold water.
- In a large skillet, heat 1 tablespoon of the oil over medium heat and sauté the arugula until wilted. Remove with a slotted spoon and set aside.
- Wipe out the pan and add another tablespoon of oil. Sauté the onion over medium heat until soft and translucent, about 3 minutes. Add the garlic and sauté an additional minute. Add the wine and simmer 2 minutes. Add the chicken broth, basil, and tomatoes. Simmer 2 minutes. Add salt and pepper to taste.
- Transfer the pasta to the skillet and bring to a simmer. Add cooked chicken. Simmer another 2 to 3 minutes or until the chicken is warm and the pasta is tender. The pasta will absorb some of the liquid. Add some of the reserved pasta water or more chicken broth if the mixture seems dry. Return the arugula to the pan and toss with the grated cheese or serve the cheese on the side.

Shortcuts:

- Use Perdue Shortcut Italian Chicken strips or gluten-free rotisserie chicken.
- Buy Dorot brand frozen chopped garlic and basil. These are premeasured, just pop out one cube per teaspoonful or use chopped garlic in a jar and ¾ teaspoon dried basil.
- Progresso chicken broth is gluten-free.

6 ounces gluten-free short-cut pasta, such as penne, elbows, or rigatoni (see Pantry, page 275)

3 tablespoons extra virgin olive oil

¾ cup washed baby arugula or baby spinach

1 small onion, chopped

2 teaspoons chopped garlic

½ cup white wine

1 cup gluten-free chicken broth (see Pantry, page 277)

1 to 2 teaspoons chopped fresh basil

one 14.5-ounce can petite-diced tomatoes, drained

Salt and pepper

1½ cups cubed cooked chicken or other cooked meat

⅓ to ½ cup grated Parmesan, Romano, or Asiago cheese

Spaghetti with Roasted Meatballs

MAKES 4 SERVINGS

Roasted meatballs, meatballs of any kind, were a lot of work until companies began offering gluten-free bread crumbs. Now I can save my slices of bread for toast and sandwiches and still make these.

- ▶ Preheat the oven to 400°F. Line a baking sheet with aluminum foil or parchment paper.
- ▶ Combine the ground meat, bread crumbs, shredded Parmesan, egg, basil, oregano, red pepper flakes, garlic powder, and salt and pepper in a large bowl. Roll into 1-inch balls and arrange in a single layer on the prepared baking sheet.
- ▶ Bake for 15 minutes. Transfer the meatballs to a medium saucepan. Add the marinara sauce. Cover and simmer.
- ▶ Heat a large pot of salted water and cook the spaghetti just until al dente. Drain and transfer to a large serving platter. Spoon the sauce and meatballs over the pasta and serve with the grated Parmesan cheese.

VARIATION: Sauté mushrooms and onions and add to the marinara sauce and meatballs.

1 pound ground dark turkey meat, ground beef, or chicken

½ cup gluten-free bread crumbs (see Pantry, page 272)

⅓ cup shredded Parmesan cheese

1 large egg, lightly beaten

1 teaspoon dried basil

½ teaspoon dried oregano

Pinch of red pepper flakes

¼ teaspoon garlic powder

Salt and pepper to taste

one 24-ounce jar good-quality gluten-free marinara sauce (see Pantry, page 276)

10 ounces rice or corn spaghetti

Grated Parmesan cheese

Basket of Muffins, Quick Breads, and Scones, see recipes beginning on page 63

Challah Bread, page 40

Parker House Rolls, page 48

Croissants, page 41

Jen's Deluxe
Granola, page 91

Cherry White Chocolate Scones, page 75

Orange Blueberry Quick Bread, page 74

Potato and Cheese Pierogi, page 138

Pot Stickers, page 109

Susan's Baked Pasta, page 143

Shrimp in Garlic Sauce, page 166

Stir-Fried Chicken with Walnuts, page 168

Grilled Scallion Bread (Asian Pizza), page 60

Condensed Cream of Mushroom Soup, page 122

Wraps, pages 119–120

Dipped Biscotti, 176

Black and Whites, page 188

Chocolate Coconut Crème Bundt Cake, page 206

Vanilla Blueberry Bundt Cake, page 228

Orange Chocolate Mousse Cake, page 222

Lemon Walnut Squares, page 183

Mini Tartlets with
Key Lime Filling,
page 240

German Chocolate Cupcakes with Coconut Pecan Frosting, pages 219 and 254

Hostess-Style Chocolate Cupcakes, page 217

Chocolate Shortbread, page 196

Chocolate Teddy Grahams,
page 245

Susan's Baked Pasta

MAKES 10 TO 12 SERVINGS

This dish is the ultimate Make and Take recipe. It hails from a friend, Susan Pietrogallo, whose roots were shaken to the core when her daughter was diagnosed with celiac disease. After a moment of panic, Susan simply made over all her family favorites so the entire family could continue to share in the bounty of her Italian kitchen. She makes her sauce from scratch. In the interest of time, I use a good-quality marinara sauce. Use any pasta you have on hand, including lasagna noodles.

- ▶ In a large saucepan, heat 1 tablespoon of the olive oil over medium heat. Break up the sausage and sauté in two batches until cooked. Remove with a slotted spoon and drain on paper towels. Set aside.
- ▶ Wipe out the pan and heat the remaining tablespoon olive oil over medium heat. Sauté the onions and garlic until caramelized.
- ▶ Combine the sausage, onions, garlic, tomatoes, and marinara sauce and simmer, covered for 30 to 60 minutes. Add a small amount of water if the sauce becomes too thick. Set aside.
- ▶ In a large bowl, combine the ricotta, eggs, parsley, and 1 cup of the Parmesan cheese.
- ▶ Cook the pasta in a large pot of boiling salted water for half the time specified on the package. Drain and rinse in cold water. Return to the pot and toss with 2 cups of the sausage and sauce mixture. Spread out evenly so the pasta does not continue to cook. Set aside.

2 tablespoons olive oil

2 pounds ground sausage (a combination of hot and sweet), casing removed

2 medium onions, chopped

2 garlic cloves, minced

one 28-ounce can crushed tomatoes

one 32-ounce jar good-quality marinara sauce (see Pantry, page 276)

one 2-pound container ricotta or low-fat ricotta cheese

3 large eggs

⅓ cup chopped fresh parsley

2 cups grated Parmesan or Romano cheese (about 8 ounces)

12 ounces corn or brown rice spirals, penne, or other cut pasta

1 to 2 cups shredded mozzarella cheese (about 4 to 8 ounces)

continues

continued

▶ Preheat the oven to 350°F. Set a 9 x 13-inch Pyrex casserole or baking dish on an aluminum foil–lined baking sheet.

▶ Ladle 1 cup of the sausage and sauce mixture in the bottom of the pan. Spread evenly over the bottom of the pan. Add half the pasta and top with half the ricotta cheese mixture. Ladle 2 cups of the sauce over the cheese. Repeat, finishing with the sausage and sauce mixture. Top with the mozzarella and ½ to 1 cup of the Parmesan cheese.

▶ Bake 30 to 40 minutes or until bubbly. Serve hot with extra Parmesan cheese.

▶ Refrigerate any extra sauce. It will keep well for several days.

Toasted Quinoa Oriental Pilaf

Dairy-free and *Egg-free*

MAKES 4 TO 6 SERVINGS

The nutty flavor of quinoa blends well with these Asian flavors. Serve this as a side dish with fish and chicken or, for a complete meal, add 1 cup cubed, cooked chicken to the quinoa after it cooks. This pilaf makes great leftovers. Enjoy cold or reheated briefly in the microwave.

▶ Toast the almonds in a dry skillet over medium heat; set aside.

▶ In a medium saucepan, toast the quinoa over medium heat for 5 minutes, or until fragrant and golden, stirring frequently. Add the orange juice. Stir the broth and salt into the quinoa and bring to a boil. Reduce the heat to low. Cover and simmer for 15 to 17 minutes.

▶ Combine the soy sauce, vinegar, sugar, sesame oil, ginger, and green onions together in a bowl. Pour over the quinoa and stir to mix. Return to a simmer. Fold in the vegetables, if using and add the toasted almonds. Serve warm.

¼ cup sliced almonds

1½ cups quinoa, rinsed and drained well

2 tablespoons orange juice

2½ cups plus 1 tablespoon chicken or vegetable broth, or water (see Pantry, page 277)

¼ teaspoon salt

2 tablespoons gluten-free soy sauce (see Pantry, page 276)

1 tablespoon rice vinegar

1 teaspoon sugar

1 teaspoon toasted (dark) sesame oil

1 teaspoon peeled grated ginger

2 green onions, thinly sliced diagonally

¾ cup mixed vegetables, optional, such as cubed steamed carrots, roasted asparagus, slivered sautéed snow peas

Beef and Beer

A Flemish Stew

Dairy-free and *Egg-free*

MAKES 6 TO 8 SERVINGS

This hearty, flavorful dish hails from Belgium. It's a stew, yes. But, not Grandma's traditional chunky vegetable variety. The rich flavors of caramelized onion, robust ale, and red currant jelly make this a culinary treat that challenges the taste buds to identify the origins of the flavors. Sadly, this complex dish was out of reach for many years, missing a key element—beer—that was not gluten-free. Today there are as many gluten-free beers as there are brews and you can choose from hearty light beer or dark ale when you make this dish. Serve with slices of gluten-free baguettes (page 44) or over gluten-free noodles. Accompany with buttered carrots and, of course, more of the same beer that goes into the pot.

▶ Preheat the oven to 350°F.

▶ In a large ovenproof Dutch oven, sauté the bacon in 1 tablespoon of the olive oil until golden. Remove with a slotted spoon and set aside to drain on paper towels.

▶ Pat the beef cubes dry with a paper towel. Heat 1 tablespoon of the olive oil in the pot and cook the beef in small batches until browned on all sides, adding more olive oil as needed. Transfer to a plate using a slotted spoon.

▶ Place the onions and the remaining olive oil in the pot and cook over low heat until soft and slightly golden, about 10 minutes. Add the garlic and brown sugar and mix well. Add the vinegar and cook an additional 2 minutes.

4 thick slices bacon, cut into cubes

¼ cup olive oil, more as needed

2½ pounds beef stew (chuck) meat, cut into 1-inch cubes

3 large onions, coarsely chopped

2 garlic cloves, minced

2 tablespoons brown sugar

2 tablespoons red wine vinegar

3 tablespoons white or brown rice flour

one 12-ounce bottle gluten-free beer

1 cup gluten-free beef broth (see Pantry, page 277)

2 bay leaves

3 to 4 fresh parsley sprigs

2 teaspoons dried thyme

Salt and pepper to taste

2 to 3 tablespoons red currant jelly

continues

continued

▶ Return the beef and the bacon to the pot along with any collected juices. Sprinkle the rice flour over the meat and toss to coat. Add the beer and beef broth, stirring constantly until blended. Add the bay leaves, parsley, and thyme. Check the flavors and add salt and pepper as needed. Bring to a simmer. Remove from the heat, cover, and bake for 2 hours.

▶ Stir in the jelly to taste, adding more if you like a sweeter flavor, less if you prefer the robust, slightly bitter beer notes. Return the pot to the oven and cook for 15 minutes longer.

▶ This can be cooked in a crockpot. Brown the meat and sauté the onions before placing the ingredients in the crockpot. Set between 170°F to 190°F and cook for 5 hours.

Tip: *Gluten-free beer is fermented from the hops of sorghum or rice. For this dish, I prefer to use Greens Light Ale. Its robust European roots seem to call to this Flemish recipe. But I also like Redbridge Beer and a host of others: New Grist, Bard's Tale, and Rampo Valley among them.*

Charred Vietnamese Chicken with Lemon Sauce

Dairy-free and *Egg-free*

MAKES 2 SERVINGS

After eating a more elaborate version of this dish at Zinc Restaurant in New Haven, Connecticut, I asked chef/owner, Denise Appel for the recipe. She serves this with black (purple) rice and a more complex variation of this lemon sauce with Stir-Fry Asian Vegetables (page 118). For the home cook, this version is less complicated without sacrificing a bit of flavor.

▶ Make the marinade: Combine the sesame oil, fish sauce, vinegar, honey, red pepper flakes, garlic, and black pepper in a large shallow dish. Add the chicken and marinate, covered in the refrigerator, for at least 1 hour and up to 24 hours.

▶ Make the Lemon Sauce: Combine the lemon juice, sugar, salt, and pepper in a small saucepan. Bring to a simmer over medium heat. Remove from the heat; set aside.

▶ Preheat a grill to medium or the broiler. Remove the chicken from the marinade, discarding the marinade. Grill or broil the chicken with the skin side facing the heat for 2 to 3 minutes. Turn the chicken over and grill or broil for 7 to 10 minutes, until the juices run clear. Let rest for 3 minutes. Remove the chicken from the bone and cut into thin diagonal slices. Fan out over a platter. Top with the Lemon Sauce.

▶ Accompany with Stir-Fry Asian Vegetables on page 118 and a large bowl of steamed white or purple rice.

Chicken Marinade

3 teaspoons toasted (dark) sesame oil

2 teaspoons fish sauce

1 teaspoon rice vinegar

1 teaspoon honey

½ teaspoon crushed red pepper flakes

1 teaspoon chopped garlic

¼ teaspoon ground black pepper

2 bone-in skin-on chicken breast halves

Lemon Sauce

Juice of 2 large lemons

2 tablespoons sugar

1 teaspoon kosher salt

½ teaspoon ground black pepper

Chicken Marsala

Simple one-to-one substitutions, like replacing flour with rice flour, made for an easy makeover of this old family recipe. Quick and delicious, this dish is perfect for buffets and is a terrific Make and Take dish. Be careful not to overcook the chicken when reheating.

1 large egg

¼ cup rice flour, more as needed

½ teaspoon salt

⅛ teaspoon pepper

2 boneless skinless chicken breasts (about 1½ pounds), sliced into ½-inch-thick strips

2 tablespoons unsalted butter or non-dairy buttery spread

2 tablespoons olive oil

¾ pound button mushrooms, stems removed, caps sliced thinly

¼ cup marsala wine or dry sherry

¾ cup plus 2 tablespoons gluten-free chicken broth (see Pantry, page 277)

1 tablespoon cornstarch

¼ cup half-and-half or non-dairy substitute

▶ Preheat the oven to 350°F. Lightly oil a 9 x 13-inch glass baking dish.

▶ Beat the egg in a shallow bowl. On a plate, combine the flour, salt, and pepper. Dip the chicken in the egg, then in the flour to coat both sides.

▶ Heat 1 tablespoon each of the butter and oil in a sauté pan over medium heat. Sauté the chicken on both sides just until browned. Place the chicken in a single layer in the baking dish.

▶ In the remaining butter and oil, sauté the mushrooms until soft. Add the wine and simmer until reduced by half. Add ¾ cup chicken broth and bring the liquid to a simmer. Combine the remaining chicken broth and cornstarch and stir into the simmering liquid. Stir to thicken.

▶ Remove from the heat. Add the half-and-half. Pour over the chicken. Bake for 20 minutes or until the mixture is bubbly. Serve with rice. (A mixture of white and wild rice goes nicely.)

Chicken Wellington

The mystique of Beef Wellington has always haunted me. Perhaps it was the elegance, the elaborate presentation at restaurants, or perhaps it was the fact that this dish was off-limits. These days the pastry-wrapped packages can be right here on my plate thanks to this delicious gluten-free rendition. In restaurants, the recipe is often served with a sauce of mushrooms, onions, dry sherry, and chicken stock. However, I like them just as they are.

▶ Prepare the nearly puff pastry. Wrap in plastic wrap and set aside while preparing the chicken.

▶ Season the chicken breasts with salt and pepper. Melt the butter in a skillet over medium heat and brown the breasts on both sides until almost completely cooked. Transfer to a plate.

▶ In the same skillet, heat the olive oil. Sauté the onion, mushrooms, and garlic until the mushrooms are soft and the onions begin to brown slightly. Add the parsley and herbes de Provence. Stir and remove from the heat.

▶ Preheat the oven to 375°F. Line two baking sheets with aluminum foil that has been lightly sprayed with vegetable spray.

▶ Cut the edges of a quart-size plastic bag and lay flat. Place ¼ of the dough on one side of the bag and fold over the other half. Roll the dough into a 7-inch square. This will just about fill the surface of the baggie. Repeat with the remaining pastry dough.

1 recipe Nearly Puff Pastry Crust (page 98)

4 small boneless skinless chicken breast halves

Salt and pepper to taste

1 tablespoon butter or non-dairy buttery spread

1 tablespoon olive oil

1 large onion, finely chopped

½ pound cremini mushrooms or other mushroom, sliced

2 garlic cloves, minced

2 tablespoons minced fresh parsley

2 teaspoons herbes de Provence or ¾ teaspoon each dried thyme, rosemary, and tarragon

1 ounce cream cheese or soy cream cheese, softened

2 tablespoons Dijon mustard

1 large egg, lightly beaten for egg wash

continues

continued

▶ Turn out the dough onto the lined baking sheets. Set a chicken breast in the center of each square of dough. Combine the cream cheese and Dijon mustard in a small bowl and brush the tops of the chicken breasts with a small amount of the mixture. Top with 2 to 3 tablespoons of the mushroom mixture.

▶ Brush the edges of the dough with the egg wash. Gently fold the dough over the chicken, cutting away any excess dough. Seal gently and patch any broken spots with leftover dough. Brush with the egg wash. Decorate with leaves cut out of leftover dough if desired.

▶ Bake for 20 to 25 minutes or until the tops are golden. Remove from the oven and let cool slightly. Gently transfer to individual plates. The dough is fragile and will break apart with too much handling. It doesn't matter however. These are still delicious!

Chock Full of
Chicken Pot Pie

MAKES 6 SERVINGS

My mother made chicken pot pie all the time and the memory of the casserole, sauce oozing through the crust, steam coming from the slits in the top, still fills my head and my tummy. She used a gluten-filled piecrust, but this version is just as wonderful. It uses an equally yummy crust topping and calls up those delicious memories.

▸ Heat the oil in a large skillet over medium heat. Add the carrots, parsnips, celery, onion, and potato and sauté for 10 minutes, stirring frequently. Add the garlic and sauté for 1 minute. Add the thyme, parsley, peas, and salt and pepper. Sprinkle the rice flour over the vegetables, mix well, and cook for 30 seconds. Add the chicken broth and sherry and stir until the mixture is thickened. Fold in the chicken and spoon the mixture into a 9-inch deep-dish pie pan, filling to the top.

▸ Preheat the oven to 375°F. Line a baking sheet with parchment paper or aluminum foil.

▸ Roll the dream crust between sheets of plastic wrap into a circle about 12 inches round and about ⅛ inch thick. It should be thin but still have enough structure to lift off the plastic easily without crumbling. Some tearing is inevitable. Tears can be patched with leftover dough.

3 tablespoons olive oil

2 large carrots, diced

3 medium parsnips, diced

2 celery stalks, diced

1 medium onion, chopped

1 large potato, peeled and diced

2 teaspoons minced garlic

1 teaspoon dried thyme

2 to 3 tablespoons chopped fresh parsley, or 1 tablespoon dried parsley

1 cup frozen peas

Salt and freshly ground pepper to taste

6 tablespoons rice flour

2½ cups gluten-free chicken broth (see Pantry, page 277)

2 tablespoons dry sherry

4 cups cubed cooked chicken

½ recipe Dream Crust (page 232)

1 egg, beaten with 1 tablespoon water for egg wash

continues

continued

▶ Brush the outside rim of the pie pan with the egg wash. Gently ease the crust over the top of the pan. Crimp the dough around the edges, trimming any excess dough. Brush the top with egg wash and cut three slits in the top. Set on the baking sheet and bake for 40 to 50 minutes, until the mixture is bubbly and the crust has browned.

Shortcuts:

▶ Buy cooked rotisserie chicken (check ingredients).
▶ In place of Dream Crust, use a prepared pie shell. Whole Foods Market Gluten-Free Bakehouse and Gillian's Food brands are good. Roll flat and set over the chicken mixture.

Tip: *Any leftover filling and crust can be made into an individual pot pie.*

Crab-Free Crab Cakes

Shellfish-free and *Dairy-free*

MAKES TEN 3-INCH CRAB CAKES

This recipe was born of necessity. I love crab cakes but my husband is allergic to crab, and of course I can't have the cracker meal or bread crumbs that most cakes contain. I solved the problem by using Old Bay Seasoning, gluten-free crackers, and cod to combine the essence and texture without any of the offending ingredients. Using cod instead of crab has other benefits, too. It's less expensive and less time-consuming. (No need to pick through a pound of crabmeat.)

▶ Preheat oven to 400°F.

▶ Place the cod in a baking dish. Sprinkle with ½ teaspoon of the Old Bay and ½ of the lemon juice. Let stand 10 minutes.

▶ Roast the cod for 6 to 10 minutes or until the fish flakes apart easily. Remove from the oven and set aside.

▶ In a medium sauté pan, heat 2 teaspoons olive oil over medium heat. Add the shallot and green pepper and sauté for about 2 minutes or until vegetables are soft. Add the garlic and sauté briefly. Transfer to a mixing bowl and let cool slightly.

▶ Use a slotted spatula to lift the cod out of the baking dish. (Leave behind as much of the cooking liquid as possible.) Add the fish to the vegetable mixture and mash slightly. Small pieces of fish should still be visible.

1 pound cod loin or fillet, rinsed and patted dry

1 to 1½ teaspoons Old Bay Seasoning

Juice of 1 lemon

Olive oil

1 shallot, peeled and chopped

1 medium red or green bell pepper, seeded and chopped

1 teaspoon minced garlic

1 teaspoon horseradish

⅓ cup light mayonnaise or egg-free mayonnaise (see Pantry, page 275)

¾ cup ground cracker crumbs or bread crumbs (see Pantry, page 272), or ½ cup potato starch

Salt and pepper to taste

Aioli Sauce (page 155), tartar sauce, and lemon wedges for serving

continues

continued

▶ Combine the horseradish, the remaining ½ to 1 tea-spoon Old Bay, the mayonnaise, and the remaining lemon juice in a small bowl. Add to the fish mix-ture. Add the cracker crumbs and salt and pepper and mix well.

▶ Wipe out the sauté pan. Heat 2 teaspoons olive oil over medium heat. Scoop ⅓ cup of the cod mixture into the palm of your hand and form into 3-inch patties. Arrange 4 to 5 cakes in the pan and cook until brown and crispy on both sides, about 4 to 5 minutes per side. Repeat until all the cakes are cooked. Serve warm with Aioli Sauce, tartar sauce, or wedges of lemon.

Aioli Sauce

MAKES ½ CUP

▶ Combine all the ingredients in a small bowl. Chill, covered, until ready to serve.

½ cup light mayonnaise or egg-free mayonnaise (see Pantry, page 275)

3 teaspoons crushed garlic

Juice of ½ lemon

Dash of cayenne pepper

Cranberry Stuffed Chicken Breasts

Egg-free

MAKES 3 SERVINGS

I'm always on the lookout for company dishes that are easy, elegant, and not gluten-challenged. This is one. It was inspired when I saw an ad for a cooking contest for Ocean Spray. Although I never entered the contest, I thought these would surely have been a winner. Chopped apple or currants can replace the cranberries.

▶ Preheat the oven to 350°F. Line a baking sheet with aluminum foil that has been lightly sprayed with vegetable spray.

▶ Pat the chicken with paper towel and sprinkle with salt and pepper. Using your finger tips, gently separate the skin from the meat, leaving the edges intact. Set aside.

▶ In a large skillet, heat 2 tablespoons of the olive oil over medium heat. Add the onion and sauté until soft but not brown. Add the sausage and sauté until no longer pink. Add the vinegar and simmer 1 minute. Remove from the heat and add the cranberries, pecans, and cheese, stirring just until the cheese begins to soften.

▶ Stuff a generous portion of the mixture under the skin of each breast. Set on the baking sheet and brush the tops with remaining tablespoon olive oil. Sprinkle with additional salt and pepper. Bake for 20 to 25 minutes, until the juices run clear when pierced with a fork. Serve with the sauce.

▶ To make the sauce: In a small saucepan, sauté the shallots in the olive oil over medium heat until soft and opaque. Add the sherry and simmer until reduced by half. Add ¾ cup chicken broth and simmer 3 minutes. Combine the remaining ¼ cup broth with the cornstarch to make a slurry. Add half the slurry to the simmering liquid and stir until the mixture thickens. For a thicker sauce, add the remaining cornstarch mixture.

---

3 boneless skin-on chicken breast halves

Salt and pepper to taste

3 tablespoons olive oil

1 medium onion, peeled and finely chopped

3 links mild chicken sausages, casings removed, sausage crumbled

3 tablespoons red wine vinegar

1½ cups dried cranberries

¾ cup toasted pecans, coarsely chopped

1 cup grated sharp cheddar cheese (about 4 ounces)

Sauce

2 large shallots, minced

1 tablespoon olive oil

2 tablespoons dry sherry

1 cup chicken broth

2 tablespoons cornstarch or arrowroot

Tip: For this recipe, you'll need raw chicken sausage available in most supermarket meat departments. Make sure to check the ingredients before purchasing.

General Tso's Chicken

Dairy-free

MAKES 3 SERVINGS

A favorite Asian classic, General Tso's Chicken, has always been off-limits to those of us who are gluten-free as the trademark of this dish is the battered and fried chicken pieces that meld into a sweet and spicy sauce. Now this easy, yummy dish is as close as your own wok. While it calls for thigh meat, breast meat can easily be substituted.

▶ Combine garlic, ginger, green onions, and red pepper flakes in a bowl; set aside.

▶ Make the marinade: Combine the egg, cornstarch, and black pepper in a large bowl. Add the chicken pieces and coat with the marinade. Let stand 30 minutes at room temperature.

▶ Make the sauce: Combine the fish sauce, vinegar, water, and sugar in a small bowl and set aside.

▶ Heat 3 tablespoons of oil in a wok or large frying pan over medium-high heat. When the oil begins to smoke, add the chicken in small batches. Sauté until golden brown. Remove to a paper towel–lined dish and set aside.

▶ Pour off all the leftover oil. Heat 1 tablespoon oil over medium-high heat and add the garlic mixture. Sauté briefly. Return the chicken to the wok and add the sauce. Stir for 1 minute. Serve with steamed rice.

Shortcut:

▶ Instead of chopping ginger and garlic, use Dorot Brand frozen cubes of minced ginger and garlic (see Pantry, page 277).

Tip: *All ingredients can be chopped and assembled ahead of time and cooked just before serving.*

2 large garlic cloves, minced

2 teaspoons minced fresh ginger

2 green onions (white and light green parts only), chopped

¼ to ½ teaspoon red pepper flakes

Marinade

1 large egg, lightly beaten

2 tablespoons cornstarch

Freshly ground black pepper

6 to 8 boneless skinless chicken thighs, cut into 1-inch cubes

Sauce

1½ tablespoons fish sauce (see Pantry, page 276)

2 tablespoons rice vinegar

2 tablespoons water

1 tablespoon sugar

Vegetable oil for stir frying

Jeremy's Fish Tacos

My son, Jeremy, came home from college one day and asked if I would make Fish Tacos like he had eaten in a Mexican restaurant in New York. He described the taste and texture. Then he gave me hints about what might have been in the delicious sauce. Here's what we came up with. It's a recipe he requests every time he comes home. I suspect that means he approves.

▶ Preheat the oven to 200°F.

▶ Rinse and pat the fish fillets dry. Combine the flour and taco seasoning mix in a shallow dish. Beat the eggs with the warm water in a separate bowl. Dip the fish pieces in the egg, then dredge in the flour. Repeat for a crunchy exterior.

▶ In a large skillet, heat the oil over medium-high heat. Fry the fish until crispy on both sides. Remove to a cookie sheet. Wrap the tortillas in foil and place the fried fish and tortillas in the oven while making the sauce.

1 pound flounder fillets or mahi mahi, cut into 6 serving-size pieces

¾ cup corn flour or rice flour

3 teaspoons taco seasoning mix (see Pantry, page 277)

2 large eggs

1 tablespoon warm water

2 to 3 tablespoons olive oil

6 corn tortillas (see Pantry, page 277)

continues

continued

▶ Make the sauce: In a medium saucepan, heat the olive oil over medium heat. Add the shallot and tomatillos and sauté until softened, about 2 minutes. Add the garlic and sauté briefly. Add the chilies and the chicken broth and simmer until the liquid is reduced by half. Remove from the heat and stir in the sour cream and yogurt.

▶ To serve: Place one fish fillet in the center of a warmed tortilla. Sprinkle with cheese if desired, and top with a spoonful of the sauce.

Shortcut:

▶ Use 2 cubes of Doret Brand minced frozen garlic (see Pantry, page 277).

Avoiding Eggs? *Replace the eggs and water with flax gel or ½ cup of milk of choice.*

Avoiding Dairy? *Replace the sour cream and yogurt with ½ cup unflavored soy, coconut, or rice yogurt. Replace the cheese with dairy-free cheese.*

Tomatillo Sauce

1 tablespoon olive oil

1 large shallot, minced

3 tomatillos, peeled and chopped

2 garlic cloves, minced

one 4½-ounce can chopped mild green chilies

¾ cup gluten-free chicken broth (see Pantry, page 277)

⅓ cup reduced-fat sour cream

⅓ cup plain yogurt

Shredded cheddar cheese, optional

Oven-Fried Chicken Nuggets

When Jeremy was a child, we couldn't buy gluten-free chicken nuggets. So I came up with this recipe, which he loved. I made one or two batches each week and kept them in the freezer, along with personal pizzas and cookie dough. Today Moms need not do all that preparation as many companies sell quick, kid-friendly foods. Nevertheless, making these yourself will save money and control the nutritional makeup of the food your children eat. In addition, they are easy and yummy.

4 cups gluten-free dried bread crumbs or cracker crumbs (see Pantry, page 272)

2 teaspoons dried thyme

1 teaspoon freshly ground black pepper

1 teaspoon dried basil

1 teaspoon dried oregano

1½ teaspoons ground cumin

1 teaspoon garlic powder

½ teaspoon salt

¼ teaspoon cayenne pepper

1 large egg, or flax gel

1 tablespoon olive oil

1¼ cups low-fat buttermilk, soy milk, or rice milk

6 boneless skinless chicken thighs or 4 boneless skinless chicken breast halves, cut into 1 x 2-inch strips

▶ Preheat the oven to 425°F. Line a baking sheet with parchment paper or aluminum foil and coat with vegetable spray.

▶ Combine the bread crumbs, thyme, black pepper, basil, oregano, cumin, garlic powder, salt, and cayenne pepper in a large bowl; set aside.

▶ In a medium bowl, whisk together the egg, olive oil, and buttermilk. Add the chicken pieces and let sit for 10 minutes. Remove the chicken and coat with the bread crumb mixture. Press any lose crumbs into the meat. Place on a baking sheet.

▶ Bake for 20 to 25 minutes, until golden and cooked through, turning once halfway through baking. The thigh meat will take about 5 minutes longer to cook than breast meat. Serve warm with Jeremy's Favorite Dipping Sauce (page 161) or with ketchup.

▶ Freeze leftovers and reheat in a 350°F oven for 10 minutes.

Shortcut:

▶ Buy chicken breasts that are already filleted.

Jeremy's Favorite Dipping Sauce

▶ Combine all the ingredients in a small bowl.

½ cup ketchup

1 to 2 tablespoons mustard

1 to 2 teaspoons gluten-free soy sauce (see Pantry, page 276)

Dash of garlic powder

Quick Eggplant Parmesan with Ground Beef

MAKES 6 SERVINGS

I'm forever trying to find one-dish meals that are perfect to serve the family or at a potluck. Here's one that fits all the requirements. Because the eggplant is baked and not fried, it is healthier than traditional eggplant Parmesan, and faster, too. The meat can be omitted for a hearty vegetarian dish.

▶ Preheat the oven to 400°F. Line two baking sheets with parchment paper. Butter a 9 x 13-inch baking dish.

▶ Combine the bread crumbs and Italian herbs on a medium plate. Crack the eggs into a shallow bowl and beat lightly. Dip each eggplant slice in the egg, then coat with bread crumbs. Set on the baking sheets and bake 10 minutes. Turn and bake an additional 10 minutes or until tender.

▶ Heat the olive oil in a medium frying pan. Sauté the ground beef and garlic until the beef is cooked through. Drain and set aside.

▶ Cover the bottom of the prepared baking dish with 1 cup of the marinara sauce. Arrange a layer of eggplant slices over the sauce. Layer half the beef over the eggplant slices, then sprinkle evenly with half the mozzarella cheese and ¼ cup of the Parmesan cheese. Continue layering with 1½ cups sauce and the remaining eggplant, beef, and mozzarella. Sprinkle with ¼ cup Parmesan cheese and then the remaining sauce. Top with the remaining 2 tablespoons Parmesan cheese. Bake 30 minutes or until bubbly. Serve warm.

1 cup gluten-free dried bread crumbs (see Pantry, page 272)

3 teaspoons dried Italian herbs

2 large eggs

1 large eggplant (about 1¾ pounds), cut into ¼-inch-thick slices

1 to 2 tablespoons olive oil

1 pound lean ground beef, chicken, or turkey

2 garlic cloves, minced

5½ cups good-quality marinara sauce

1⅓ cups mozzarella cheese

½ cup plus 2 tablespoons grated Parmesan cheese

Roasted Turkey with Orange Maple Glaze and Corn Bread Stuffing

MAKES 8 TO 10 SERVINGS

This turkey, stuffing, and gravy grace my Thanksgiving table every year. For maximum flavor, let the bird steep in the seasoning mixture overnight and make the corn bread stuffing a day in advance. But do not stuff the turkey until just before it goes into the oven, or bake separately and reheat just before serving.

▸ Remove the giblets from the cavity of the turkey and use to prepare the gravy on page 125.

▸ Make the Seasoning Mixture: Combine the coarse salt, seasoned salt, poultry seasoning, dry mustard, paprika, and nutmeg in a small bowl. Rub over the entire turkey and into the cavities. Place in a roasting pan, cover with plastic wrap, and refrigerate overnight.

▸ Preheat the oven to 400°F. Lightly oil a small casserole dish.

▸ Make the glaze: Combine the orange juice, oil, and maple syrup in a small bowl. Brush the turkey with the glaze.

▸ Stuff the turkey with the corn bread stuffing. Place the remaining stuffing in the casserole dish; cover and set aside.

one 12- to 14-pound turkey, fresh or frozen (thawed), rinsed and patted dry

Seasoning Mixture

2 to 3 tablespoons coarse salt

2 teaspoons seasoned salt (such as Lawry's brand)

¾ teaspoon poultry seasoning

¾ teaspoon dry mustard

½ teaspoon paprika

¼ teaspoon ground nutmeg

Glaze

½ cup orange juice, more as needed

¼ cup extra virgin olive oil

2 tablespoons maple syrup or honey

Corn Bread Stuffing (page 133)

continues

continued

- ▶ Truss the bird or cover the stuffed cavities with aluminum foil to prevent burning. Bake for 20 minutes. Reduce the oven temperature to 325°F and roast 3 to 3½ hours, basting* frequently, until a meat thermometer inserted into the thickest part of the thigh registers 180°F.
- ▶ Bake the remaining stuffing for 30 minutes.
- ▶ Remove the turkey from the oven and let stand 10 minutes before carving. Remove the stuffing to a serving dish and slice the turkey. Serve with Roasted Turkey Gravy on page 125.

*Baste the turkey with chicken stock until enough juices collect in the pan to use as a basting liquid.

Tips: *The cooking time will be slightly less if the turkey is not stuffed. Begin checking after 3 hours.*

My preference is Empire kosher turkeys. They are brined, which adds flavor and tenderizes the meat. Reduce the amount of coarse salt added to the seasoning mixture if using a brined turkey.

Santa Fe Enchiladas

Egg-free

MAKES 4 SERVINGS

I've always loved enchiladas, but most enchilada sauces contained some wheat. Today several companies make good enchilada sauce and many are gluten-free, making possible this and many other Southwest dishes.

▶ Preheat the oven to 350°F. Grease a 9 x 13-inch Pyrex baking pan.

▶ Heat 1 tablespoon of the oil in a small skillet over medium heat. Add the onion, chilies, cumin, chili powder, and salt and sauté for 3 minutes. Remove from the heat and place in a medium bowl with the ricotta, corn, and 1¼ cups mozzarella. Mix until combined. Set aside.

▶ In a deep skillet or wide shallow saucepan, warm the enchilada sauce over low heat. Using tongs, dip 2 tortillas at a time in the hot sauce until softened. Allow the excess sauce to drip off and place the tortillas into the prepared baking pan.

▶ Spread ¼ cup ricotta filling onto each tortilla. Roll and place seam side down in the pan. Repeat until all the tortillas have been prepared. Drizzle with 1 cup of the remaining enchilada sauce and sprinkle with the remaining mozzarella cheese. Bake for 15 to 20 minutes, until bubbly. Set the oven to broil and broil the enchiladas for 3 minutes, or until the tops have browned.

1 tablespoon vegetable oil

1 small onion, chopped (about ⅓ cup)

one 4-ounce can chopped mild green chilies

1 teaspoon ground cumin

1 teaspoon chili powder

½ teaspoon salt

one 15-ounce container whole-milk or reduced-fat ricotta cheese

1¼ cups frozen corn kernels, thawed

2 cups grated mozzarella cheese (about 8 ounces)

two 10-ounce cans hot or mild enchilada sauce (see Pantry, page 275)

twelve 6-inch gluten-free corn tortillas (see Pantry, page 277)

Tip: *Rice, beans, and guacamole make wonderful side dishes to this meal.*

Avoiding Dairy? *Replace the ricotta cheese with refried beans and use dairy-free mozzarella cheese (see Simple Substitutions, page 267).*

Shrimp in Garlic Sauce

Dairy-free

MAKES 4 SERVINGS

No need to wait for a Chinese New Year celebration to make this delicious dish. It will impress your guests and make your taste buds sing. If you can't have shrimp, try using cubes of uncooked chicken breast or firm tofu, cubed.

▶ Make the marinade: Combine the salt, sugar, sesame oil, pepper, cornstarch, and egg whites in a large bowl. Add the shrimp and toss to coat. Let stand for 30 to 60 minutes.

▶ Make the batter: Combine the egg yolks, cornstarch, and water in a small bowl; set aside.

▶ Make the vegetable mixture: Combine the green pepper, ginger, scallions, garlic, and red pepper flakes in a medium bowl; set aside.

Marinade

½ teaspoon coarse salt

¼ teaspoon sugar

1 teaspoon toasted (dark) sesame oil

Freshly ground pepper

½ tablespoon cornstarch

2 egg whites, beaten until frothy (reserve yolks for batter below)

1⅓ pounds large shrimp (21 to 30 per pound), peeled and deveined

Shrimp Batter

2 egg yolks, lightly beaten

3 tablespoons cornstarch

2 teaspoons water

Vegetable Mixture

½ green bell pepper, cut into ¼-inch cubes

½-inch-long piece fresh ginger, peeled and minced

2 scallions (white and light green parts only), minced

3 garlic cloves, peeled and minced

¼ to ½ teaspoon red pepper flakes

continues

continued

▶ Make the seasoning mixture: Combine the vinegar, sugar, broth, ketchup, salt, and sesame oil in a small bowl; set aside.

▶ Heat 1 cup of vegetable oil in a wok or deep frying pan over medium-high heat until the oil is very hot. Drain the shrimp from the marinade, discarding the marinade. Dip in the batter and then drop into the oil a handful at a time. Cook for 2 minutes, turning once. Remove with a slotted spoon and place on a paper towel to drain. Repeat until all the shrimp are cooked.

▶ Drain off all but 2 tablespoons of the oil. Return the wok to medium-high heat and add the vegetable mixture. Toss for 1 minute. Stir in the seasoning mixture. Add the shrimp and toss to coat. Heat briefly. Serve immediately with steamed white rice.

Seasoning Mixture

2 tablespoons rice vinegar

2 tablespoons sugar

2 tablespoons gluten-free chicken broth (see Pantry, page 277)

3 tablespoons ketchup

1 teaspoons salt

1 teaspoon toasted (dark) sesame oil

1 cup vegetable oil for deep frying

Stir-Fried Chicken with Walnuts

Dairy-free and *Egg-free*

MAKES 4 SERVINGS

This family-style dish has it all: protein, vegetables, and a tangy sauce. It was a dish I loved to teach to my Chinese cooking students years ago because the ingredients are readily available—there is nothing weird to buy—and because this was an Asian recipe that was within my own reach when I replaced the soy sauce with my own gluten-free version.

▸ Make the marinade: Combine the sherry, salt, sugar, and cornstarch in a large bowl. Place the chicken in the marinade and toss. Set aside while preparing the remaining ingredients, about 30 minutes.

▸ Make the sauce: Combine the ketchup, soy sauce, salt, sugar, vinegar, sesame oil, molasses, and broth; set aside.

▸ Make the sugared walnuts: Heat 2 tablespoons oil in a wok. When hot, add the walnuts. Stir-fry until the nuts darken. Add the sugar. Toss briefly and remove with a slotted spoon. Discard the remaining oil and wipe out the wok.

▸ Heat 2 tablespoons oil and add ⅓ of the chicken. Stir fry until the chicken turns golden brown. Remove with a slotted spoon. Set aside on a plate. Repeat until all of the chicken is cooked, adding additional oil as needed.

continues

Marinade

1 teaspoon dry sherry

½ teaspoon kosher salt

½ teaspoon sugar

1 tablespoon cornstarch

1 whole boneless skinless chicken breast, cut into 1-inch cubes

Sauce

¼ cup ketchup

2 teaspoons wheat-free soy sauce (see Pantry, page 276)

½ teaspoon kosher salt

2 tablespoons sugar

2 tablespoons rice wine vinegar

1½ teaspoons toasted (dark) sesame oil

1 teaspoon molasses

¼ cup gluten-free chicken broth

Sugared Walnuts

2 tablespoons vegetable oil

¾ cup walnut halves

3 teaspoons sugar for coating walnuts

continues

continued

▶ Heat 2 more tablespoons of oil in the wok. When hot, add the ginger, garlic, and scallions. Toss briefly. Add the carrots and toss for 1 minute. Add the bell pepper and cook for an additional 2 minutes. Add the chicken, the sauce, and the snow peas. Heat until the liquid comes to a boil. If the sauce is too thin, stir in a mixture of cornstarch and water to thicken. Simmer briefly. Remove from the heat and add the sugar-coated walnuts. Serve with white or brown rice.

▶ Walnuts can be omitted if someone doesn't like them or can't have nuts.

Shortcut:

▶ Buy Dorot brand frozen minced garlic and ginger cubes (see Pantry, page 277). Replace the bell pepper, carrots, and snow peas with a bag of frozen stir-fry vegetables, thawed before using.

continued

4 to 6 tablespoons vegetable oil for frying

1 walnut-size piece fresh ginger, peeled and minced

2 garlic cloves, minced

2 green onions (white and light green parts only), chopped

2 carrots, peeled and cut into julienne strips

1 red bell pepper, seeded and cut into julienne strips

½ pound snow peas, trimmed

Turkey Tetrazzini

MAKES 4 SERVINGS

This is one of the best ways to use up leftover turkey, introduce a menu that is something other than roasted turkey or chicken, and bring comfort food to the table. Add frozen broccoli cuts (thawed) or chopped spinach (see below) for variation.

▶ Heat the oil in large skillet over medium heat. Sauté the green onions and mushrooms until the mushrooms are soft. Add the turkey and stir. Add the sherry, broth, and cream and bring to a simmer. Add the cornstarch mixture and stir to thicken. Add the spaghetti and cheese and mix well.

▶ Transfer to a 9 x 13-inch casserole dish and top with additional cheese. Place under the broiler 4 to 6 minutes, until the top is brown and bubbly.

VARIATION: For Turkey Florentine Tetrazzini, add ¼ teaspoon freshly ground nutmeg and 2 tablespoons lemon juice. Fold in one 10-ounce package frozen chopped spinach, thawed and drained, or add 1 to 2 cups frozen broccoli cuts, thawed and cooked for 3 minutes in a microwave.

1 tablespoon olive oil

3 green onions (white and light green parts only), chopped

2½ cups sliced mushrooms

2 cups cubed cooked turkey or chicken

3 tablespoons dry sherry

1 cup gluten-free chicken broth (see Pantry, page 277)

¼ cup light cream, fat-free evaporated milk, soy milk, or rice milk

2 tablespoons cornstarch mixed with ¼ cup chicken broth or water

8 to 10 ounces rice or corn spaghetti, cooked al dente, rinsed and drained

½ cup grated Parmesan cheese, plus more for topping

Sweet Treats

A Note on Gluten-Free Desserts

The world is full of sweet treats from bars to cookies, from cakes to tarts. Fortunately, they are especially easy to make over and nothing is lost in translation. Simply replace flour with a blend of gluten-free flours and these delicious desserts can be yours. I use my Cake and Pastry Flour in many of the recipes here. It's healthier and lighter than the ubiquitous rice flour based combos. But you can use any basic formula. If it contains gum and salt, you'll need to omit them from my recipes. So dig out family recipes and old church and synagogue cookbooks and substitute boldly.

I should note that the recipes here are revised considerably from the mainstream recipes that inspired them, but when you are on your own, simply replace the flour and you'll have great success.

Almond Lemon Biscotti

MAKES 20 TO 24 BISCOTTI

What could be more delightful than sipping coffee and nibbling biscotti in an outdoor café? The coffee and the café have always been within reach, but the sleek biscotti was more elusive until I created this gluten-free version. Now my image of a romantic café is complete. This formula is inspired by several recipes and leans heavily on eggs for its texture.

- ▶ Preheat the oven to 325°F. Line a baking sheet with parchment paper that has been lightly sprayed with vegetable spray.
- ▶ Combine the flour blend, baking powder, lemon zest, and salt in a bowl; set aside.
- ▶ In a separate bowl, beat the eggs on medium speed until they have doubled in volume and turned light yellow, about 4 to 5 minutes. Add the sugar and beat to combine. Add the butter, oil, vanilla, and almond extract and beat until mixed. Add the dry ingredients and beat on low until blended. Fold in the almonds.
- ▶ Spoon the dough onto the prepared baking sheet and form into a 15 x 4½-inch log. Bake for 30 minutes, or until the edges are lightly browned. Allow to cool for 15 minutes.
- ▶ Transfer the log to a cutting board. With a very sharp knife, slice diagonally into twenty to twenty-four ½-inch-wide slices. Lay flat and bake until golden on the bottom, about 10 minutes. Turn and bake an additional 7 minutes. Cool completely and store at room temperature in an airtight container. These will keep 5 to 7 days or may be frozen.

3 cups Cake and Pastry Flour (page 16)

1½ teaspoons baking powder

½ teaspoon lemon zest, or dried lemon peel

¼ teaspoon salt

3 large eggs, at room temperature

1 cup sugar

¼ cup unsalted butter or non-dairy buttery spread, softened

¼ cup vegetable oil

1½ teaspoons vanilla extract

½ teaspoon almond extract

1 cup chopped blanched almonds, toasted

Avoiding Nuts? Omit *the almond extract and almonds and substitute ⅔ cup chopped dried cranberries or pumpkin seeds or ½ cup Perky's Crunchy Rice or Flax Cereal (see Pantry, page 274).*

Vanilla or Chocolate Biscotti

Dairy-free

MAKES 30 TO 40 BISCOTTI

I wanted to create a biscotti that did not crumble or lose its shape as gluten-free pastries are apt to do. This seemed like a tall order until I discovered this biscotti inspired by several recipes from traditional Italian bakers.

Note that the basis of this recipe is the eggs beaten to ribbon stage. An egg substitution will not work. However people who have a sensitivity to eggs, rather than an anaphylactic reaction, can try using duck eggs.

▶ Preheat the oven to 350°F. Line a baking sheet with parchment paper.

▶ Combine the flour blend, baking powder, xanthan gum, and salt in a medium bowl. Blend well with a fork. Set aside.

▶ Beat the eggs and sugar together in a mixing bowl on medium speed until doubled in volume and pale yellow, about 5 to 7 minutes. Add the vanilla and almond extracts and the oil and beat just to combine. Sprinkle ⅓ of the dry ingredients over the egg mixture and fold in. Repeat until all of the flour is incorporated. Fold in the nuts, if using.

▶ Drop the dough in two lines along the length of the cookie sheet, leaving plenty of space between the logs. Use a spatula to mound the dough up and make the logs narrow (about 2 inches by 8 inches). You may need to repeat a couple of times to form the logs, as the dough will spread somewhat. The dough may also be spooned into a lightly oiled 12 x 5¼-inch biscotti pan or two 8½ x 4½-inch loaf pans. Quickly place in the oven.

2 cups Basic Blend (page 17)

1 teaspoon baking powder

¾ teaspoon xanthan gum

¼ teaspoon salt

3 large eggs, at room temperature

¾ cup sugar

3 teaspoons vanilla extract

1½ teaspoons almond or orange extract

2 tablespoons vegetable oil

½ cup toasted ground almonds or other nuts, optional

continues

continued

- Bake for 18 to 20 minutes or until light golden on top. Remove from the oven and slide the parchment paper with the biscotti onto a wire rack to cool for about 10 minutes.
- Transfer the logs to a cutting board and cut diagonally into ½-inch slices. Place the biscotti cut side down on the baking sheet and bake 10 to 15 minutes, until dry, turning them halfway through baking. Cool completely and store in an airtight container.

FOR CHOCOLATE BISCOTTI: Replace ¼ cup blend with ¼ cup unsweetened cocoa powder and add as part of the dry ingredients.

For a festive finish, dip half of each cooled biscotti in ½ cup melted chocolate or white chocolate combined with 1 tablespoon vegetable oil. Decorate with colorful sprinkles. Let harden on wax paper before storing. To keep this recipe dairy-free, refer to the dairy-free chocolate section in Simple Substitutions, page 269.

Blonde Brownies

Dairy-free

MAKES 16 BROWNIES

Since my mother introduced me to this dessert when I was a child, the combination of brown sugar, pecans, and chocolate chips has always beckoned me. These rich, chewy squares are always a hit and no one ever guesses that they are gluten-free.

- ▶ Preheat the oven to 350°F. Grease an 8-inch square pan with vegetable spray or line with lightly oiled aluminum foil.
- ▶ Stir together the flour blend, and baking powder in a small bowl. Set aside.
- ▶ Beat the oil, the brown sugar, and the granulated sugar in a medium bowl on medium speed until smooth. Add the eggs, water, and vanilla and beat well. Add the dry ingredients and stir to thoroughly combine. Fold in the pecans, if using, and chocolate chips. Spread the batter evenly into the prepared pan.
- ▶ Bake for 30 to 32 minutes or until a toothpick inserted into the center comes out with a few moist crumbs sticking to it. Allow to cool completely in the pan on a wire rack before cutting into squares.

Tip: For a celebratory touch, sprinkle 2 cups of chocolate chips evenly over the top as the brownies come out of the oven. Use a rubber spatula to smooth the chocolate evenly over the bars.

VARIATION: Replace the pecans and chocolate chips with ¼ cup roasted pumpkin seeds and ¾ cup chopped dried cherries.

1¼ cups Cake and Pastry Flour (page 16)

½ teaspoon baking powder

6 tablespoons vegetable oil

¾ cup packed light brown sugar

½ cup granulated sugar

2 large eggs, or flax gel (see Simple Substitutions, page 268)

¼ cup water

2 teaspoons vanilla extract

¾ cup toasted pecans, optional

½ cup semi-sweet chocolate chips (for dairy-free see Simple Substitutions, page 269)

Tips for Success

Struggling to get the first bar or brownie out of the pan? Line a baking pan with aluminum foil and lightly oil the surface. When the baked bars have cooled you can lift the entire contents out of the pan and cut the bars on a cutting board. Freeze briefly before cutting for added ease. This also saves on cleanup.

Do not bake bars, cookies, or biscotti on dark or non-stick pans. This can cause the bottoms to burn and pastry to be soggy.

Store in an airtight container at room temperature for up to three days or wrap well and freeze for four to six months. Refrigeration causes bars, cookies, and biscotti to dry out.

Killer Brownies

MAKES 24 TO 30 BROWNIES

My tester, Janet Alquist (age twelve), made this recipe and declared the brownies to be "awesome." She suggests spraying a rubber spatula with PAM to help even out the batter. These are a chocolate lover's dream come true.

▶ Put the oven rack in the middle position and preheat the oven to 350°F. Lightly oil a 9 x 13-inch baking pan with vegetable spray.

▶ In a microwaveable dish, combine the unsweetened chocolate with butter. Heat on medium high until the butter is melted, about 1 to 2 minutes. Stir until the mixture is smooth. Repeat, heating in 20-second intervals, until the chocolate is melted. Keep a close eye on it as overheated chocolate can become lumpy.

▶ Beat the eggs with the sugar in a mixing bowl on medium speed until light yellow and doubled in volume, about 5 minutes. Add the vanilla and beat to combine.

▶ Add the melted chocolate to the egg mixture and beat on low speed just to combine, about 30 to 60 seconds. Fold in the flour blend, walnuts, if using, and chocolate chips.

▶ Bake for 30 minutes, until a toothpick inserted into the center comes out slightly moist. Cool completely before cutting into squares. These cut more easily if frozen for 1 hour. Cut brownies may be stored in the freezer.

8 ounces unsweetened chocolate, broken into pieces

½ pound (2 sticks) unsalted butter or non-dairy buttery spread, cut into pieces

4 large eggs

2 cups sugar

2 teaspoons vanilla extract

2 cups Cake and Pastry Flour (page 16)

1 cup chopped walnuts, optional

1 cup semi-sweet chocolate chips

Avoiding Eggs? Replace the eggs with 1 cup of puréed silken tofu or add 1 teaspoon baking powder and 1 cup unsweetened applesauce, or 1 cup soy or coconut yogurt. Beat just to combine with the sugar.

VARIATIONS:
- Add 2 teaspoons espresso powder to the flour blend.
- Add white chocolate chips in place of the semi-sweet chocolate chips.

Healthy Oat Bars

Dairy-free

MAKES 24 BARS

These bars are loaded with fiber and nutrients. Since they are not too sweet, they are perfect for breakfast or snacking and they taste so good, even the kids will enjoy them.

▶ Preheat the oven to 350°F. Lightly grease a 9 x 13-inch baking pan.

▶ Soak the raisins in warm water to soften, about 10 minutes, then drain. Set aside.

▶ Whisk together the oats, oat flour, sorghum flour, buckwheat flour, tapioca starch, almond flour, xanthan gum, salt, baking soda, baking powder, cinnamon, and brown sugar in a large bowl.

▶ In a medium bowl, combine the oil, eggs, syrup, and vanilla. Add to the dry ingredients, mixing with a fork or wooden spoon until blended. Fold in the raisins. Spread the batter into the prepared baking pan.

▶ Bake for 20 to 25 minutes, until golden. Cool on a wire rack. Cut into bars or squares. Serve immediately or wrap and store at room temperature or in the freezer.

½ cup raisins

1⅓ cups quick-cooking rolled oats (see Pantry, page 274), or 1 cup quinoa flakes

½ cup oat flour or sorghum flour

½ cup sweet white sorghum flour

½ cup plus 2 tablespoons buckwheat flour

½ cup tapioca starch/flour or cornstarch

⅓ cup almond flour

1½ teaspoons xanthan gum

½ teaspoon salt

1 teaspoon baking soda

1 teaspoon baking powder

1½ teaspoons ground cinnamon

1⅔ cups light brown sugar, not packed

⅔ cup canola oil or other vegetable oil

2 large eggs

¼ cup maple syrup or honey

2 teaspoons vanilla extract

Key Lime Bars

MAKES 16 TO 20 BARS

An early version of this recipe appeared on Gluten-Free Pantry's website, glutenfree.com, using GFP's Cake & Cookie mix for the crumbs. These days I use homemade graham-style crumbs or, when I'm short on time, commercial gluten-free graham cracker or cookie crumbs. This recipe is easy and delicious and will become part of your repertoire as it has become part of mine.

▶ Make the crust: Preheat the oven to 350°F. Lightly grease a 9 x 13-inch baking pan.

▶ In a food processor, process the graham cracker crumbs, butter, and sugar until finely ground. Press into the pan.

▶ Bake for 5 to 8 minutes, until the edges begin to brown. Cool slightly. Maintain the oven temperature.

▶ Make the filling: Beat the cream cheese in medium bowl with an electric mixer on medium speed until light and fluffy. Gradually beat in the condensed milk and egg yolks until smooth. Beat in the lime juice. Spread over the crust.

▶ Bake for 35 minutes, or until the center is set. Cool for 30 minutes. Cover loosely and refrigerate for at least 3 hours, or until chilled.

▶ Cut into bars. Store, covered, in the refrigerator. Serve the bars as is or with a dollop of whipped cream and slices of lime.

Crust

2¼ cups graham cracker–style crumbs (page 235) or commercial gluten-free graham or sugar cookie crumbs (see Pantry, page 273)

⅓ cup butter or non-dairy buttery spread, melted

3 tablespoons sugar

Filling

two 8-ounce packages reduced-fat cream cheese or soy cream cheese, softened

two 14-ounce cans low-fat sweetened condensed milk or dairy-free version (see page 267)

3 large egg yolks

¾ cup key lime juice (such as Nellie & Joe's brand)

Shortcut:

▶ Grind premade gluten-free cookies in a food processor to yield 2¼ cups.

Avoiding Eggs? Omit and add 2 tablespoons corn or potato starch to the filling mixture. Beat well.

Dairy-free? Replace condensed milk with an equal amount of cream of coconut or see page 267 to make dairy-free condensed milk.
Use soy cream cheese and add 2 tablespoons corn or potato starch.
Use Earth Balance Dairy-Free Spread in the crust.

Lemon Walnut Squares

MAKES 24 SQUARES

I've adapted my favorite parts of several recipes to create these yummy lemon squares. I make them every year for my son's birthday and mail them to his office. They never make it home. For best results, do not replace the eggs with an egg substitute.

▶ Make the crust: Preheat the oven to 350°F. Line a 9 x 13-inch pan with aluminum foil. Spray with vegetable spray.

▶ Combine the rice flour, sorghum flour, cornstarch, xanthan gum, and salt together in a bowl. Stir well with a fork to blend. Remove 5 tablespoons of the flour mixture to a separate bowl and set aside.

▶ In the bowl of a food processor, combine the ¾ cup walnuts, 1½ cups of the rice flour blend, the butter, and brown sugar. Pulse until the mixture resembles coarse meal. Remove ¾ cup of the mixture and place in a separate bowl. Press the remaining mixture into the bottom and 1 inch up the sides of the prepared pan.

▶ Bake 10 to 12 minutes, until the edges are light brown.

▶ Make the filling: Beat the eggs, sugar, lemon juice, reserved flour blend, and baking powder in a bowl and pour over the baked crust. Sprinkle the reserved ¾ brown sugar mixture over the top and cover evenly with the walnuts.

▶ Bake 25 to 30 minutes, until just set and the top has begun to brown. Cool and refrigerate.

Crust

¾ cup plus 2 tablespoons rice flour

½ cup sorghum or chickpea flour

½ cup cornstarch or potato starch

1 teaspoon xanthan gum

¼ teaspoon salt

¾ cup coarsely chopped walnuts, toasted

8 tablespoons (1 stick) cold unsalted butter or non-dairy buttery spread, cut into pieces

½ cup lightly packed light brown sugar

Lemon Filling

4 large eggs

1½ cups sugar

Juice of 4 large lemons (about ¾ cup)

5 tablespoons rice flour blend (from crust recipe)

1 teaspoon baking powder

½ cup coarsely chopped walnuts, toasted

Tips: For best handling, freeze one hour before cutting into squares. Lift out of the pan using the edges of the aluminum foil. These bars are best if made one day prior to serving.

To make juicing the lemons easier, cut in half and place in a glass bowl. Microwave for 2 minutes. Let cool before juicing.

Peanut Butter Bars

MAKES 24 TO 30 BARS

When a version of this recipe appeared in the *Hartford Courant* several years ago I had to try it. After all, what could be wrong with a recipe that calls for chocolate and peanut butter? In place of the four and sugar, I used a Gluten-Free Pantry Cake and Cookie Mix. The results were stunning. Then I made it with the Cake and Pastry Four Blend and the results were even better—a bit lighter and less granular. Either way, you are sure to get rave reviews. Get out the milk. You are in for a treat!

▶ Make the crust: Preheat the oven to 350°F. Lightly oil a 9 x 13-inch baking pan.

▶ In a mixer, combine the sugar, flour blend, baking powder, and baking soda and mix just to blend. Add the peanut butter, butter, and eggs and mix until the dough forms a ball. The mixture will be crumbly. Remove 1 cup of the dough and set aside. Press the remaining dough into the bottom and 1 inch up the sides of the prepared pan.

▶ Make the filling: In a microwave-safe bowl, combine the chocolate chips, condensed milk, and butter. Microwave on medium heat for 1 to 2 minutes, until the chips have melted. Stir until smooth.

▶ Pour the melted chocolate over the dough in the pan. Crumble the reserved dough and sprinkle over the chocolate filling.

▶ Bake for 24 to 28 minutes or until the chocolate is no longer shiny. The surface will look wrinkled. Remove from the oven. Cool completely or refrigerate before cutting into bars.

Shortcut:

▶ Replace the dry ingredients in the crust with one 15- to 16-ounce package of commercial gluten-free white cake mix, such as Gluten-Free Pantry brand Old Fashioned Cake and Cookie Mix.

Crust

1 cup sugar

1¾ cups Cake and Pastry Flour (page 16)

1 teaspoon baking powder

½ teaspoon baking soda

1 cup all-natural unsweetened peanut butter (smooth or crunchy)

8 tablespoons (1 stick) unsalted butter or non-dairy buttery spread, melted

2 large eggs

Filling

1 cup semi-sweet chocolate chips

one 14-ounce can sweetened condensed milk or low-fat sweetened condensed milk (see page 267 for dairy-free version)

2 tablespoons unsalted butter or non-dairy buttery spread

Raspberry Dazzle Bars

MAKES 9 TO 12 BARS

The original recipe for these decadent bars belonged to my grandmother. But I can't give Grandma all the credit. A variation of this recipe appears on the Nestlé Toll House website. The blend of white chocolate and raspberry jam in a yummy short crust is a tantalizing favorite with kids of all ages.

- Preheat the oven to 325°F. Lightly oil a 7½ x 11-inch square baking pan.
- Melt the butter in a microwave-safe bowl on medium high for 1 minute; stir. Add half the chocolate chips and stir gently to soften. Let stand.
- Beat the eggs in a large mixing bowl on medium speed until foamy. Add the sugar and beat until lemon-yellow, about 5 minutes. Gently stir in the butter mixture. Add the vanilla extract. Add the cake flour blend to the butter and egg mixture. Beat at low speed to combine.
- Spread ⅔ of the mixture into the prepared pan and bake for 15 to 17 minutes, until light golden brown around the edges. Cool briefly on a wire rack.
- Heat the jam in a small microwave-safe bowl for 30 seconds or until spreadable and spread over the warm crust. Stir the remaining chips into the remaining batter. Drop spoonfuls of the batter over the jam.
- Bake 30 minutes or until the edges are browned. Cool completely and cut into squares.

½ cup unsalted butter or non-dairy butter spread

2 cups white chocolate chips

2 large eggs

½ cup sugar

1 teaspoon vanilla extract

1¼ cups Cake and Pastry Flour (page 16)

½ cup seedless raspberry jam

Sir Isaac Fig Bars

MAKES 20 BARS

Fig Newtons were a favorite of mine before I became gluten-free. When I spotted a fruit bar recipe that included figs as the filling, I knew I could transform it without sacrificing anything by way of flavor or texture. I've made this recipe with dried apricots and apples as well and the results are equally yummy.

▶ In a medium saucepan, soak the dried figs in 1 cup water for 1 hour. If using fresh figs, soak in ½ cup water.

▶ In a large bowl, beat 1 cup of the sugar with the butter until soft and fluffy. Add the egg, milk, and vanilla and beat well.

▶ In another bowl, combine the flour blend and xanthan gum. Mix well with a fork and add to the butter mixture. Beat until the mixture resembles a coarse meal. Refrigerate for 1 hour.

▶ Add the remaining ¾ cup sugar to the figs in the saucepan and cook over medium heat until it reaches the consistency of jam, stirring frequently. After 15 minutes, mash the figs until the consistency is smooth. Add a little more water if necessary to render a spreadable texture. Let cool until just warm to the touch.

▶ Preheat the oven to 350°F. Coat a 9 x 13-inch Pyrex baking dish with vegetable spray.

▶ Divide the dough in half. Place one half between two sheets of plastic wrap and roll out to ¼ inch thick. Remove the top sheet of plastic and place the dough into the bottom of the baking dish. Spoon the fig mixture over the dough, spreading evenly. Roll out the remaining dough and place over the figs. Don't worry if the dough tears. Just piece it back together.

▶ Bake for 30 minutes or until the top is golden. Let cool and cut into squares.

1 pound dried figs or 2 pounds fresh figs, diced

½ to 1 cup water

1¾ cups sugar

½ cup butter or non-dairy buttery spread, at room temperature

1 large egg, or flax gel

1 tablespoon milk, soy milk, or rice milk

1 teaspoon vanilla extract

1¾ cups plus 1 tablespoon Self-Rising Flour (page 16)

1 teaspoon xanthan or guar gum

Shortcut:

▶ Instead of preparing the fig mixture, use either fig, apricot, or other jam. Spread a generous layer over the pastry, cover with the second pastry layer, and bake as directed.

S'mores Bars

MAKES 24 BARS

This kid-friendly treat is ideal picnic food. The combination of chocolate, graham crackers, and marshmallows makes an irresistible dessert that's reminiscent of the campfire treat. The availability of commercial graham cracker–style crumbs cuts the preparation time considerably.

- ▶ Heat the oven to 350°F. Line a 9 x 13-inch baking pan with aluminum foil, or lightly oil a 9 x 13-inch baking pan.
- ▶ Beat the butter and sugar in a large bowl until light and fluffy. Add the eggs and vanilla and beat well. Mix together the flour blend, graham cracker crumbs, baking powder, xanthan gum, and salt. Add to the butter mixture, beating until blended.
- ▶ Press half the dough into the prepared pan. Sprinkle the chocolate chips over the dough, and then sprinkle with the marshmallows. Scatter bits of the remaining dough over the marshmallows, pressing to cover the marshmallows. Don't worry if some of the marshmallows are showing.
- ▶ Bake for 25 to 30 minutes, until lightly browned. Cool completely in the pan on a wire rack. Use the edges of the foil to lift the bars out of the pan. Set on a smooth surface and cut into bars, or cut into squares in the pan.

Shortcut:

- ▶ Use commercially prepared gluten-free graham cracker crumbs or grind gluten-free graham crackers in a food processor (see Pantry, page 273).

---

12 tablespoons (1½ sticks) unsalted butter or non-dairy buttery spread, softened

1¼ cups sugar

2 large eggs

2 teaspoons vanilla extract

2 cups Basic Blend (page 17)

1¼ cups gluten-free graham cracker–style crumbs (page 236 or see note below)

2 teaspoons baking powder

1½ teaspoons xanthan gum

¼ teaspoon salt

1½ cups semi-sweet chocolate chips

4 cups mini marshmallows (see Pantry, page 274)

Black and Whites

MAKES THREE DOZEN 3-INCH COOKIES

My friend, Debbie, who was recently diagnosed with celiac disease, handed me a recipe for Black and Whites and asked if I could make it over for her. These New York traditions are also called Half-Moon Cookies although the texture is more like a soft cake. One half is frosted with vanilla icing and the other with chocolate. Debbie thought they were wonderful. I think you'll agree.

▶ Make the cookies: Preheat the oven to 350°F. Line two cookie sheets with parchment paper.

▶ In a medium bowl, combine the flour blend and baking powder and set aside.

▶ In a large bowl, cream the sugar, shortening, and butter, beating until light and fluffy. Beat in the honey. Add the eggs one at a time, beating after each addition, just until incorporated. Add the dry ingredients alternately with the milk, beginning and ending with the dry ingredients and mixing until each addition is just incorporated. Add the vanilla and lemon juice and beat to combine.

▶ Use a #30 scoop or ⅛-cup measure and scoop the dough onto the cookie sheets, leaving about 2 inches between each. Lay a piece of plastic wrap on top of the dough and smooth into 3-inch circle. These do not spread.

▶ Bake 12 to 15 minutes or until the bottoms are golden and the tops are puffed. Do not overbake. Remove and cool completely on a rack before frosting.

Cookies

4¼ cups Cake and Pastry Flour (page 16)

2½ teaspoons baking powder

1⅓ cups sugar

½ cup (4 ounces) organic vegetable shortening

12 tablespoons (1½ sticks) unsalted butter or non-dairy buttery spread, room temperature

3 tablespoons honey

4 large eggs, at room temperature

⅔ cup milk, soy milk, or rice milk

2 teaspoons vanilla extract

2 teaspoons lemon juice

continues

continued

▶ Make the icing: In a small bowl, combine the confectioners' sugar, light corn syrup, vanilla, lemon juice, and 2 to 3 tablespoons water. Stir to combine, adding a little more water if the icing is too thick to spread. Transfer half the icing to another bowl and set aside.

▶ Turn the cookies flat sides up, and spread half of each cookie with the vanilla frosting. Return to the wire rack to harden.

▶ Microwave the chocolate on low heat just until melted. Stir in the corn syrup, if necessary to produce a smooth consistency. Add to reserved frosting, adding additional corn syrup if needed to create spreadable consistency.

▶ Once the vanilla frosting has hardened, spread the chocolate frosting over the other half of each cookie, adding a tiny bit of warm water from time to time to keep the frosting smooth and spreadable.

Icing

6 cups confectioners' sugar, sifted

⅓ cup light corn syrup

1 teaspoon vanilla extract

2 teaspoons lemon juice

¼ to ⅓ cup hot water

4 ounces bittersweet or semi-sweet chocolate, chopped into small pieces

1 to 2 teaspoons corn syrup, optional

Celebration Chocolate Chip Cookies

MAKES FORTY-EIGHT 3-INCH COOKIES OR 1 GIANT COOKIE

My sister-in-law makes a giant chocolate chip cookie instead of a birthday cake. She decorates it with candy or writes notes in frosting. I wanted a birthday cookie for my birthday so I created this gluten-free version. These are equally good using dairy-free options, but the cookies spread a little bit more.

- ▶ Preheat the oven to 375°F. Line two cookie sheets with parchment paper.
- ▶ Beat the butter in a large bowl until light and fluffy. Add both kinds of sugar and beat well. Add the whole eggs and egg yolk and the vanilla and beat until combined.
- ▶ In a separate bowl, combine the flour blend, xanthan gum, baking soda, and salt. Add to the butter mixture and beat just to combine. Fold in the chocolate chips.
- ▶ Drop the dough by rounded spoonfuls onto the cookie sheets, leaving room between the cookies as they spread. Bake for 10 to 12 minutes, until the edges are golden. Remove from the oven and let stand on the baking sheets for 1 minute to set. Use a spatula to remove the cookies to a cooling rack.

½ pound (2 sticks) unsalted butter, at room temperature

1 cup granulated sugar

½ cup lightly packed light brown sugar

2 large eggs plus 1 yolk

2 teaspoons vanilla extract

2 cups Basic Blend (page 17)

1 teaspoon xanthan gum

1 teaspoon baking soda

¼ teaspoon salt

2 cups semi-sweet chocolate chips (about 24 ounces)

continues

continued

GIANT CELEBRATION COOKIE: Preheat the oven to 350°F. Lightly oil a 12-inch pizza pan. Spread the cookie dough evenly in the pan and bake for 27 minutes. Cool completely. Place on a cardboard cake round for support if transporting, or leave in the pan and decorate with messages written in frosting and additional chocolate chips, M&M's, or other decorations.

Avoiding Dairy? Replace the butter with 8 tablespoons non-dairy spread and 8 tablespoons organic shortening.

Freeze the Dough: Scoop the dough onto a parchment paper–lined cookie sheet. Don't worry if the balls touch. Freeze for 2 hours or overnight. Transfer the frozen dough to a zip-top bag and keep frozen. Remove as needed and bake from the frozen state. Add 2 to 3 minutes to the baking time.

Chocolate Chip Caramel Cookies

MAKES ABOUT 60 COOKIES

A few years ago, I spotted a recipe for these in an issue of *Ladies' Home Journal*. Being a sucker for chocolate and caramel, I went to work on revising the recipe. I replaced the flour with my own blend, added a little potato flour for structure, and made other alterations. These cookies were such a hit that they've become a regular at my own gluten-free holiday cookie swaps.

- ▶ Preheat the oven to 325°F. Line two cookie sheets with parchment paper.
- ▶ Whisk together the flour blend, potato flour, baking soda, and salt in a small bowl. In another bowl, beat the butter and sugar on high speed until light and fluffy, about 2 minutes. Add the yolks one at a time, beating well after each addition. Add the vanilla and honey and beat until combined.
- ▶ Add the flour mixture and beat on low speed until just combined. Fold in the chocolate chips. Chill the dough for about 2 hours or until firm.
- ▶ Roll the dough into one-inch balls and press a piece of caramel in the center of each. Place the cookies about 1 inch apart on cookie sheets and and freeze for 15 minutes.
- ▶ Bake for 13 to 15 minutes, until golden. Set the cookie sheets on wire racks to cool. Store in single layers separated by wax paper in a sealed container at room temperature for up to one week.
- ▶ May be frozen.

2 cups plus 2 tablespoons Basic Blend (page 17)

2 tablespoons potato flour

2¼ teaspoons baking soda

⅛ teaspoon salt

12 tablespoons (1½ sticks) unsalted butter or non-dairy buttery spread, softened

¾ cup sugar

3 large egg yolks, at room temperature

1½ teaspoons vanilla extract

1½ teaspoons honey

½ cup mini semi-sweet chocolate chips

Caramel candies, cut into quarters

Chocolate Crinkles

Dairy-free

MAKES 36 COOKIES

These are called crinkles because of the lines that form on the top as they bake, making them look a little crinkly. The centers are dense and chocolaty like a truffle. For a real treat, just before eating microwave a cookie for 20 seconds to warm and soften the center.

- Preheat the oven to 350°F. Line two cookie sheets with parchment paper.
- Combine the flour blend, xanthan gum, 1½ cups of the confectioners' sugar, the cocoa powder, and salt in a large bowl. Mix with a fork to blend.
- In a medium saucepan, combine the chocolate and vegetable oil and warm over low heat until the chocolate is melted, stirring frequently. Do not allow it to boil or the chocolate will scorch. Add the brown sugar, honey, and vanilla and mix until the brown sugar is dissolved. Remove from the heat and cool slightly.
- Whip the eggs with a whisk until foamy. Add to the chocolate mixture and mix well. Pour into the dry ingredients and mix with a spoon until completely blended and no dry mix is visible. The dough will be thick.
- Pour the remaining cup confectioners' sugar into a bowl. Roll the cookie dough into 1-inch balls and dredge in the sugar. Set 1 inch apart on the cookie sheets.
- Bake for 10 minutes, or until tops are almost firm when tapped. Let stand on the cookie sheets for 2 minutes, then transfer to a wire rack to cool completely and store in an airtight container for up to three days. The cookies may be frozen.

---

2 cups Basic Blend (page 17)

1 teaspoon xanthan or guar gum

2½ cups confectioners' sugar

⅓ cup unsweetened cocoa powder

¼ teaspoon salt

3½ ounces unsweetened chocolate, chopped

3½ tablespoons vegetable oil

1¼ cups packed light brown sugar

⅓ cup honey

1½ tablespoons vanilla extract

2 large eggs

Chocolate Roll-Out Cookies

MAKES 24 TO 36 COOKIES

Reindeer-shaped cookies decorated in royal icing jumped out at me from a magazine and right into my gluten-free imagination. The result was these cut-out cookies that I've made into everything from witches to Christmas trees and dreidels. A soft bite and rich chocolate flavor make these perfect for all holidays, or any day!

- ▶ Combine the flour blend, rice flour, cocoa powder, xanthan gum, salt, baking powder, and baking soda in a large bowl and whisk to blend.
- ▶ Place the chocolate in a microwave-safe bowl and heat in the microwave on medium for 1 minute. Stir and repeat until melted. Do not overheat.
- ▶ In another large bowl, beat the butter at medium speed until light and fluffy, 1 to 2 minutes. Add the sugar and beat another 2 minutes, or until pale. Add the egg and beat until blended. On low speed, add the vanilla and melted chocolate. Add the flour mixture and beat to blend. Form the dough into a ball. The dough may be refrigerated overnight at this point. Return to room temperature before rolling out.
- ▶ Preheat the oven to 350°F. Line two baking sheets with parchment paper.
- ▶ Divide the dough into three pieces. Roll out each piece between two pieces of plastic wrap to an even ¼-inch thickness. Remove the top sheet of the plastic and cut out cookie shapes using your favorite cookie cutters. Gather the remnants of the dough and form another ball, then roll to ¼-inch thickness and cut out more cookies. Repeat until all the dough is used. Use a spatula to transfer the cookies to the baking sheets and place 2 inches apart.

2 cups plus 2 tablespoons Basic Blend (page 17)

½ cup sweet rice flour

¼ cup unsweetened Dutch processed cocoa powder

¾ teaspoon xanthan gum

½ teaspoon salt

½ teaspoon baking powder

¼ teaspoon baking soda

½ cup semi-sweet chocolate chips

½ pound (2 sticks) unsalted butter or 1 cup non-dairy buttery spread, at room temperature

1½ cups sugar

1 large egg

1 teaspoon vanilla extract

continues

continued

- If the dough becomes too warm to handle, lift the cookies with the plastic wrap onto a cookie sheet and chill for a few minutes until the cookies are easy to remove.
- Bake for 9 to 11 minutes, or until the edges are slightly dark. Do not overbake or the cookies will become crispy once they cool.
- Decorate with confectioners' or royal icing on page 258.
- These cookies can be stored at room temperature for five days or in the freezer for up to four weeks.

Shortcut:

- For easy decorating, sprinkle decorative sugar or sprinkles on the cookies before baking.

Chocolate Shortbread

Egg-free

MAKES 24 TO 30 SQUARES

My cousin Bette makes a gluten-filled version of this shortbread for every occasion because it's easy and made from ingredients that are usually on hand. By replacing the all-purpose flour with a basic gluten-free blend, this has become the go-to recipe for last minute occasions in my house, too.

- ½ pound (2 sticks) unsalted butter, at room temperature
- 1¼ cups confectioners' sugar
- 2 teaspoons vanilla extract
- 2 cups Basic Blend (page 17)
- 1 teaspoon xanthan gum
- ½ teaspoon salt
- 1½ cups semi-sweet chocolate chips
- ¾ cup chopped toasted pecans or walnuts, optional

- ▶ Preheat the oven to 325°F. Line a 9 x 13-inch pan with aluminum foil. Lightly oil the foil.
- ▶ Beat together the butter, sugar, and vanilla until blended. In a separate bowl, combine the flour blend, xanthan gum, and salt. Add to the butter mixture and beat on low to combine. Press into the bottom of the prepared pan.
- ▶ Bake for 35 minutes, or until the top is golden brown. Remove from the oven and sprinkle the chocolate chips evenly over the top. Let melt and spread with a rubber spatula. If the chocolate does not melt, return to the oven briefly. Sprinkle evenly with the pecans and press into the chocolate. Cool completely.
- ▶ Use the foil to lift the cookies onto a cutting board. Cut into squares or other shapes. These handle more easily if frozen for 1 to 2 hours before cutting.

Shortcut:

- ▶ Use any all-purpose gluten-free flour blend, but omit the salt and gum if they are already added to the blend.

Ginger Giants

Dairy-free

MAKES 12 TO 15 COOKIES

This award-winning cookie was created by Bob Spector at Nature's Grocer in Vernon, Connecticut, and is reprinted with his permission. Laced with tiny bits of ginger, these soft molasses cookies belong in the "unforgettable" category. My tester, Beverly, agreed. She called them "fabalicious." They are great crumbled as a quick crust for ice cream pie, too, but chances are, you won't have any extra lying around once you've bitten into one Ginger Giant.

½ cup canola or other vegetable oil

¼ cup unsulphured molasses

1 cup sugar

2 tablespoons chopped crystallized ginger

1 large egg

2 cups Cake and Pastry Flour (page 16)

½ cup chickpea flour or quinoa flour

1½ tablespoons baking soda

1½ teaspoons xanthan gum

1 teaspoon ground ginger

Pinch of salt

Additional sugar for rolling cookies

▶ Combine the oil, molasses, sugar, ginger, and egg in a medium bowl. In a large bowl, mix the flour blend, chickpea flour, baking soda, xanthan gum, ginger, and salt together. Add the wet ingredients to the dry ingredients and beat on medium-low until the mixture is smooth, about 1 minute.

▶ Preheat the oven to 350°F. Line two baking sheets with parchment paper.

▶ Cover a plate with a thin layer of sugar. Use a ¼-cup scoop to scoop out the dough and roll in the sugar until coated. Place on the cookie sheets about 2 inches apart as cookies will spread a little. Press down slightly to form even circles.

▶ Bake about 12 minutes, or until the edges are slightly browned. Remove and cool completely.

continues

continued

VARIATION:

Lemon Ginger Ice Cream Sandwiches

- ▶ Combine 1 cup of the sugar and the lemon juice. Add more sugar until the mixture reaches spreading consistency. Set aside.
- ▶ Soften vanilla, ginger, or lemon ice cream. Spread a generous layer over the bottom of one cookie. Place a second cookie, bottom side down over the ice cream. Frost with lemon icing. Freeze briefly or store in the freezer until ready to serve. If stored in the freezer, let sit at room temperature for 10 minutes to soften before serving.

Lemon Icing
1 to 2 cups confectioners' sugar

Juice of 1 lemon

Orange Pecan Cookies

MAKES 48 MEDIUM COOKIES

I was searching for a cookie that would travel well in the summer heat, which meant no chocolate or meringue. I turned to one of my favorite cookie experts, Maida Heatter, and I proceeded to convert one of her recipes for a gluten-free kitchen. The cookies are crisp and chewy and hold up well for three days without freezing. These make giant saucer cookies that look lovely on a plate.

- ▶ Preheat the oven to 325°F. Line two to four cookie sheets with parchment paper.
- ▶ Spread the chopped pecans over the surface on one sheet and toast for 5 minutes, shaking the pan once or twice so they don't burn. Remove from the oven. Raise the oven temperature to 400°F.
- ▶ In a medium bowl, combine the flour blend, baking powder, and baking soda. In a large mixing bowl, cream the butter. Add both kinds of sugar and beat until the mixture is smooth. Add the orange peel, the extracts, and the eggs and beat well. Add the flour mixture, a little at a time, and beat on low until combined. Use a wooden spoon to fold in the toasted pecans.
- ▶ Use a teaspoon or a small scoop to scoop the balls onto the cookie sheets, leaving about 2 inches between cookies. Bake two cookie sheets at a time, 10 to 11 minutes, rotating the pans once during baking. Transfer the cookies to cool on a wire rack.

VARIATION: Replace the orange extract and pecans with 1 cup chocolate chips or toffee crunch pieces.

---

1 cup pecans, coarsely chopped

3 cups Cake and Pastry Flour (page 16)

1½ teaspoons baking powder

½ teaspoon baking soda

12 tablespoons (1½ sticks) unsalted butter or non-dairy buttery spread, at room temperature

1 cup packed light or dark brown sugar

1 cup granulated sugar

2 teaspoons dried orange peel or 1 tablespoon grated fresh orange zest

1 teaspoon vanilla extract

½ teaspoon orange extract

2 large eggs

Avoiding Eggs? Use a flax gel equivalent or puréed silken tofu (see Simple Substitutions, page 268).

Avoiding Dairy? Replace 1½ sticks of butter with 6 tablespoons organic shortening and 6 tablespoons non-dairy buttery spread.

Pinwheel Cookies

MAKES 48 COOKIES

Chocolate or vanilla? When you can't decide, here's another childhood recipe that will never force you to choose. The "logs" of unbaked cookies keep nicely in the freezer so you can slice and bake as needed. They will fill your desire for chocolate and vanilla at once. As with most chocolate cookies, be careful not to overbake.

▶ Beat the butter and cream cheese together until fluffy. Add the sugar and beat until light and fluffy. Combine the flour blend, baking powder, and baking soda in a separate bowl and stir to mix. Add to the butter mixture and beat on low speed until combined.

▶ Add the whole egg, the egg white, and the vanilla and beat until the dough is smooth. Remove half the dough and set aside. Add the cocoa powder and the egg yolk to the remaining half of the dough in the mixing bowl and beat until smooth.

▶ Roll out each portion of the dough between sheets of plastic wrap to an even ¼-inch thickness (about 9 x 15-inches). Remove the top sheet of plastic and lay the chocolate dough on top of the vanilla dough, leaving ¼ inch of the vanilla dough showing on all edges. Pat and patch the chocolate layer as necessary. Gently roll the dough jelly-roll fashion, peeling away the plastic wrap as you roll. Wrap in plastic and chill for 1 hour.

▶ Preheat the oven to 350°F. Line two cookie sheets with parchment paper or lightly oil.

▶ Slice the cookies ¼ inch thick. Lay on the prepared cookie sheets. Bake 10 to 12 minutes, just until the edges are slightly brown. The baked cookies and the prepared dough may be frozen. Logs of dough will keep up to three days in the refrigerator or three months in the freezer.

6 tablespoons unsalted butter, softened

6 tablespoons regular or low-fat cream cheese, softened

1⅓ cups sugar

2½ cups Cake and Pastry Flour (page 16)

1½ teaspoons baking powder

¾ teaspoon baking soda

1 large egg

1 large egg, separated

2 teaspoons vanilla extract

⅓ cup unsweetened cocoa powder

Avoiding Dairy?

Replace the butter with organic shortening and use soy cream cheese in place of regular cream cheese.

Roll-Out Sugar Cookies

MAKES 18 TO 24 COOKIES

We had several variations of sugar cookie recipes when I owned Gluten-Free Pantry. I tested them all and selected the best cookie in the bunch for this book. It was not an easy job, that's for sure. However, this recipe won our hearts. I am sure you will agree!

- ▶ Cream the butter and sugar in a large bowl on medium-high speed until light and fluffy. Add the egg and vanilla and beat for 1 minute. In a separate bowl, combine the flour blend, rice flour, xanthan gum, salt, and baking powder and mix with a fork. Add gradually to the butter mixture, beating on low speed until combined. Shape the dough into a ball and flatten into a disk. Cover with plastic wrap and chill for 3 hours or overnight.
- ▶ Preheat the oven to 375°F. Line two cookie sheets with parchment paper.
- ▶ Roll the dough between two pieces of plastic wrap to ¼ inch thick. Remove the top sheet of plastic and cut out cookies using your favorite cutters. Gather the remnants of dough and form another ball, then roll to ¼-inch thickness and cut out more cookies. Repeat until all the dough is used. Use a spatula to transfer the cookies to the cookie sheets.
- ▶ If the dough becomes too warm to handle, lift the cookies and the plastic wrap onto a cookie sheet and chill for a few minutes until the cookies are easy to remove.
- ▶ Bake 8 to 10 minutes, until the edges are light brown. Cool on a wire rack
- ▶ Decorate with confectioners' or royal icing on pages 258 and 259.

½ pound (2 sticks) unsalted butter, softened

⅔ cup sugar

1 large egg

2 teaspoons vanilla extract

2 cups Basic Blend (page 17)

½ cup sweet rice flour

½ teaspoon xanthan gum

½ teaspoon salt

½ teaspoon baking powder

continues

continued

Shortcuts:

▶ Before baking these cookies, sprinkle with colored sugar. This touch gives your cookies a perfect finish without the icing.

▶ One of my testers, Brooke Mommsen, rolled this dough into a 1-inch round log. She wrapped and refrigerated the dough then cut it into ¼-inch-thick slices, sprinkled the tops with colored sprinkles, and baked as above. The results were delicious and with far less fuss.

Cakes and Cupcakes

It's challenging to make over desserts in the cake and cupcake department. Something is often lost when rice flour replaces wheat flour and that's often the light and airy texture. So many desserts smack of a certain graininess that is barely masked by sugar and chocolate and frosting. The blends used here aim for a light texture that fools most. People who can eat wheat are surprised and delighted. I don't tell them how far gluten-free has come. I simply smile and say, "What did you expect?"

Once you have successful recipes like these in your repertoire, you can dress them up with any number of frostings and fillings. Scoop out a bit of cupcake and pipe preserves or frosting into the center for a tasty surprise. Or spoon half the batter into each muffin cup, drop a dollop of preserves or a chocolate kiss in the center and cover with more batter.

Slice through the center of a cake to create thin layers and spread chocolate mousse or buttercream mixed with toasted ground almonds between the layers. Once these are stacked and the cake is frosted, sprinkle toasted almonds or chocolate shavings around the sides and top. The presentation is lovely and professional looking. And it's a great way to hide any mistakes.

Most of all, imagine that every cake and cupcake is for you and celebrate.

Auntie's Apple Cake

Dairy-free

MAKES 10 TO 12 SERVINGS

Years ago, my husband's aunt made an apple cake for the Jewish New Year. Alas, I couldn't taste it, but the compliments she received touched my soul where good food lives. This version uses my Cake and Pastry Flour blend, reduces the oil, and replaces it with additional orange juice. Delicious—and lower in calories.

3 to 4 cups peeled, thinly sliced Granny Smith or McIntosh apples (about 3 large)

5 tablespoons plus 2 cups sugar

5 teaspoons ground cinnamon

3 cups Cake and Pastry Flour (page 16)

3 teaspoons baking powder

1 teaspoon dried orange peel

4 large eggs

¾ cup vegetable oil

¾ cup orange juice

▶ Preheat the oven to 375°F. Lightly oil a tube pan.

▶ Toss the apples with 5 tablespoons of the sugar and the cinnamon; set aside.

▶ In a large mixing bowl, combine the flour blend, the remaining 2 cups sugar, the baking powder, and orange peel. Toss with a fork to combine. In a separate bowl, combine the eggs, oil, and juice. Pour the wet ingredients into the dry ingredients and mix until smooth.

▶ Spread one third of the batter over the bottom and slightly up the sides of the prepared pan. Cover with half the apple mixture. Spread with another one third of the batter. Use a spatula to smooth the batter over the apples. Cover with the remaining apples and the remaining batter. Smooth the top of the cake so the batter fills in around the apples.

▶ Bake for 30 minutes. Cover with aluminum foil and bake another 15 to 20 minutes, until the top of the cake is firm to the touch. Remove from the oven and cool in the pan set on a wire rack for 1 hour. Remove to a serving plate. Cut and serve.

Shortcut:

▶ A commercial all-purpose blend can be used. Just omit the gum and salt if they are already included in the mix.

Chocolate Angel Food Cake

Dairy-free

MAKES 12 SERVINGS

Although I like an ooey, gooey dessert as much as the next person, I think this angel food cake could be my all-time favorite. It's yummy without loading on the calories. Serve with sliced strawberries and whipped cream or ice cream and chocolate syrup, or enjoy as is. If using a stand mixer, prepare this using the whisk attachment.

▶ Preheat the oven to 375°F.

▶ Sift the flour, cocoa powder, and ¾ cup of the sugar into a bowl. Set aside.

▶ Beat the egg whites at low speed in a large mixing bowl until foamy, about 5 minutes. Add the vanilla, cream of tartar, and salt. With the mixer on medium speed, add the remaining ¾ cup sugar in a slow, steady stream. Beat an additional 5 to 7 minutes, until the whites are shiny and form stiff peaks.

▶ Sift one third of dry ingredients over the egg whites and gently fold in with a rubber spatula. Repeat until all the flour mixture has been incorporated. Scrape the batter into an ungreased non-stick aluminum 10-inch tube pan. Smooth the top and gently tap the pan onto the counter to remove any air pockets.

▶ Bake 40 to 45 minutes, until tiny cracks appear on the top and the cake springs back to the touch. Invert the pan onto a wire rack if the pan has feet or invert the center tube of the pan onto the neck of bottle to cool completely.*

▶ To unmold, run a thin knife around the side of the pan and the tube and gently push the base up if using a two-piece pan or invert the cake onto a serving plate.

* I prefer using a rack in case the cake falls out as it cools which a number of people have told me happens when they make angel food cake. I've not had that experience with this cake, but it's better to be safe than sorry.

1 cup Cake and Pastry Flour (page 16)

5 tablespoons unsweetened cocoa powder

1½ cups sugar

12 large egg whites, at room temperature

1½ teaspoons vanilla extract

1½ teaspoons cream of tartar

¼ teaspoon salt

VARIATION: To make vanilla angel food cake, omit the cocoa powder and use 1¼ cups of flour blend.

Chocolate Coconut Crème Bundt Cake

MAKES 12 SERVINGS

A Bundt cake is a circle of cake surrounding an open center, like a gathering of friends around a sumptuous dish. But slice into this cake for the biggest surprise of all—the coconut crème center. This is one recipe you'll want to share with your circle of friends. And no one will guess it's gluten-free.

▶ Make the filling: Using a stand mixer fitted with the whisk attachment or a handheld mixer, beat the egg whites and salt on low speed until foamy, about 5 minutes. Add the confectioners' sugar and beat at high speed until the stiff peaks form. In a bowl, mix the coconut with the flour blend. Fold into the egg whites. Fold in the vanilla and chocolate chips and set aside.

▶ Make the cake: Preheat the oven to 350°F. Spray a 10-cup Bundt pan with vegetable spray.

▶ Combine the flour blend, cocoa powder, baking powder, and baking soda in a bowl; set aside.

▶ Using the paddle attachment on a stand mixer or a handheld mixer, beat the butter and sugar until fluffy. Add the eggs and egg yolk one at a time, beating after each addition. While the mixer is on low speed, add the flour mixture alternately with the milk, beginning and ending with the flour mixture and mixing until each addition is just incorporated.

Coconut Crème Filling

2 large egg whites

Pinch of salt

½ cup confectioners' sugar

1½ cups sweetened flaked coconut

2 tablespoons Cake and Pastry Flour (page 16)

1 teaspoon vanilla extract

1 cup semi-sweet chocolate chips

Cake

2⅓ cups Cake and Pastry Flour (page 16)

⅔ cup unsweetened cocoa powder, sifted

2 teaspoons baking powder

1 teaspoon baking soda

¾ cup unsalted butter or non-dairy buttery spread, softened

1¾ cups sugar

3 large eggs plus 1 egg yolk

1 cup milk, soy milk, or rice milk

continues

continued

▸ Spoon one third of the batter into the bottom of the prepared pan. Smooth the top with a rubber spatula. Spoon the coconut filling over the batter, making sure that the filling does not touch the sides of the pan. Smooth, patting the mixture down slightly. Spoon the remaining batter over the filling and smooth the top.

▸ Bake for 45 to 50 minutes, until a tester inserted into the center comes out clean and the top springs back to the touch. Let cool in the pan for 10 minutes, then loosen the edges and invert the cake onto a serving plate. Cool completely.

▸ Make the glaze: Melt the butter in a medium saucepan over medium heat. Add the confectioners' sugar, cocoa powder, milk, and vanilla. Remove from the heat and whisk until blended and smooth. Add more sugar or milk, if needed, to reach desired consistency. Drizzle over the cooled cake, letting the glaze run down the sides. Store at room temperature.

Shortcut:

▸ Prepare the batter of a commercial chocolate cake mix according to the package directions and assemble and bake according to the Bundt cake recipe. You will need roughly 4¾ cups dry mix to have enough batter for this cake.

VARIATION: Makes 3 dozen cupcakes. Assemble according to the directions above, filling three 12-cup muffin tins with the batter and filling, being careful not to overfill the cups. Bake 18 to 20 minutes. Spoon the glaze over the cooled cupcakes.

Chocolate Glaze

4 tablespoons unsalted butter or non-dairy buttery spread

1½ cups confectioners' sugar

3 tablespoons unsweetened cocoa powder, sifted

3 to 4 tablespoons milk, or soy or rice milk

1 teaspoon vanilla extract

Chocolate Ginger Cake
with Ginger Glaze

MAKES 8 TO 10 SERVINGS

This may win the longest-title-in-the-book award. However, the recipe is so good it deserves this honor, and others! The glaze packs a ginger "punch." Adjust the amount to suit personal taste. Add ¼ cup chopped crystallized ginger to the batter if you are a true ginger lover.

- ▶ Make the cake: Preheat the oven to 350°F. Lightly grease a 10-inch springform pan.
- ▶ Combine the milk and cider vinegar in a small bowl; set aside.
- ▶ Combine the chocolate, oil, molasses, and butter in a small saucepan over medium heat and cook until melted, stirring often. Remove from the heat and set aside.
- ▶ In a large mixing bowl, combine the flour blend, both sugars, baking powder, baking soda, ginger, cinnamon, and nutmeg. In a separate bowl, mix together the eggs, milk mixture, and vanilla. Stir into dry ingredients, mixing until combined. Add the melted chocolate mixture to the batter and beat until the mixture is smooth.
- ▶ Spoon the batter into the prepared pan and bake for 40 to 50 minutes, until a toothpick inserted in the center comes out clean. Cool on a wire rack. Run a knife around the side of the pan to release the cake. Remove the side of the springform pan. Set the cake with the bottom of the pan on a serving plate and cool completely.
- ▶ Make the glaze: Combine confectioners' sugar, water, vanilla, and ginger in a bowl and mix well. Taste and add more ginger if necessary. Drizzle the glaze over the cooled cake.

Chocolate Ginger Cake

1 cup milk, soy milk, or rice milk

2 teaspoons cider vinegar

3 ounces unsweetened chocolate

½ cup vegetable oil

½ cup light molasses

4 tablespoons unsalted butter or non-dairy butter spread

1¾ cups Cake and Pastry Flour (page 16)

1¼ cups granulated sugar

½ cup packed light brown sugar

2 teaspoons baking powder

½ teaspoon baking soda

4 teaspoons ground ginger

2 teaspoons ground cinnamon

1½ teaspoons nutmeg

2 large eggs

1½ teaspoons vanilla extract

Ginger Glaze

1 cup confectioners' sugar

¼ cup warm water

½ teaspoon vanilla extract

2 to 3 teaspoons ground ginger, or to taste

Cinnamon Plum Cake

MAKES 8 SERVINGS

Elegant and easy, this recipe was inspired by one that I saw in *Bon Appétit* several years ago. The first time I made it for company, everyone was surprised when I served myself a piece. If you don't have fresh plums, try peaches, apricots, or nectarines or use frozen, thawed fruit.

▶ Preheat the oven to 350°F. Lightly oil a 9-inch springform pan. Combine the cake flour blend, baking powder, and xanthan gum in a bowl; set aside.

▶ Beat ¾ cup of the sugar and butter in a mixing bowl until fluffy. Add the dry ingredients and lemon zest and beat until crumbly. Add the eggs one at a time, beating after each addition. Add the lemon juice and beat just to incorporate. Spread the batter evenly in the prepared pan.

▶ Arrange the plum slices on top of the batter so that they touch and form concentric circles that cover the batter. Press into the batter lightly. Don't worry if the slices are not perfect. The cake will partially cover the fruit as it bakes. Combine the remaining 3 tablespoons sugar and the cinnamon and sprinkle over the batter.

▶ Bake 55 to 60 minutes, until golden and a tester inserted into the center comes out clean. Run a knife along the side of the pan to release and remove the side of the pan. Serve slightly warm or at room temperature with whipped cream or ice cream.

1¼ cups Cake and Pastry Flour (page 16)

1½ teaspoons baking powder

1 teaspoon xanthan gum

¾ cup plus 3 tablespoons sugar

8 tablespoons (1 stick) unsalted butter or non-dairy buttery spread, at room temperature

1½ teaspoons finely grated lemon zest

2 large eggs or egg substitute (see page 268)

1 tablespoon fresh lemon juice

5 to 6 plums halved and each half cut into 4 slices

¾ teaspoon ground cinnamon for topping

Whipped cream or ice cream

Dairy-Free Black Cherry Cheesecake

MAKES 10 TO 12 SERVINGS

My friend Connie sent me a blueberry cheesecake recipe from an issue of *Bon Appétit*. When I heard that several guests at a Memorial Day gathering were severely lactose intolerant, I raced to the store to pick up dairy-free replacements for cream cheese and sour cream. I added cherries because they are delicious and juicy at that time of year. The result was this light dessert that made everyone happy. If you are not avoiding dairy, you could use equal amounts of regular cream cheese and sour cream. This should be prepared the day before it is served.

- ▶ Make the crust: Preheat the oven to 375°F. Spray the bottom and sides of a 9-inch springform pan with vegetable spray. Wrap the outside of the pan with heavy-duty foil.
- ▶ In a medium bowl, combine the graham cracker crumbs and buttery spread. Mix with a fork until the crumbs are moist. Press the crumb mixture firmly onto the bottom and 2 inches up the side of the prepared pan.
- ▶ Bake about 8 minutes, or until the crust begins to brown. Transfer the crust to a rack and cool. Maintain the oven temperature.
- ▶ Make the filling: Using an electric mixer, beat the cream cheese and confectioners' sugar in a large bowl until well blended. Beat in the tapioca starch. Add the eggs one at a time, beating just until combined. Beat in the sour cream and vanilla. Pour the filling into the cooled crust.

Crust

2 cups plus 2 tablespoons gluten-free graham cracker–style crumbs (see Pantry, page 273)

6 tablespoons non-dairy buttery spread or other dairy-free spread, melted

Filling

three 8-ounce packages soy cream cheese, at room temperature (see Simple Substitutions, page 266)

½ cup confectioners' sugar (see page 268 for corn-free confectioners' sugar)

2 tablespoons tapioca starch/flour

4 large eggs

one 12-ounce container soy sour cream (see Simple Substitutions, page 266)

2 teaspoons vanilla extract

continues

continued

▶ Place the springform pan into a roasting pan. Set on the center rack of the oven and pour enough hot water into the roasting pan to come 1 inch up the sides of the cheesecake pan.

▶ Bake for about 1 hour, until the cheesecake is just set in the center and the top is slightly puffed and golden brown. A sharp knife inserted into the center of the cake should come out with thickened mixture on the tip. Turn off the oven. Let the cheesecake stand in the oven for 1 hour with the door closed. Remove from the oven and cool completely. Refrigerate at least 2 hours uncovered, then cover and refrigerate overnight.

▶ Make the topping: In a large glass bowl, warm the cherry spread in a microwave for 45 seconds, or until softened. Add the cherries and stir gently to coat.

▶ Run a sharp knife around the edge of the cheesecake to loosen and release the side of the pan. Set the cake with the bottom of the pan on a serving plate. Spoon the topping over the cake, spreading evenly. Chill at least 1 hour and up to 4 hours.

Topping

½ cup fruit-sweetened black cherry spread

2 cups pitted cherries, halved, or one 12-ounce package frozen pitted cherries, thawed and drained

Featherlight White Cake

MAKES 8 TO 10 SERVINGS

Every collector has a list of acquisitions they *must* have. I'm no exception. As a collector of gluten-free recipes, a light and airy white cake is high on my list. To create it, I went to the experts to see what formulas and techniques they applied. Inspired by a mélange that included King Arthur Bakers, an old Pillsbury Cookbook, and a White Lily Flour primer, I came up with the recipe below. The Cake and Pastry Flour blend is a critical ingredient to this recipe's success.

▶ Preheat the oven to 350°F. Lightly grease or oil two 9-inch cake pans and dust with rice flour.

▶ Combine the cake flour blend and baking powder in a bowl and set aside.

▶ In a separate bowl, blend the sugar and butter until soft and fluffy. Add the eggs one at a time, beating to incorporate. Beat in the vanilla. Add the flour mixture alternately with the milk in three batches, beating after each addition.

▶ Divide the batter evenly between the two pans. Smooth the tops and bake on the center rack for 28 to 30 minutes, until a wooden toothpick inserted in the center comes out clean. Let cool in the pans on a wire rack for 10 minutes. Remove from the pans and cool completely before frosting.

2¾ cups Cake and Pastry Flour (page 16)

1 tablespoon baking powder

1½ cups superfine sugar (granulated is okay)

12 tablespoons (1½ sticks) unsalted butter or dairy-free buttery spread, at room temperature

3 large eggs, at room temperature

1½ teaspoons vanilla extract

1 cup 2% milk, soy milk, or rice milk

Frosting of your choice (page 254 or see below)

VARIATIONS:

• To make a chocolate cake, use 2½ cups flour blend and ⅓ cup unsweetened cocoa powder.

• To jazz up your cake, in place of vanilla extract, use ¾ teaspoon lemon extract and add 2 teaspoons grated lemon zest. Frost with Simple Confectioners' Sugar Frosting (page 259), replacing the milk with 2 tablespoons of lemon juice. Spread apricot or raspberry jam between the cake layers and frost with the frosting of your choosing.

• For more ideas, see frosting recipes beginning on page 254.

Gingerbread

MAKES 12 TO 20 SQUARES

Doesn't everyone need a good gingerbread recipe? The combination of several mainstream recipes, this rich and spicy gingerbread is delicious served warm with vanilla ice cream, whipped cream, or Crème Anglaise Sauce (page 260). Orange juice and buttermilk help make this cake moist and balance out the fragrant spices. A version of this first appeared in *Living Without* magazine.

▶ Preheat the oven to 350°F. Coat a 9 x 13-inch pan with vegetable spray.

▶ In a medium saucepan, combine the molasses, brown sugar, and butter. Set over low heat until the butter melts, stirring once or twice. Remove from the heat and cool.

▶ In a large mixing bowl, combine the flour blend, baking powder, baking soda, ginger, cinnamon, nutmeg, and cloves. Whisk to blend. Add the buttermilk, orange juice, eggs, and molasses mixture to the dry ingredients. Beat on medium speed until smooth. Transfer the batter to the prepared pan.

▶ Bake for 25 to 30 minutes, until a toothpick inserted in the center comes out clean.

1 cup light molasses

½ cup packed light brown sugar

8 tablespoons unsalted butter or non-dairy buttery spread

2¾ cups Cake and Pastry Flour (page 16)

2½ teaspoons baking powder

1 teaspoon baking soda

2 teaspoons ground ginger

½ teaspoon ground cinnamon

½ teaspoon freshly grated or ground nutmeg

¼ teaspoon ground cloves

¾ cup buttermilk, soy milk, or rice milk

¼ cup orange juice

2 large eggs, lightly beaten

Avoiding Eggs? Replace with 2 tablespoons flax meal soaked in 6 tablespoons hot water until the mixture thickens.

Grandma's Sour Cream Coffee Cake

I was reminded of how much I missed this old family favorite when fellow celiacs Judy Kissane and Mary Champagne brought a gluten-free version to one of our support group meetings. I revised their version and Grandma's using the Cake and Pastry Flour.

▶ Preheat oven to 350°F. Lightly oil a 9-inch springform pan.

▶ Cream the butter and sugar in a mixing bowl on medium-high speed. Add the eggs one at a time, blending well after each addition. Blend in the vanilla.

▶ In a separate bowl, combine the flour blend, baking powder, and baking soda. Add to the wet mixture and beat on low to combine. Fold in the sour cream.

▶ Smooth half the batter over the bottom of the prepared pan. Spread ½ cup of the streusel over the batter. Spread the remaining batter over the layer of streusel. Sprinkle the remaining streusel over the top.

▶ Bake 45 to 50 minutes, until a cake tester inserted in the center of the cake comes out clean. Cool 10 minutes in the pan. Remove the rim of the pan and cool completely on a wire rack. Transfer the cake to a cake plate and serve.

Shortcut:

▶ Replace the dry ingredients (including sugar) with Gluten-Free Pantry Cake and Cookie Mix or another 15-ounce white or yellow cake mix. Add to the butter and proceed with the recipe as above.

---

8 tablespoons (1 stick) unsalted butter, softened

1 cup sugar

2 large eggs

2 teaspoons vanilla extract

2 cups Cake and Pastry Flour (page 16)

2 teaspoons baking powder

1 teaspoon baking soda

1 cup low-fat sour cream or yogurt

1 cup Streusel Crumb Topping (page 236)

Egg-Free and Dairy-Free Coffee Cake

This version of Grandma's Coffee Cake is not reserved just for those avoiding eggs and dairy. Everyone will enjoy it. Moist and flavorful, it showcases the wonders of vegan baking.

▶ Preheat the oven to 325°F and lightly oil a 9-inch springform pan.

▶ Combine the sugar, flour blend, baking powder, and baking soda in a large bowl. Set aside.

▶ Combine the soy yogurt, vegetable oil, and applesauce in a mixing bowl and beat until smooth. Add the dry ingredients and beat until smooth.

▶ Spoon half the batter over the bottom of the prepared pan and smooth to the edges of the pan. Cover with half of the streusel mixture. Spoon the remaining batter over the streusel and smooth to the edges. Sprinkle the remaining streusel over the top.

▶ Bake 55 to 60 minutes, until cake tester comes out clean and center springs back when gently touched. Cool 10 minutes in the pan. Remove the rim of the pan and cool completely on a wire rack. Serve.

1 cup sugar

2 cups Cake and Pastry Flour (page 16)

2 teaspoons baking powder

1 teaspoon baking soda

1½ cups soy yogurt (vanilla or peach yogurt work well)

6 tablespoons vegetable oil

4 tablespoons unsweetened applesauce

1 cup Streusel Crumb Topping (page 236); use non-dairy buttery spread

Honey Cake

Dairy-free

MAKES 10 TO 12 SERVINGS

This recipe was inspired by a recipe I saw in *Gourmet* several years ago. It is filled with the flavor of warm spices and sweetness. Try it served with a dollop of freshly whipped cream and chopped candied ginger.

▶ Put the oven rack in the middle position and preheat to 350°F. Generously oil a 10-cup Bundt or tube pan.

▶ In a large bowl, whisk together the flour blend, cinnamon, baking soda, and cloves. In a separate bowl, lightly beat the eggs on medium speed. Add the honey, sugar, oil, coffee, and water and beat until blended. Add the dry ingredients and beat until well combined. Pour the batter into the pan.

▶ Bake for 45 to 50 minutes, until a tester inserted in the center comes out clean. Cool in the pan on a rack for 20 minutes and then turn out onto the rack to cool completely. The cake may be kept in an airtight container at room temperature for one week.

2½ cups Self-Rising Flour (page 16)

2 teaspoons ground cinnamon

½ teaspoon baking soda

½ teaspoon ground cloves

3 large eggs

1 cup honey

1 cup sugar

⅔ cup vegetable oil

½ cup brewed coffee

¼ cup water

Hostess-Style Chocolate Cupcakes

MAKES 24 CUPCAKES

Several steps are involved in making these cupcakes, but they are fun to build and each step brings you closer to a cupcake that could truly pass for the real deal. One bite will send you back to your gluten-filled childhood.

▶ Make the cake: Preheat the oven to 350°F. Spray twenty-four 3-inch muffin cups with vegetable spray.

▶ Blend the self-rising flour, cocoa powder, and baking soda in a bowl with a fork and set aside.

▶ In a medium bowl, beat the softened butter on medium-high speed until fluffy. Add the sugar and beat 1 minute. Add the eggs and vanilla and beat until blended. Add the flour mixture and beat until smooth and incorporated. Add the buttermilk and vinegar and beat to combine.

▶ Fill the prepared muffin cups halfway with the batter. Bake for 20 to 22 minutes, or until a cake tester comes out clean. Let cool in the pans for 10 minutes, then turn onto a wire rack and cool completely before filling.

▶ Make the filling: Beat the butter, 2 cups of the confectioners' sugar, marshmallow fluff, and 1½ tablespoons of the cream until fluffy. Add additional confectioners' sugar until the consistency is thick and fluffy.

Cake

2 cups plus 2 tablespoons Self-Rising Flour (page 16)

⅔ cup unsweetened cocoa powder

1 teaspoon baking soda

¾ cup (1½ sticks) unsalted butter or non-dairy buttery spread, softened

1⅔ cups sugar

3 large eggs, at room temperature

1½ teaspoons vanilla extract

1 cup low-fat buttermilk, soy milk, or rice milk

1 teaspoon cider vinegar

Filling

6 tablespoons unsalted butter or non-dairy buttery spread, softened

2 to 3 cups confectioners' sugar

¼ cup marshmallow fluff

1½ tablespoons plus 1 teaspoon heavy cream, coconut milk, or soy milk

continues

continued

▶ In a small bowl, combine ½ cup of the filling with the remaining 1 teaspoon cream and reserve for the topping. Scrape the remaining filling into a pastry bag fitted with a ¼-inch round tip. Gently insert the tip of the pastry bag about ½ inch into the top of each cupcake and lightly squeeze some of the filling into the cupcake. You may also use a cupcake corer to hollow out the center of each cupcake and fill.

Ganache

▶ Make the ganache: Heat the cream in a small saucepan over low heat until it begins to steam, stirring constantly so the cream does not scorch. Remove from the heat and stir in the chocolate until melted and the mixture is smooth. Add the butter and stir until smooth.

▶ Dip the top of each cupcake into the mixture. Set on a baking sheet and refrigerate for 5 to 10 minutes.

▶ Spoon the reserved filling mixture into a pastry bag fitted with a #2 or #3 round tip or a plastic zip-top bag with a small corner snipped off and pipe curlicues across the center of each cupcake. Refrigerate for 10 minutes. The cupcakes will keep in refrigerator for up to three days.

VARIATION: This makes a wonderful cake, too. Spoon the batter into two 8- or 9-inch round cake pans and bake for 30 to 34 minutes, depending on the size of the pan. The cakes are done when a cake tester inserted into the center comes away clean. Spread the filling between the layers and frost the top and sides with the ganache. Decorate with curlicues.

Ganache

¼ cup heavy cream, coconut milk, or soy milk

4 ounces semi-sweet or bittersweet chocolate, chopped

1 tablespoon unsalted butter or non-dairy butter spread, softened

Light-as-Air Cupcakes

MAKES 24 CUPCAKES

You will be spoiled by this versatile recipe and the many frostings it can wear. Light and airy, as the name suggests, these cupcakes will bring smiles to everyone who tries them.

▶ Preheat the oven to 375°F. Lightly grease or oil two 12-cup muffin tins or line with paper liners.

▶ Combine the cake flour and baking powder; set aside.

▶ In a separate bowl, beat the sugar and butter until light and fluffy. Add the eggs one at a time, beating to incorporate. Blend in the vanilla. Add the flour mixture alternately with the milk in three batches, beginning and ending with the dry ingredients and mixing until each addition is just incorporated.

▶ Spoon the batter evenly into the muffin cups, filling a little more than half full. Smooth the tops and bake on the center rack for 18 to 20 minutes, until a wooden toothpick inserted in the center comes out clean. Let cool in the pans on a wire rack for 10 minutes. Remove from the pans and cool completely before frosting.

2¾ cups Cake and Pastry Flour (page 16)

1 tablespoon baking powder

1½ cups superfine sugar (granulated is okay)

12 tablespoons (1½ sticks) unsalted butter or non-dairy buttery spread, at room temperature

3 large eggs, at room temperature

1½ teaspoons vanilla extract

1 cup milk, soy milk, or rice milk

VARIATIONS:

• To make chocolate cupcakes, replace 6 tablespoons Cake and Pastry Flour Blend with ½ cup unsweetened cocoa powder.

• For jazzier cupcakes, try Hidden Treasure Cupcakes: Spoon 2 tablespoons of Light-as-Air Cupcakes batter into the bottoms of the muffin cups. Place a scant teaspoon of apricot or strawberry jam in the center and pour the remaining batter into the muffin cups, filling the cups a little more than half full. Bake as above. Cool and frost with orange, lemon, or vanilla confectioners' sugar frosting on page 259.

Lemon Raspberry Layer Cake with Lemon Cream Cheese Frosting

MAKES ONE 9-INCH, 2-LAYER CAKE, SERVING 10 TO 12

I tested Bundt, pound, and pudding cakes before I decided to include this lovely cake in the book. A combination of buttermilk and lemon turns this into a tangy, light, and moist cake. Filling with raspberry jam balances the tart with a touch of sweet. Bake the cake layers ahead and freeze for easier handling.

▶ Make the cake: Preheat the oven to 350°F. Lightly grease two 9-inch round cake pans and dust with rice flour. Tap out any excess flour.

▶ In a mixing bowl, whisk together the flour blend, baking powder, baking soda, and lemon zest. Set aside.

▶ In a large mixing bowl, cream the butter and sugar for 2 minutes, or until light and fluffy. Add the eggs one at a time, beating to incorporate after each addition. Add the lemon juice, then add the flour mixture alternately with the buttermilk in 3 batches, beginning and ending with the flour and beating after each addition.

▶ Divide the batter between the two cake pans and smooth the tops. Bake for 35 to 37 minutes, until a cake tester comes out clean and the center springs back to touch. Let cool for 10 minutes on a wire rack. Run a knife around the edges of the pans and invert onto the rack to cool completely.

Cake

Rice flour for dusting

2¾ cups Cake and Pastry Flour (page 16)

2 teaspoons baking powder

½ teaspoon baking soda

1 tablespoon grated fresh lemon zest or 1½ teaspoons dried lemon peel

½ pound (2 sticks) unsalted butter or non-dairy buttery spread, at room temperature

1¾ cups sugar

4 large eggs

2 tablespoons fresh lemon juice

1 cup low-fat buttermilk

⅓ to ½ cup seedless raspberry jam

continues

continued

► Line the edges of a cake plate with strips of wax paper and center one layer, top side down, onto a cake plate with the edges overlapping the wax paper. (You should be able to easily remove the pieces of wax paper after frosting the cake.) Heat the raspberry jam in the microwave for 30 seconds or until spreading consistency.

► Spread a generous layer of raspberry jam over the cake and top with the second cake layer, top side down. Chill while preparing the frosting.

► Make the frosting: Combine the Cream Cheese Frosting, lemon zest, and lemon juice in a mixing bowl and beat until smooth. Frost the sides and top of the cake or the tops of the cupcakes with the frosting. Garnish with raspberries and chill until ready to serve.

THIS CAKE MAKES TERRIFIC CUPCAKES: Divide half the batter between two 12-cup muffin tins and spoon a dollop of raspberry jam into the center of each cupcake. Top with the remaining batter for a spectacular treat.

Frosting

1 recipe Cream Cheese Frosting (page 255)

1 teaspoon lemon zest

1 tablespoon lemon juice

Fresh raspberries, for garnish

Orange Chocolate Mousse Cake

MAKES ONE 9-INCH, 3- OR 4-LAYER CAKE

This cake was inspired by Chelsea Clinton's gluten-free wedding cake, a nine-tier white cake with a chocolate mousse filling and luscious fondant frosting. The orange flavoring is my touch, and I use buttercream in place of fondant. It's much easier to handle. And about those nine layers? Don't you think three or four is enough?

▶ Prepare the Featherlight Cake according to the recipe and divide the batter among either two or three 9-inch round cake pans. If using two cake pans, slice the baked and cooled layers horizontally in half, making four layers.

▶ Make the filling: In a medium saucepan, melt the chocolate chips with the butter and ½ cup orange juice over low heat. Remove from the heat and stir in the vanilla. Scrape into a mixing bowl. Add the confectioners' sugar and beat until fluffy.

▶ In a separate bowl using clean beaters, beat the cream until stiff. Fold into the mixture. Cover and chill in the refrigerator

▶ Make the frosting: Cream the butter on medium speed until soft and fluffy. Add 3½ cups of the confectioners' sugar and beat for 1 to 2 minutes, until fluffy and doubled in volume. Beat in the orange extract, vanilla, and half-and-half for 3 minutes. Check the consistency and add more sugar if needed for spreading. Set aside ¾ cup of the frosting for decorating.

1 recipe Featherlight White or Chocolate Cake (page 212)

Chocolate Mousse Filling

16 ounces semi-sweet chocolate chips

6 tablespoons unsalted butter

½ cup orange juice, heavy cream, or coconut milk

2 teaspoons vanilla extract

2 cups confectioners' sugar

2 cups cold heavy cream

Buttercream Frosting

½ pound (2 sticks) unsalted butter

3 to 4 cups confectioners' sugar, more for stiffer frosting

½ teaspoon orange extract

2 teaspoons vanilla extract

1 to 2 tablespoons half-and-half

continues

continued

- ▸ To assemble: Set one cake layer on a cake plate.* Spread with an even layer of filling, no more than ¼ inch thick. Repeat with the remaining cake layers and filling. Frost the top and sides with a generous layer of the frosting. Do not worry about crumbs. Refrigerate the cake for 1 hour. Even out the frosting and cover the crumbs with another layer of buttercream.
- ▸ Spoon reserved ¾ cup frosting into a pastry bag fitted with a decorative tip of your choice. Pipe the frosting around the edges and decorate the center with sliced oranges or edible flowers.
- ▸ Chill the cake for at least 6 hours. Bring to room temperature before serving.

*The halved layers will be more fragile. Use two large spatulas to handle them and prevent them from breaking. However, broken pieces can be *glued* back together with mousse and will not show when frosted.

Shortcut:

- ▸ Use commercial chocolate or yellow cake mix to make two or three layers of cake (see Pantry, page 273).

Pumpkin Orange Brandy Layer Cake

MAKES 8 TO 10 SERVINGS

This cake is light and richly flavored with warm spices and a hint of orange. Last time I served this, everyone, gluten-free or not, came back for seconds. The layers freeze well. Because it is so easy to assemble and transport, I often store well-wrapped cake layers in my freezer for last minute gatherings.

- ▶ Make the cake: Preheat the oven to 350°F. Lightly grease two 8-inch round cake pans.
- ▶ Beat the eggs, sugar, and oil on medium speed until light lemon in color, about 5 minutes. Blend in the canned pumpkin and vanilla.
- ▶ Mix together the flour blend, baking soda, baking powder, cinnamon, nutmeg, and cloves in a separate bowl. Blend with a whisk. Add to the pumpkin mixture and gently stir until no flour is visible.
- ▶ Divide the batter evenly between the two pans. Bake for 25 to 28 minutes, until a toothpick inserted in the center comes out clean. Let cool for 10 minutes in the pans before turning onto a wire rack to cool completely.
- ▶ Make the filling: Heat the marmalade in the microwave on high for 30 to 40 seconds. Stir in the brandy, if using, and let cool for 5 minutes.
- ▶ Make the cream cheese frosting according to the recipe, substituting ½ teaspoon orange extract for the vanilla.
- ▶ To assemble: Set one cake layer on a cake plate. Place strips of wax paper or paper towels underneath the edge of the cake to catch any overflow of frosting. Spread with an even layer of filling. Top with the second layer. Spread the top and sides of the cake with the frosting. Sprinkle the orange zest over the top for a lovely presentation. Remove the wax paper before serving.

Cake

3 large eggs

2 cups sugar

¾ cup vegetable oil

one 15-ounce can solid-pack pumpkin

2 teaspoons vanilla extract

2 cups Cake and Pastry Flour (page 16)

1¼ teaspoons baking soda

¾ teaspoon baking powder

½ teaspoon ground cinnamon

¼ teaspoon ground nutmeg

⅛ teaspoon ground cloves

Filling

⅓ cup good-quality orange marmalade

2 teaspoons brandy, optional

Frosting

Cream Cheese Frosting (see page 255)

½ teaspoon orange extract

Zest of 1 orange for decorating

Tip: *Freeze the cake layers before frosting. Assembling and frosting while the cake is still frozen will reduce crumbs and produce a smoother finish.*

Quick Low-Fat Lemon Cheesecake

MAKES 8 SERVINGS

This falls into the have-your-cake-and-eat-it-too category. Although this is lower in calories, it doesn't sacrifice anything in taste. The crust would be great with Chocolate Orange Mousse Filling on page 222 or an instant pie and pudding filling.

▶ Preheat the oven to 350°F. Spray the bottom of an 8-inch springform pan with vegetable spray.

▶ Make the crust: Toss the cookie crumbs with the melted butter and press into the bottom of the springform pan. Bake for 8 minutes. Remove from the oven. Lower the oven temperature to 300°F.

▶ Make the filling: In a large bowl, beat the cream cheese until fluffy. Slowly add the condensed milk, beating until smooth. Add the egg whites, egg, lemon juice, vanilla, and lemon zest. Beat until the mixture is thoroughly blended.

▶ Add the cornstarch to the batter and stir until very smooth. Pour the batter into the prepared pan. Bake for 55 to 65 minutes, until the center is set. Cool the cheesecake completely, then store in the refrigerator.

Crust

1½ cups ground vanilla or lemon shortbread cookies (see Pantry, page 272)

3 tablespoons melted butter

Filling

two 8-ounce packages reduced-fat cream cheese, or one 8-ounce package each reduced-fat and non-fat cream cheese, at room temperature

one 14-ounce can fat-free or low-fat sweetened condensed milk

4 large egg whites

1 large egg

⅓ cup freshly squeezed lemon juice

1 teaspoon gluten-free vanilla

2 teaspoons freshly grated lemon zest

⅓ cup cornstarch

Sacred Banana Cake

MAKES 8 TO 12 SERVINGS

This cake was asked for religiously by customers at the private kitchen where I worked years ago. Every time we had over-ripe bananas, it was my job to make it. The cake looked luscious and disappeared quickly. I brought the recipe into my own test kitchen, tinkered a bit, and created this gluten-free version. After one heavenly bite, you'll know why it is called "sacred."

▶ Preheat the oven to 350°F. Lightly grease two 8-inch round cake pans and dust lightly with rice flour.

▶ Combine the butter and brown sugar in a mixing bowl and cream until light and fluffy. Add the eggs, vanilla, and mashed bananas and beat well. In a separate bowl, combine the flour blend, baking powder, and baking soda. Add to the butter mixture and beat until thoroughly mixed.

▶ Divide the batter between the prepared pans. Bake for 25 to 30 minutes, until a cake tester inserted in the center comes away clean. Let cool on a wire rack for 10 minutes. Turn the cakes out onto a rack and cool completely.

▶ Frost with Cream Cheese Frosting or the dairy-free variation (page 255).

10 tablespoons unsalted butter or non-dairy buttery spread, at room temperature

1½ cups packed light brown sugar

2 large eggs

1 teaspoon vanilla extract

1 cup mashed ripe bananas (about 3)

1¾ cups Cake and Pastry Flour (page 16)

2 teaspoons baking powder (see Simple Substitutions, page 267, for corn-free baking powder)

1 teaspoon baking soda

The Best Carrot Cake

MAKES 12 SERVINGS

I tried nearly a dozen recipes for carrot cake and none produced a cake with the right taste and texture. Some were very sugary, while others were saturated with too much oil. So I went back to a basic spice cake recipe I always loved and used it as my foundation, adding grated carrots and pineapple for part of the moisture. The results were just right.

- ▶ Preheat the oven to 350°F. Lightly spray two 8- or 9-inch round cake pans with vegetable spray.
- ▶ Combine the flour blend, baking soda, baking powder, cinnamon, nutmeg, and cloves in a bowl; set aside. In a large mixing bowl, beat the sugar, vegetable oil, and eggs at low speed until smooth, then beat at high speed for 3 minutes. Add the flour mixture and beat on low speed to blend. Add the buttermilk or reserved pineapple juice and beat until smooth. Fold in the carrots, pineapple, raisins, and walnuts, if using.
- ▶ Divide the batter between the cake pans. Bake on the center rack for 33 to 38 minutes, until the cake begins to pull away from the sides of the pan and a toothpick inserted in the center comes away clean. Remove to a wire rack and cool for 15 minutes. Turn the cakes out onto a rack to cool completely.
- ▶ Frost with Cream Cheese Frosting on page 255.

2½ cups Cake and Pastry Flour (page 16)

1½ teaspoons baking soda

¼ teaspoon baking powder

1½ teaspoons ground cinnamon

¼ teaspoon ground nutmeg

¼ teaspoon ground cloves

1¾ cups sugar

1 cup vegetable oil

3 large eggs

¼ cup buttermilk or reserved pineapple juice

2 cups grated carrots (about 4 medium)

one 8-ounce can crushed pineapple, well drained, juice reserved

¾ cup raisins

½ cup chopped walnuts, optional

Avoiding Eggs? *To make this egg-free, substitute ¾ cup puréed silken tofu for the eggs.*

Avoiding Dairy? *Frost with the dairy-free variation of Cream Cheese Frosting on page 255.*

Vanilla Blueberry Bundt Cake

MAKES 10 TO 12 SERVINGS

Inspired by a recipe by Dorie Greenspan and a crop of fresh, local blueberries, this magnificent cake is as pretty as it is luscious. I serve it on a glass cake stand with vanilla glaze draping over the crowns of the cake and a glint of the fruit peeking from the frosting's edges. When blueberries are not in season, I use frozen blueberries, raspberries, or chocolate chips. Originally, I made this with Gluten-Free Pantry's Cake and Cookie Mix, which is still a great shortcut when company is waiting and the clock is ticking.

▶ Preheat the oven to 350°F. Lightly oil a 10-cup Bundt or tube pan.

▶ Combine the flour blend, baking powder, and baking soda and set aside.

▶ In a large mixing bowl, beat the butter until fluffy. Add the sugar and beat to incorporate. Add the eggs and vanilla and beat well until the mixture is light and fluffy, about 1 minute. Add the flour mixture and beat until blended. Fold in the sour cream and mix to combine. Gently fold in the blueberries.

▶ Spoon into the prepared pan and bake for 55 minutes, or a toothpick inserted in the center comes away clean. Cool for 10 minutes in the pan and then turn onto a wire rack, and cool completely. Frost with the vanilla glaze, if desired.

▶ This freezes well. (Do not frost before freezing.)

▶ Make the glaze: Combine the confectioners' sugar, water, and vanilla in a bowl. Add additional confectioners' sugar 1 tablespoon at a time, if the glaze is too thin. If the glaze is too thick, add additional water.

2½ cups Cake and Pastry Flour (page 16)

2 teaspoons baking powder

½ teaspoon baking soda

14 tablespoons (1¾ sticks) unsalted butter or non-dairy buttery spread, softened

1½ cups sugar

3 large eggs plus 1 egg white, lightly beaten

2 teaspoons gluten-free vanilla

1½ cups reduced-fat sour cream, plain yogurt, or soy or coconut yogurt

1 cup fresh blueberries or frozen berries (unthawed)

Vanilla Glaze

¼ cup confectioners' sugar

2 to 3 teaspoons warm water

1 teaspoon gluten-free vanilla extract

continues

continued

Shortcut:

▶ Use 4 cups of a commercial gluten-free cake mix in place of the flour and sugar here. If the mix contains baking powder, omit it from the above ingredients.

VARIATION: In place of the blueberries, fold in 1 cup fresh or frozen raspberries or ¾ cup chocolate chips.

Zucchini Quinoa Cake

MAKES 12 SERVINGS

This recipe first appeared in *Living Without* magazine. It was inspired by an abundance of zucchini and a curiosity about baking with quinoa. The recipe is a cross between carrot cake and zucchini bread. It may sound too healthy to be delicious, but you'll be sneaking seconds and thirds.

▶ Preheat the oven to 325°F. Lightly oil a 10- or 12-cup Bundt pan.

▶ Combine the flour blend, quinoa flakes, baking powder, baking soda, cinnamon, and nutmeg in a bowl; set aside.

▶ In a large mixing bowl, beat the butter until fluffy. Add the brown sugar and beat until the mixture is light and fluffy. Add the eggs one at a time, mixing well after each addition. Add the vanilla and beat to combine. On low speed, add the dry ingredients alternately with the buttermilk, beginning and ending with the dry ingredients and mixing until each addition is just incorporated. Fold in the zucchini and nuts, if using. (The batter will be thick.)

▶ Spoon the batter into the prepared pan and smooth out to fill all the crevices in the pan. Bake for 60 to 65 minutes, until golden and a toothpick inserted in the center comes out clean. Cool on a rack for 10 minutes then invert onto a serving plate and cool completely.

▶ Frost with Cream Cheese Frosting, or simply dust with confectioners' sugar or serve as is.

▶ If using flax gel, add the mixture all at once.

2½ cups Cake and Pastry Flour (page 16)

1 cup quinoa flakes

2 teaspoons baking powder

1 teaspoon baking soda

1 teaspoon ground cinnamon

½ teaspoon freshly grated or ground nutmeg

12 tablespoons (1½ sticks) unsalted butter or dairy-free buttery spread, at room temperature

1½ cups packed light brown sugar

3 large eggs or flax gel (see Simple Substitutions, page 268)

2 teaspoons vanilla extract

¾ cup low-fat buttermilk, vanilla soy milk, or other dairy-free milk

2 cups finely grated zucchini

¾ cup chopped nuts, optional

Cream Cheese Frosting (page 255), optional

Confectioners' sugar for dusting, optional

Notes on Gluten-Free Pie Making

The category of pies was the last holdout in my gluten-free culinary explorations. I thought they were difficult, too crumbly, and too dry—simply not worth the bother. Now I know how wrong I was. Don't miss out on this American tradition like I did.

In traditional piecrusts, bakers always warn that overworking the crust will build up gluten and create a tough pastry. That's not a problem when working with gluten-free dough. The trick here is the right proportion of fat and liquid to dry ingredients. Using high protein flour also helps add a natural amount of elasticity. Handling the dough through sheets of plastic wrap prevents the crust from breaking and crumbling. It also helps in transferring the dough to the pie pan. Although some breakage is inevitable, handling through plastic wrap also helps with repairs. Just press and smooth the broken pieces back together. Tears will not be visible after the crust bakes.

Double-crust pies are always more challenging with gluten-free piecrusts because it is more difficult to smooth the torn pieces back together over a chunky filling. Sometimes it results in more tears. Instead, try cutting strips of dough and laying them in lattice fashion over the pie filling. Or sprinkle a crumb topping such as the Streusel Crumb Topping on page 236 over the filling.

I provide some of my favorite filling recipes here, but you can use your own family recipes once you've mastered the easy and delicious techniques.

Dream Crust
(Flaky Piecrust)

MAKES TWO 9-INCH PIECRUSTS

This crust has everyone fooled. It is tender and flaky with no hint of the grittiness that, according to gluten-filled tasters, is characteristic of many gluten-free foods. It's used in many recipes throughout this book. However, if you are short on time, use a commercial piecrust, such as Whole Foods Market Gluten-Free Bakehouse or Gillian's Food.

- In the bowl of a food processor, combine the flours, sugar, and baking powder. Pulse to combine. Add the butter and shortening and pulse until the mixture resembles coarse meal. Add the eggs, vinegar, and 2 tablespoons of water and pulse to combine. Add more water, a few drops at a time, until the flour holds together. Remove the dough to a work surface and form into a ball.
- Divide the dough in half. Roll each piece of dough between sheets of plastic wrap into a 12-inch circle. The dough round should be thin but still have enough structure to lift off of the plastic easily without crumbling. Some tearing is inevitable. Tears can be patched with leftover dough.
- Gently flip over onto a 9-inch pie pan. Press into the pan, crimp the edges, and prick the bottom with a fork. Set on a baking sheet for ease of handling.
- Fill with the pie filling of your choice and bake according to the recipe instructions, or prebake for 25 minutes in a 375°F oven if using for pudding fillings.

2 cups Cake and Pastry Flour (page 16)

½ cup amaranth flour

2 tablespoons potato flour

1 tablespoon sugar

1½ teaspoons baking powder

6 tablespoons cold unsalted butter, cut into small pieces

6 tablespoons organic shortening, cut into pieces

2 large eggs

2 teaspoons cider vinegar

2 to 3 tablespoons cold water

Tips: When processing the dough, you are looking for a smooth not crumbly texture, but it should not be wet as that will lead to a tougher crust. Don't scoop out of food processor with fingers. The blade is sharp.

To freeze: The crust can be rolled out, set in a pie shell, wrapped in plastic wrap, and frozen. Thaw for 15 minutes before using.

Graham Cracker Crust

Egg-free

MAKES ONE 9-INCH PIECRUST

This easy crust begs for an easy filling. Try the Chocolate Mousse Filling on page 238 or use a gluten-free instant pie filling and add your favorite berries or sliced bananas.

> 1½ cups gluten-free graham cracker crumbs (page 235 or see Pantry, page 273)
>
> 4 tablespoons butter or non-dairy buttery spread, melted
>
> ¼ cup sugar

▶ Preheat the oven to 350°F. In a medium bowl, combine the crumbs, butter, and sugar and mix to moisten. Press into the bottom and 1½ inches up the sides of a 9-inch springform pan.

▶ Bake 8 to 10 minutes, or until the edges are slightly golden. Let cool before adding the filling of your choice.

VARIATIONS:

• To make a Cookie Crumb Crust, replace the graham cracker crumbs with an equal amount of ground gluten-free chocolate, vanilla, or ginger cookies.

• For a quick Passover dessert, press 2 cups of crushed macaroons into a springform or tart pan and fill with the Chocolate Mousse Filling on page 238. Chill and serve with whipped cream or non-dairy whipped topping.

• To make a Quick Mud Pie: Line a 9-inch springform pan, pie plate, or tart pan with Chocolate Cookie Crumb Crust. Bake as above and cool. Soften 2 pints of vanilla ice cream or dairy-free frozen dessert and spoon into the cooled crust. Drizzle with Chocolate Sauce (page 251 or a commercial brand) and freeze. Bring to room temperature for 15 minutes before serving. Top with whipped cream or non-dairy topping and sprinkle chocolate cookie crumbs on top.

Tartlet Crust

MAKES 30 MINI TARTLETS

This versatile crust—a cross between a traditional pie-crust and a short crust—turns an ordinary quiche or fruit tart into an extraordinary dish. It is used in the Mini Quiches (page 104) and the Mini Tartlets with Key Lime Filling (page 240).

- Spray thirty metal or silicone mini muffin cups with vegetable spray.
- In a food processor fitted with the steel blade, add the flours, gum, confectioners' sugar, and salt. Pulse to combine. Add the butter and pulse until the mixture resembles coarse meal. Add the egg and vanilla and pulse until the dough forms a ball.
- Press 2 teaspoons of dough evenly into the bottom and up the sides of each muffin cup. Pierce the bottoms with a fork. Cover with plastic wrap and refrigerate for 1 hour or overnight.
- Preheat the oven to 350°F. Bake the tarts for 10 minutes or until the edges are golden brown. Remove to a wire rack and cool for 10 minutes.
- Add the filling of your choice and bake according to the recipe.
- For a savory crust, replace 3 tablespoons confectioners' sugar with 2 teaspoons granulated sugar and 1½ tablespoons cornstarch.

¾ cup sorghum flour

⅓ cup white rice flour

¼ cup tapioca starch/flour

1½ teaspoons xanthan or guar gum

3 tablespoons confectioners' sugar, sifted

¼ teaspoon salt

8 tablespoons (1 stick) cold unsalted butter or non-dairy buttery spread, cut into ½-inch pieces

1 large egg, lightly beaten

1 teaspoon vanilla extract

Tip: If using dairy-free buttery spread, freeze the cut pieces for 15 minutes before proceeding with the recipe.

VARIATION: Press the dough into a 9-inch pie or tart pan to about ⅛ inch thick. Wrap any leftover dough in plastic and refrigerate. The dough will keep for several days or can be stored in the freezer for up to three months.

Graham Cracker-Style Crumbs

Egg-free

MAKES 4¼ CUPS

When all I need are graham cracker crumbs, this recipe is a godsend. However, if time is short, try using a commercial gluten-free graham cracker–style product (see Pantry, page 273). Use these in any recipe that calls for graham cracker crumbs.

▸ Preheat the oven to 325°F. Line one 11 x 18-inch pan or two smaller baking sheets with parchment paper or aluminum foil.

▸ Place the flour blend, chickpea flour, powdered milk, brown sugar, cinnamon, and ginger in the bowl of a food processor fitted with the metal blade.

▸ Pulse to blend. Combine the honey, ½ cup water, oil, and vanilla in a separate bowl and drizzle into the bowl of the food processor. Pulse until the mixture is moist and pulls away from the sides of the bowl. Add up to 2 tablespoons additional water, a little at a time, if necessary.

▸ Spread the mixture evenly over the prepared pan and bake for 10 minutes. Stir, using a wooden spoon, to break into pieces. Bake 10 minutes longer, or until golden brown, stirring occasionally to break up the pieces and brown evenly. Do not overbake. Set aside to cool.

▸ Grind in a food processor until the cookies are fine crumbs and store in an airtight container. These will keep for several weeks.

2½ cups Self-Rising Flour (page 16)

½ cup chickpea or other bean flour

½ cup powdered dry milk or powdered milk substitute (see Simple Substitutions, page 265)

¼ cup packed light brown sugar

½ teaspoon ground cinnamon

¼ teaspoon ground ginger

¼ cup honey

½ cup plus 2 tablespoons water

2 tablespoons vegetable oil

2 teaspoons vanilla extract

Streusel Crumb Topping

MAKES 3½ CUPS OR 3 CUPS IF NUTS ARE OMITTED

Great for topping any fruit pie or crisp. This is also layered into Grandma's Sour Cream Coffee Cake on page 214.

- ▶ Combine the flour, brown sugar, cinnamon, allspice, cloves, salt, and pecans, if using, in a large bowl. Mix well. Add the butter and use your fingertips to mix just until crumbly.
- ▶ To use as a topping for an apple pie, crumble 2 cups of crumb topping over the apples. Bake at 350°F, or until the apples are bubbly. If the edge of the piecrust browns too quickly, cover loosely with aluminum foil.

¾ cup rice flour

1 cup packed brown sugar

1 tablespoon ground cinnamon

½ teaspoon ground allspice

¼ teaspoon ground cloves

½ teaspoon salt

½ cup ground pecans, walnuts, or almonds, optional

6 tablespoons unsalted butter or non-dairy buttery spread, at room temperature, cut into pieces

Tip: *Make a double batch and store in the refrigerator for three weeks or freezer for three months.*

Cranberry Apple Pie

MAKES 8 SERVINGS

The gluten-filled version of this recipe (originally from *FamilyFun* magazine) is a tradition with my friend Oksana and her family. I offered to create a gluten-free recipe so her son Mikey, a celiac, could enjoy this holiday dessert along with the rest of the family. There's no doubt this will be a tradition with both families from now on.

- ▶ Preheat the oven to 400°F. Roll out the crust and line a 9-inch pie pan. Crimp the edges and set on a cookie sheet for easy handling.
- ▶ Thinly slice the apples along the short side. Combine the sliced apples, sugar, cinnamon, lemon juice, and rice flour in a large bowl. Add the cranberries and toss. Gently spoon the filling into the prepared pie shell and smooth the top.
- ▶ Bake for 30 minutes. If the crust browns too quickly, cover the edges with strips of aluminum foil.
- ▶ Make the topping: While the apple mixture is baking, combine the rice flour, cornstarch, xanthan gum, and cinnamon in a bowl. Add the butter using your fingertips until the mixture resembles coarse meal.
- ▶ Spread the topping evenly over the apple mixture. Reduce the oven temperature to 375°F and bake an additional 30 minutes, or until the top is golden and the fruit bubbles around the edges.
- ▶ Cool and serve. The pie may also be covered with plastic wrap and refrigerated for up to two days. Return to room temperature before serving.

one 9-inch Dream Crust (see page 232)

2½ cups peeled, cored, and quartered apples (McIntosh or Granny Smith or a mixture of both)

⅔ cup sugar

1 teaspoon ground cinnamon

1 tablespoon lemon juice

2 tablespoons rice flour

2 cups fresh cranberries, rinsed and drained

Crumb Topping

¼ cup rice flour

¼ cup cornstarch or tapioca starch

½ teaspoon xanthan gum

½ teaspoon ground cinnamon

4 tablespoons cold butter or non-dairy buttery spread, cut into small pieces

Dairy-Free Chocolate Mousse Pie

MAKES 8 SERVINGS

Easy and delicious, this pie will be enjoyed by all, but will be a special treat for those with allergies to gluten and dairy. It can be made egg-free, as well.

▶ Make the crust: Preheat the oven to 350°F. Spray the bottom and sides of a 9-inch pie pan with vegetable spray.

▶ In a medium bowl, combine the almonds, cinnamon, sugar, and salt. Add the melted butter and mix well. In small bowl, whisk the egg until foamy. Add to the almond mixture and mix well. Pat the mixture into the bottom of the pie pan.

▶ Bake for 12 to 15 minutes, until lightly browned. If the crust rises, pierce with a fork and press down. Let cool.

▶ Make the filling: Melt the chocolate with the butter in the microwave on medium power. Stir to combine. Let cool slightly, but do not let the chocolate solidify. Fold in the whipped topping and vanilla.

▶ Pour the filling over the cooled crust. Smooth the top with a spatula and garnish with the almonds. Chill for 2 hours or overnight. Serve and enjoy.

Crust

1½ cups finely ground almonds or almond flour

2 teaspoons ground cinnamon

3 tablespoons sugar

Pinch of salt

3 tablespoons non-dairy buttery spread, melted

1 large egg

Filling

10 ounces semi-sweet or bittersweet chocolate

4 tablespoons non-dairy buttery spread

one 8-ounce container dairy-free whipped topping, such as Cool Whip

2 teaspoons vanilla extract

¼ cup toasted sliced almonds

Avoiding Eggs? *The egg may be omitted.*

Grandma's Pecan Pumpkin Pie

MAKES 8 TO 10 SERVINGS

Grandma was known for the array of pies she made for every holiday, but none was requested more often than this pumpkin pie. This gluten-free version rivals her original. Start with the Dream Crust on page 232 or use a commercial gluten-free piecrust or a piecrust mix.

▶ Preheat the oven to 400°F.

▶ Combine the pecans, ⅓ cup of the sugar, and butter. Press into the bottom of the piecrust with the back of a spoon. Set the piecrust on a baking sheet and set aside.

▶ Beat the eggs in a bowl until frothy. Add the pumpkin, the remaining ⅔ cup brown sugar, salt, mace, cinnamon, ginger, cloves, half-and-half, and cornstarch. Beat until well-blended.

▶ Pour the filling into the piecrust and bake 10 minutes. Reduce the oven temperature to 350°F and bake for 50 minutes, or until a knife inserted near the center comes out clean. Cool completely. Refrigerate until ready to serve, or cover with plastic wrap and store in the refrigerator for up to two days.

▶ Serve with a dollop of whipped cream or a scoop of vanilla ice cream, if desired.

⅓ cup finely chopped pecans

1 cup packed brown sugar

2 tablespoons butter or margarine, softened

1 unbaked 9-inch Dream Crust (page 232)

2 large eggs

1 cup canned solid-pack pumpkin

½ teaspoon salt

½ teaspoon mace

½ teaspoon ground cinnamon

½ teaspoon ground ginger

¼ teaspoon ground cloves

1 cup half-and-half

1½ teaspoons cornstarch

Whipped cream or ice cream, optional

Mini Tartlets with Key Lime Filling

MAKES 30 TARTLETS

This is the dessert version of the Mini Quiches (page 104). Both are elegant and will fool guests into believing you were baking all day. In reality, this is an easy, foolproof recipe that can be done a day ahead. The crust can be formed and kept in the refrigerator for up to three days.

- ▶ Spray thirty metal or silicone mini muffin cups with vegetable spray.
- ▶ Press 2 teaspoons of the tartlet dough evenly into the bottom and up the sides of each cup. Pierce the bottoms with a fork. Cover with plastic wrap and refrigerate for 1 hour or overnight.
- ▶ Preheat the oven to 350°F. Bake the tartlets for 10 minutes, or until the edges are golden brown. Remove to a wire rack and cool for 10 minutes. Maintain the oven temperature.
- ▶ Whisk together the sweetened condensed milk and egg yolks in a bowl. Add the lime juice and whisk until well combined. The mixture will thicken slightly.
- ▶ Set the mini muffin cups on baking sheets for easy handling. Spoon a scant tablespoon of the filling into each tartlet shell, or enough to fill each tartlet without overflowing. Bake for 15 to 20 minutes, until the filling is set. Cool completely on a wire rack, then chill for several hours before serving.
- ▶ Decorate with a dollop of whipped cream and lime zest or thin slices of lime.

VARIATION: Pour the key lime filling into a baked 9-inch graham-style cracker crust (page 233) and bake 20 to 25 minutes or until the center is set.

---

1 recipe Tartlet Crust (page 234)

one 14-ounce can regular or low-fat sweetened condensed milk

4 large egg yolks

10 tablespoons bottled key lime juice, such as Nellie and Joe's

Whipped cream

Lime zest or slices

Avoiding Dairy? See page 267 for the dairy-free sweetened condensed milk formula or replace the condensed milk with an equal amount of cream of coconut. Use dairy-free buttery spread in place of the butter.

This section is by no means an afterthought. I prefer to think of it as the place for little gems that could not be captured in any other category. Among those jewels, you'll find whoopie pies, doughnuts, toaster tarts, teddy grahams, and an assortment of frostings. And, if you are anything like I am, I always start at the back when I pick up a book.

Apple Clafouti

MAKES 8 SERVINGS

This is an Alsatian pudding that is traditionally served during cherry season in France, but I make this delightful dessert any time of the year using fresh apples, peaches, or cherries, depending on which fruit is available at the time.

- ▶ Toss the apples with 2 tablespoons of the sugar; set aside.
- ▶ Preheat the oven to 350ºF. Butter a 9-inch deep-dish pie pan. Line the bottom and sides of the pan with the apple slices.
- ▶ Beat the eggs, milk, cinnamon, if using, salt, vanilla, flour blend, and baking powder together in a large bowl until smooth, about 1 minute.
- ▶ Pour one third of the batter over the fruit and bake for 15 minutes, or just until the fruit is set. Add the remaining batter and bake for 50 minutes. Serve warm dusted with powdered sugar, or with ice cream or Crème Anglaise Sauce.

3 cups peeled and thinly sliced McIntosh apples (3 to 4 medium)

2 tablespoons plus ½ cup sugar

3 large eggs

1½ cups milk, soy milk, or rice milk

½ teaspoon ground cinnamon, optional

Pinch of salt

1 teaspoon vanilla extract

1 cup Basic Blend (page 17)

½ teaspoon baking powder

Confectioners' sugar, ice cream, or Crème Anglaise Sauce (page 260)

Apple Cranberry Custard Crisp

MAKES 8 SERVINGS

This was inspired by a recipe I saw in *Bon Appétit* several years ago. I was missing some of the ingredients and substituted the granola that was sitting on my counter. The result was fantastic and using this quick fix cut the preparation time in half.

▶ Preheat the oven to 375°F. Coat a 9 x 13-inch Pyrex baking dish with vegetable spray.

▶ Make the topping: Place the granola in a zip-top bag and crush with a rolling pin until coarse crumbs. Using a fork, mix the granola and butter together in a bowl; set aside.

▶ Make the custard: Combine the eggs, yogurt, and vanilla in a bowl. Whisk in the rice flour until smooth. Set aside.

▶ For the filling: Toss the apples and cranberries with the orange juice in a large bowl. Combine the flour blend, brown sugar, and cinnamon in a separate bowl and add to the apple mixture. Mix to coat the apples.

▶ Spread the filling over the bottom of the prepared baking dish. Pour the custard over the filling. Sprinkle the topping over the filling. Bake for 50 to 55 minutes, until the apples are tender. Remove and cool for 10 minutes. Serve with ice cream or whipped cream.

Tip: I like Bakery on Main Maple Cranberry Granola. It's what I had on hand when I first made this recipe. However, you can use any gluten-free granola that's available to you.

Topping

2 cups granola with fruit and nuts

4 tablespoons (½ stick) unsalted butter or non-dairy buttery spread, at room temperature

Custard

2 large eggs

1 cup plain yogurt, soy yogurt, or coconut yogurt

1 teaspoon vanilla

1 tablespoon rice flour

Filling

8 medium apples, peeled and cut into 1-inch cubes

1 cup dried sweetened cranberries

¼ cup orange juice

⅓ cup Basic Blend (page 17)

½ cup packed light brown sugar

2 teaspoons ground cinnamon

Ice cream, dairy-free ice cream, or whipped cream

Best Ever Doughnuts

MAKES TWO DOZEN 3-INCH DOUGHNUTS

The best treat of all is diving into a slightly warm, gluten-free doughnut and coming up with a ring of powdered sugar and pleasure around your mouth. You might be tempted to dig in the moment the light, cakey treats come out of the hot oil. But let them cool slightly before you indulge. It will save burned tongues and allow the sugar to melt and adhere to the doughnuts.

- ▶ Place the flour blend, sugar, baking powder, and yeast in the bowl of a stand mixer fitted with the paddle attachment. Beat briefly to combine. Add the milk, melted butter, and eggs and beat for 5 minutes at medium speed. Let the dough rest for 20 minutes in a warm, draft-free area.

- ▶ Cut two dozen 5 x 5-inch squares of parchment paper. Spoon the dough into a pastry bag fitted with the widest tip or a plastic bag with the bottom corner cut to create a ¼- to ½-inch opening. Pipe a doughnut shaped circle onto each parchment square. (If necessary, smooth the doughnuts using plastic wrap sprayed with vegetable oil.) Set the parchment squares on baking sheets and let rise for 20 minutes in a warm, draft-free area. These will rise more if they are fried.

- ▶ In a deep skillet or electric fryer, heat the oil over medium heat until the oil reaches 350°F on a deep-fry thermometer. Gently slide 3 or 4 doughnut sheets into the oil and fry 3 to 4 minutes, until bottoms are golden brown. Use a slotted spoon to remove the paper and gently turn the doughnuts. Cook another 2 to 3 minutes. Remove to a tray lined with paper towels. Sprinkle the doughnuts with granulated sugar, confectioners' sugar, or cinnamon, or enjoy plain.

3 cups plus 3 tablespoons Bread Flour #1 (page 15)

1 cup sugar

1¾ teaspoons baking powder

7½ teaspoons instant active or active dry yeast

1¼ cups warm milk, or soy milk, rice milk, or water (105° to 110°F)

12 tablespoons (1½ sticks) unsalted butter or non-dairy buttery spread, melted

2 large eggs, lightly beaten

4 cups vegetable oil (or more) for deep-frying

Granulated sugar, confectioners' sugar, or cinnamon

Blueberry Cobbler

MAKES 8 SERVINGS

My mother was the champion of cobblers, buckles, and crisps. It seemed natural to continue that tradition, in a gluten-free way, of course. Once I started experimenting, I realized why they graced our table so often when I was young. These are easy desserts, made easier because many of the ingredients are mixed right in the baking dish. Dress this up by serving it warm with a scoop of vanilla ice cream or frozen yogurt or non-dairy frozen dessert.

▸ Preheat the oven to 350°F. In an 11 x 7-inch glass baking dish, toss the blueberries with the sugar and rice flour to coat. Sprinkle the lemon juice over the blueberries.

▸ For the topping: In a bowl, combine the flour blend, sugar, and nutmeg in a large bowl. Add the butter and mix with two forks or your fingertips until the mixture resembles coarse meal.

▸ In a separate bowl, beat the eggs with the milk and vanilla. Add to the flour mixture and stir to blend. Add an additional tablespoon of milk, if necessary, to make the mixture smooth but not runny. Drop the dough over the berries into mounds. Brush the dough with milk and sprinkle with sugar.

▸ Bake 35 to 40 minutes, until the top is golden and the fruit is bubbly. Cool for 15 minutes. Cut and serve.

VARIATIONS: Substitute 6 medium, thinly sliced peaches or peeled and sliced apples for the blueberries. Use cinnamon in place of the nutmeg for the topping. Frozen fruit works, too.

---

3 cups fresh blueberries

½ cup sugar

2 tablespoons rice flour, or cornstarch or potato starch

Juice of ½ large lemon

Topping

2 cups Self-Rising Flour (page 16)

2 tablespoons sugar

½ teaspoon freshly grated nutmeg

6 tablespoons cold unsalted butter or non-dairy buttery spread, cut into small pieces

2 large eggs

¾ cup milk, soy milk, or rice milk, plus more for brushing

1 teaspoon vanilla extract

Sugar for sprinkling

Chocolate Teddy Grahams
(Graham Cracker–Style Crackers)

Egg-free

MAKES 24 TO 30 CRACKERS

It tickles me to bring these to the table. They are adult-tasty and kid-adorable. This recipe was inspired by chocolate graham cracker recipes in the *King Arthur Flour's Baker's Catalogue*, an online recipe, and a plain graham cracker formula from *Gluten-Free Baking* doyenne, Rebecca Reilly. Chocolate and cinnamon varieties soften if covered. To make them crispy again, leave them on the counter, uncovered, overnight.

▶ Chill the butter in the freezer for 10 to 15 minutes.

▶ In the bowl of a food processor fitted with the metal blade, add the flour blend, cocoa powder, brown sugar, and baking soda. Pulse to blend, breaking up any clumps of sugar. Add the butter and pulse until the mixture resembles coarse meal. Combine the vanilla, honey, and 4 tablespoons of water and add to the mixture. Pulse until the flour is slightly moist. Add 1 tablespoon additional water in small amounts, if necessary, and pulse until the mixture stays together when pressed between two fingers.

▶ Preheat the oven to 325°F. Line two baking sheets with parchment paper.

▶ Transfer the dough to a sheet of parchment paper and knead the dough until smooth. The dough can be wrapped in plastic and refrigerated overnight at this point. Roll the dough into a rectangle about ⅛ inch thick. Use a medium teddy bear cookie cutter to cut out crackers or cut into 2 x 3-inch rectangles. If making teddy grahams, form the scraps into a ball and roll out again, cutting crackers until all the dough is used.

8 tablespoons (1 stick) cold unsalted butter, cut into small pieces

2 cups Self-Rising Flour (page 16)

½ cup unsweetened cocoa powder

¾ cup packed brown sugar

½ teaspoon baking soda

1 teaspoon vanilla extract

3 tablespoons honey

4 to 5 tablespoons cold water

Cream for brushing

Sugar for sprinkling

continues

continued

▶ Use a spatula or your fingers to transfer the crackers onto the baking sheets. Brush with cream and sprinkle with sugar. Bake for 12 to 15 minutes.

▶ Store the crackers in a plastic container (covered loosely with wax paper) at room temperature for several days.

▶ To make vanilla cinnamon grahams, replace the cocoa powder with ⅓ cup Self-Rising Flour and add 2 teaspoons ground cinnamon. Add more flour while kneading the dough if sticky.

Chocolate Whoopie Pies

MAKES 12 SERVINGS

Chances are, if you grew up in New England, you will recall this childhood treat. If you are not familiar with whoopie pies, this recipe will introduce you to a whole new category of comfort food. Reminiscent of Devil Dogs, these can also be made egg- and dairy-free. When this book went to press, the Whoopie Pie had been nominated as the official State of Maine dessert.

▶ Preheat the oven to 375°F. Line two baking sheets with parchment paper.

▶ Make the cakes: Whisk together the flour blend, sugar, cocoa powder, and baking soda in a large bowl. Combine the buttermilk, oil, vinegar, egg, and vanilla in a separate bowl. Whisk into the dry ingredients until well blended.

▶ Spoon 2-tablespoon mounds of batter about 2 inches apart onto the baking sheets. Bake for 14 to 16 minutes, until the tops feel firm to the touch and a toothpick inserted in the center of one cookie comes out clean. Cool completely on a wire rack before filling.

▶ Make the filling: Cream the butter until light and fluffy. Add the marshmallow fluff and blend for 1 minute. Slowly add 1 cup of the confectioners' sugar, the vanilla, and salt. Beat for 3 minutes, until smooth. If the mixture is not thick enough, add more confectioners' sugar, ¼ cup at a time.

▶ To assemble, generously spread the filling onto the flat side of half the cakes. Top with the remaining cakes. Wrap the pies individually in plastic wrap to store. These will keep three days at room temperature or three weeks in the freezer.

▶ To make this recipe egg-free, omit the egg and increase the buttermilk or dairy-free milk to 1 cup.

Cakes

1¾ cups Self-Rising Flour (page 16)

¾ cup sugar

⅓ cup unsweetened cocoa powder

1 teaspoon baking soda

¾ cup low-fat buttermilk, soy milk, or rice milk

⅓ cup vegetable oil

1 teaspoon cider vinegar

1 large egg

1 tablespoon vanilla extract

Filling

12 tablespoons (1½ sticks) unsalted butter or non-dairy buttery spread, at room temperature

1⅓ cups marshmallow fluff

1 to 2 cups confectioners' sugar

1 teaspoon vanilla extract

Pinch of salt

Pumpkin Whoopie Pies

MAKES 9 TO 10 SERVINGS

No longer just for kids, this adult version of an old favorite is inspired by a recipe in the *King Arthur Flour's Baker's Catalogue*. The idea of pumpkin and warm spices rolled into a whoopie pie was too tempting to ignore. Make the chocolate whoopie pies on page 247 for the kids and save these treats for yourself.

▶ Preheat the oven to 375°F. Line two baking sheets with parchment paper.

▶ Combine the flour blend, baking soda, baking powder, cinnamon, nutmeg, and cloves in a bowl; set aside.

▶ In a large mixing bowl, combine the sugar, butter, oil, and molasses and beat until smooth and fluffy. Add the eggs one at a time, beating until fluffy. Fold in the pumpkin. Add the flour mixture, one third at a time, beating well after each addition. The batter will be thick.

▶ Spoon ¼-cup mounds of the batter about 2 inches apart onto the baking sheets,. Bake 16 to 18 minutes, until the tops feel firm to the touch and a toothpick inserted in the center of one cookie comes out clean. Cool completely on a wire rack.

▶ Generously spread Cream Cheese Frosting on the flat side of half the cakes. Top with the remaining cakes. Wrap the pies individually in plastic wrap to store. These can be stored for three days in the refrigerator or three weeks in the freezer.

2½ cups Cake and Pastry Flour (page 16)

1½ teaspoons baking soda

¾ teaspoon baking powder

1½ teaspoons ground cinnamon

¼ teaspoon nutmeg

¼ teaspoon ground cloves

1¾ cups packed brown sugar

8 tablespoons (1 stick) unsalted butter or non-dairy buttery spread, at room temperature

½ cup vegetable oil

2 tablespoons dark molasses

2 large eggs

one 15-ounce can solid-pack pumpkin

1 recipe Cream Cheese Frosting (page 255)

Cranberry Tart

An easy holiday dessert, this recipe is inspired by one that the late Laurie Colwin included in a food-for-thought piece in *Gourmet* magazine. Laurie's words were nearly as delicious as her food. This has been revised for our gluten-free enjoyment but also as a tribute to the very talented Ms. Colwin.

▶ Preheat the oven to 350°F. Lightly oil or butter a 10-inch tart or pie pan.

▶ Combine the cranberries, walnuts, and sugar in a bowl. Spread evenly into the bottom of the prepared pan.

▶ Make the topping: In a large bowl, whisk together the flour, cornstarch, tapioca starch, xanthan gum, baking powder, and salt; set aside. Mix the sugar, eggs, cooled butter, and almond extract to combine. Add the flour mixture, whisking to break up any clumps. Whisk until smooth. Pour over the cranberry mixture. Bake for 35 to 40 minutes, until a cake tester comes out clean.

2 cups chopped fresh cranberries

½ cup chopped walnuts

½ cup sugar

Topping

½ cup rice flour

¼ cup cornstarch

¼ cup tapioca starch/flour

½ teaspoon xanthan gum or guar gum

½ teaspoon baking powder

¼ teaspoon salt

¾ cup sugar

2 large eggs, lightly beaten

12 tablespoons (1½ sticks) unsalted butter or non-dairy buttery spread, melted and cooled

¼ teaspoon almond extract

Profiteroles with Coffee Ice Cream and Chocolate Sauce

MAKES 12 SERVINGS OR 24 PROFITEROLES

This easy, elegant dessert is based on the cheese puff recipe on page 100. In my mind, however, this dessert is just an excuse to eat chocolate and caramel—as if anyone needed an excuse. The sauces are great by themselves spooned over ice cream. The puffs can be made ahead and frozen for up to one month.

▶ Make the cream puffs: Preheat the oven to 400°F. Line two baking sheets with parchment paper.

▶ Combine the flour, cornstarch, xanthan gum, sugar, and salt in a medium mixing bowl.

▶ Combine the milk, water, and butter in a large saucepan over medium-high heat and bring to a boil. Remove from the heat. Add the dry ingredients and beat briskly with a wooden spoon until thoroughly incorporated. Return the saucepan to the stove and reduce the heat to low. The mixture will begin to pull away from the side of the pan. Stir for 3 to 4 minutes, letting any moisture evaporate.

▶ Remove from the heat and let stand at room temperature for about 5 minutes or until cooled slightly. Add the eggs one at a time, stirring briskly after each addition until the egg is thoroughly incorporated.

▶ Form the dough into 2-tablespoon-size mounds and drop onto the baking sheets, leaving 1 to 2 inches between each puff.

▶ Bake in the oven for 15 minutes. Reduce the temperature to 350°F and bake for 30 minutes longer, rotating the pans halfway through. Turn off the oven and prop open the oven door slightly. Let the puffs cool in the oven for an additional 30 minutes.

Cream Puffs

1¼ cups white rice flour

¼ cup cornstarch

¼ teaspoon xanthan gum

2 teaspoons sugar

¾ teaspoon salt

1 cup milk or dairy-free milk

1 cup water

6 tablespoons unsalted butter or non-dairy buttery spread, cut into 1-inch pieces

4 large eggs, at room temperature

Tips: *Egg substitutes will not work. Also, avoid commercial all-purpose gluten-free baking mixes that contain xanthan or guar gum. They will produce a gummy texture.*

continues

continued

Remove the puffs from the oven and make a small slit in the side of each puff to allow the steam to escape. Let cool completely.

▶ Make the filling: Set an aluminum pan in the freezer to chill for 1 hour. Remove and cover with plastic wrap.

▶ Using a small ice cream scoop, scoop out 24 ice cream balls and set on the chilled pan. Return to the freezer.

▶ Make the Chocolate Sauce: In a small saucepan, melt the chocolate chips and butter. Bring to a simmer over medium-low heat, stirring constantly until the mixture is smooth. Stir in the cream. Whisk together the sugar, cocoa powder, and salt in a small bowl and then whisk into the chocolate mixture. Stir constantly while the mixture comes to a boil. Remove from the heat.

▶ Whisk for another minute, letting the mixture cool slightly. Add the brandy, if using, and the vanilla. Cool to room temperature before serving. This sauce can be made one week ahead and stored in the refrigerator. Reheat briefly in the microwave before serving.

▶ Make the caramel sauce: In a small saucepan, whisk together the brown sugar and salt. Add the butter and warm over low heat until the butter is melted and the sugar is dissolved. Add the heavy cream and bring to a boil, stirring to blend. Remove from the heat.

▶ Whisk for another minute, letting the mixture cool slightly. Whisk in the rum, if using, and the vanilla. Set aside. This sauce is best made just before serving and left to sit a room temperature. Storing in the refrigerator may cause the sauce to crystallize.

▶ To assemble: Cut each cream puff in half crosswise through the center. Place a scoop of ice cream between the top and bottom of each profiterole. Arrange 2 profiteroles on each serving plate and drizzle with chocolate or caramel sauce.

Filling

1 quart good-quality gluten-free coffee, vanilla, chocolate, or other flavor ice cream

Chocolate Sauce

¾ cup semi-sweet chocolate chips

¼ cup (½ stick) unsalted butter or non-dairy buttery spread

½ cup heavy cream, soy milk, or coconut milk

¾ cup sugar

¼ cup unsweetened cocoa powder

Pinch of salt

1 tablespoon brandy, optional

2 teaspoons vanilla extract

Caramel Sauce

½ cup packed light brown sugar

Pinch of salt

6 tablespoons unsalted butter or non-dairy buttery spread, cut into pieces

¼ cup heavy cream or soy or coconut milk

1 tablespoon dark rum, optional

2 teaspoons vanilla extract

Strawberry Shortcake

Egg-free

MAKES 12 SHORTCAKES

Strawberry shortcake is as American as apple pie. It seems appropriate to include a recipe for this all-time favorite in a cookbook, albeit, a gluten-free one. The addition of vinegar activates the baking soda and helps to produce a light textured shortcake. Use any fruit you have on hand. I've even made these with frozen (thawed) peaches.

▶ Heat the oven to 450°F. Line a baking sheet with parchment paper.

▶ In a large mixing bowl, combine the flour blend, baking powder, baking soda, and sugar. Cut the butter and shortening into small pieces. Using an electric mixer, beat into the flour mixture until the texture resembles coarse meal. Mix in the buttermilk and vinegar.

▶ Scoop out large spoonfuls of the dough and form into balls. Shape into 1-inch-thick rounds and place on the baking sheet. Brush with melted butter and sprinkle with sugar. Bake for 15 minutes, or until the tops are slightly golden. Let cool completely.

▶ Cut the shortcakes in half and heap the bottoms with strawberries. Cover with the tops. Serve with a dollop of whipped cream.

---

3 cups Cake and Pastry Flour (page 16)

4 teaspoons baking powder

1 teaspoon baking soda

3 tablespoons sugar

3 tablespoons cold unsalted butter or non-dairy buttery spread, cut into small pieces

3 tablespoons organic shortening or other shortening, cut into small pieces

1⅓ cups buttermilk or milk of choice

1 teaspoon cider vinegar

2 tablespoons melted butter for brushing

Additional sugar for sprinkling

3 cups sliced strawberries

Whipped cream

Toaster Tarts

MAKES 9 TARTS

This is a great way to use leftover pie or tart crust. However, these fruit-filled treats will be so well received that you will find yourself making batches of dough just to create these and pies will become an afterthought.

- ▶ Line two cookie sheets with parchment paper.
- ▶ Divide the Dream Crust dough in half and roll each piece into a 9 x 12-inch rectangle, about ⅛ inch thick. Trim the edges of both rectangles so they are the same size. Cover the dough with plastic wrap. Chill for 30 minutes while preparing the filling.
- ▶ Heat the preserves in the microwave for 30 to 60 seconds or until soft. Mix in the rice flour and vanilla until smooth. Set aside.
- ▶ Preheat the oven to 350°F.
- ▶ Remove the sheets of dough from the refrigerator. Remove the plastic wrap. Set one sheet of dough onto the counter or a cutting board.
- ▶ Using a ruler, score the sheet of dough into thirds both lengthwise and crosswise so you have nine 3 x 4-inch rectangles. Brush the egg wash over the dough. Place a heaping tablespoon of the raspberry filling onto the center of each rectangle. Gently place the second sheet over the top and press the edges around the preserves to seal the dough on all sides. Cut the dough evenly into the nine rectangles, making sure the preserves are in the center of each tart. Press the tines of a fork around the edges of each rectangle for decoration.
- ▶ Use a spatula to gently place each tart onto the prepared pans. Prick the top of each tart to release steam. Brush the tops with remaining egg wash.
- ▶ Bake for 25 to 30 minutes, until golden brown. Remove from the oven and cool on the pans.
- ▶ Make the glaze: Combine the confectioners' sugar, water, and vanilla in a small bowl. Drizzle the glaze over the tarts and serve.

1 recipe Dream Crust
  (page 232), unbaked

¾ cup raspberry preserves

2 tablespoons rice flour

1 teaspoon vanilla extract

1 large egg, lightly beaten
  for egg wash

Glaze

1 cup confectioners' sugar

3 teaspoons water, plus 1 to
  2 teaspoons more if necessary
  to reach frosting consistency

1 teaspoon vanilla extract

Coconut Pecan Frosting for German Chocolate Cupcakes

ENOUGH FROSTING FOR 24 CHOCOLATE CUPCAKES (PAGE 219) OR ONE 2-LAYER 8- OR 9-INCH CAKE (PAGE 212)

This traditional frosting turns any chocolate cake into a yummy German Chocolate dessert. Leftovers will keep in the refrigerator for up to a week.

▶ In a large saucepan, combine the confectioners' sugar, cornstarch, and salt. Stir in the cream and egg yolks and mix until smooth. Cook over medium heat, stirring continuously until the mixture begins to boil and thicken. Lower the heat and simmer for 1 to 2 minutes, stirring constantly. Remove from the heat and fold in the coconut, vanilla, and pecans. Cool before frosting the cupcakes or cake. After frosting the cupcakes, chill until the frosting hardens slightly.

1 cup plus 2 tablespoons confectioners' sugar

2 tablespoons cornstarch

¼ teaspoon salt

1 cup light cream or low-fat evaporated milk

2 large egg yolks

2 cups sweetened flaked coconut

2 teaspoons vanilla extract

1 cup pecans, toasted and coarsely chopped

1 recipe Chocolate Light-as-Air Cupcakes, baked (page 219)

Cream Cheese Frosting

MAKES 3½ CUPS, ENOUGH TO FROST
ONE 8- OR 9-INCH, 2-LAYER CAKE

▶ Beat together the cream cheese and butter in a mixing bowl until smooth. Add 4 cups of the confectioners' sugar and vanilla and beat until fluffy, scraping the side of the bowl occasionally. Add additional confectioners' sugar until desired consistency is reached. Spread the cream cheese frosting on the top and sides of a cake. Decorate as desired.

two 8-ounce packages regular or low-fat cream cheese, softened

8 tablespoons (1 stick) unsalted butter, softened

4 to 5 cups confectioners' sugar, sifted, more for stiffer frosting

1 teaspoon vanilla extract

Avoiding Dairy? Replace the cream cheese with tofu cream cheese and use non-dairy buttery spread instead of butter.

Quick Chocolate Buttercream Frosting

ENOUGH FROSTING FOR 24 CUPCAKES OR ONE 2-LAYER 8- OR 9-INCH CAKE

Mix and match your cupcake creations using this simple, decadent chocolate buttercream. Flavor the cupcakes or the frosting with orange or other extract to vary the presentation and tasty treats.

- ▶ In a medium saucepan over medium heat, melt the butter. Stir in the confectioners' sugar, cocoa powder, milk, and vanilla. Remove from the heat and whisk until blended and smooth. Add additional sugar or milk, if needed, to reach the desired consistency.
- ▶ Frost the cooled cupcakes or cake and store in a cool place or refrigerate. Store leftover frosting in the refrigerator. Bring to room temperature before using.

6 tablespoons unsalted butter or non-dairy buttery spread

4 to 4½ cups confectioners' sugar

4½ tablespoons unsweetened cocoa powder, sifted

6 to 8 tablespoons milk, soy milk, or rice milk

1½ teaspoons vanilla extract or ½ teaspoon orange extract

Raspberry Cream Frosting

ENOUGH FROSTING FOR 12 TO 18 MEDIUM CUPCAKES

Filled with raspberry jam and luscious cream cheese frosting, these cupcakes can turn the most ordinary occasion into a celebratory event. This simple technique of filling and frosting can be used to jazz-up any cupcakes or muffins.

▶ Beat the cream cheese until fluffy. Add the confectioners' sugar and beat to combine. Fold in the jam and add the food coloring, if using. Spoon half the filling into a pastry bag fitted with a medium star or round tip. Use a paring knife or cupcake corer to scoop out a small amount of cupcake from the center without cutting through to the bottom of the cupcake. Pipe the filling into each cupcake and over the top of the cupcake or frost with the remaining mixture. Top each with a raspberry, if desired.

one 8-ounce package reduced-fat cream cheese, softened

2 to 3 cups confectioners' sugar (more for stiffer frosting)

¼ cup raspberry jam

1 to 3 drops red food coloring, optional (see Pantry for natural food coloring, page 274)

Fresh raspberries, optional

12 to 18 Light-as-Air Cupcakes, baked (page 219)

No pastry bag? Cut the cupcakes in half horizontally and place a dollop of the filling between the layers. Frost and enjoy.

Royal Icing

The traditional version of this recipe is called Seven Minute Frosting and starts with unpasteurized egg whites warmed over simmering water while beating. Using pasteurized or powdered egg whites eliminates that step and food safety concerns.

3½ cups confectioners' sugar

4 large pasteurized egg whites, or powdered egg whites mixed with water to equal 4 egg whites

½ teaspoon lemon juice

▶ Using an electric mixer, beat the sugar and egg whites in a mixing bowl until thick and shiny, about 4 minutes. Add the lemon juice and beat 1 more minute. Divide the icing among bowls and add drops of food coloring to dye to desired colors, or use as is for a glorious white frosting.

Tip: *Add ½ teaspoon vanilla, mint, orange, or almond extract for flavoring, if desired.*

Simple Confectioners' Sugar Frosting

ENOUGH FROSTING FOR 12 MEDIUM CUPCAKES

▶ Beat the butter in a large bowl until fluffy using an electric mixer. Add the confectioners' sugar and beat to combine. The mixture will be crumbly. Add the milk, orange juice, and vanilla. Add additional confectioners' sugar if necessary to create a smooth, spreadable consistency.

▶ Double this recipe for a 2-layer, 8- or 9-inch cake.

3 tablespoons butter or dairy-free spread, at room temperature

2 cups confectioners' sugar, more for a stiffer consistency

2 to 3 tablespoons milk of choice

1 tablespoon orange or lemon juice

1 teaspoon vanilla

Crème Anglaise Sauce

This sauce will dress up any dessert, especially those made with apple or chocolate. Add 2 tablespoons Calvados or other apple brandy for an interesting flair to this rich, creamy sauce.

1 cup half-and-half, soy milk, or rice milk

1 teaspoon vanilla extract

3 large egg yolks

3 tablespoons sugar

- ▶ Pour the half-and-half into a heavy medium saucepan. Bring to a simmer. Remove from the heat and stir in the vanilla.
- ▶ Whisk the egg yolks and sugar in a medium bowl to blend. Gradually whisk the hot cream into the yolk mixture. Return the mixture to the saucepan and stir with a wooden spoon over low heat until the custard thickens and coats a wooden spoon so that a line remains visible when your finger is drawn across the spoon, about 5 minutes. Do not boil. Strain the sauce through a fine sieve into a bowl. Cover and chill. The sauce can be made one day in advance.

Menu Planner

I don't know about you, but every time I start to plan a meal, my mind goes blank and all the wonderful recipes I've made throughout the years are beyond my recall. Here's a great checklist of suggestions to get you started. Add your own notes and recipes to this page, too. Some of the menu ideas such as roast beef or grilled asparagus are inherently gluten-free and not included in this book.

Christmas

Condensed Cream of Mushroom Soup (page 122)
Roast Beef
Perfect Popovers (page 52)
Baked Risotto (page 128)
Baby Greens with Candied Walnuts and Bleu Cheese
Profiteroles (page 250)
Chocolate Shortbread (page 196)

Easter

Potato and Cheese Pierogi (page 138)
Grandma's Babka (page 45)
Roast Leg of Lamb
Company Pasta (page 131)
Roasted Beets with Frisée or Other Greens
Lemon Raspberry Layer Cake with Lemon Cream Cheese Frosting (page 220)

Hanukah

Potato Pancakes (page 140)
Brisket Braised in Onions and Chili Sauce

Carrots and Prunes in Honey
Broccoli Cranberry Salad (page 115)
Best Ever Donuts (page 243)

Buffet Dinner

Baked Brie with Fig Spread en Croûte (page 97)
Beef and Beer (page 146)
Fabulous Focaccia (page 59)
Buttered Noodles
Roasted Carrots
Vanilla Blueberry Bundt Cake (page 228)
The Best Carrot Cake (page 227)
Lemon Walnut Squares (page 183)

Thanksgiving

Roasted Turkey with Orange Maple Glaze (page 163)
Corn Bread Stuffing (page 133)
Corn and Smoked Bacon Cakes (page 102)
Parker House Rolls (page 48)
Roasted Asparagus with Lemon Mayonnaise Sauce
Cranberry Tart (page 249)
Grandma's Pecan Pumpkin Pie (page 239)
Dairy-Free Chocolate Mousse Pie (page 238)

Cocktail Party

Mini Quiches (page 104)
Cheese Puffs *Gougères* (page 100)
Antipasto Squares (page 95)
Mexican Pizza (page 103)
Crab-Free Crab Cakes (page 154)
Mini Brick Oven–Style Pizzas (page 57)
Hummus with Veggies
Salsa with Corn Chips
Cheese and Fruit Platters

Brunch

Cranberry Scones (page 77)
Flaky Egg-Free Biscuits with Jam and Butter (page 78)
Sausage and Goat Cheese Strata (page 94)
Jen's Deluxe Granola (page 91) with Yogurt (Milk or Coconut)
Fresh Fruit with Mint

Make and Take

I often wish someone would give me a list of reliable, delicious gluten-free one-dish meals I can call upon when I need something wonderful to bring to a pot luck gathering or serve for a buffet meal. Now, here it is—a list of recipes in this book that we can all make and take.

Antipasto Squares (page 95)
Baked Brie with Fig Spread en Croûte (page 97)
Baked Risotto (page 128)
Cheese Puffs *Gougères* (page 100)
Chicken Marsala (page 149)
Chicken Salad with Grapes, Pecans, and Blue Cheese (page 116)
Company Pasta (page 131)
Corn Bread Extraordinaire (page 72)
Deviled Chicken Crêpes (page 88)
Crêpes with Ricotta Raisin Filling (page 86)
Debbie's Applesauce Noodle Pudding (page 134)
Maple Cheddar Breakfast Casserole (page 92)
Mexican Pizza (page 103)
Quick Eggplant Parmesan with Ground Beef (page 162)
Risotto Cakes (page 111)
Risotto Squares (page 111)
Santa Fe Enchiladas (page 165)
Sausage and Goat Cheese Strata (page 94)
Susan's Baked Pasta (page 143)
Turkey Tetrazzini (page 170)

Simple Substitutions

There is always a way to replace ingredients. Can't have milk, or eggs, or nuts? Look for substitutions here that will impart similar if not the same properties to your baking and cooking.

Start with these easy guidelines for replacing milk, cheese, eggs, sour cream, yogurt, and cream cheese. Use these for all the recipes in this book and for all your other baking.

Dairy

To replace milk use an equal amount of

Almond milk
Coconut milk
Fruit juice
Hemp milk
Rice milk
Soy milk

To replace buttermilk try this easy makeover

Combine 2 teaspoons cider vinegar or lemon juice with any type of milk. Let sit 15 minutes at room temperature before using.

To replace powdered milk use an equal amount of

Ener-G NutQuik or Soy Quik Powder (Ener-g.com)
Goat Milk Powder (meyenberg.com)
Vance's Dari-Free, unflavored (vancesfoods.com)

Soy Milk Powder (modernfearn.com)
Soy Protein Isolate (modernfearn.com)

To replace whipped cream use an equal amount of

Cool Whip Imitation Whipped Cream
Healthy Top Dairy-Free Whipped Topping (mimiccreme.com)

To replace yogurt use an equal amount of

Lactose-Free Yogurt (greenvalleylactosefree.com)
Redwood Hill Farm Goat Milk Yogurt (redwoodhill.com)
Ricera Rice Milk Yogurt (ricerafoods.com)
So Delicious Coconut Yogurt (turtlemountain.com)
Unsweetened Applesauce or other fruit purée
WholeSoy Yogurt (wholesoyco.com)

To replace butter use an equal amount of

Blue Bonnet Light Margarine
Coconut oil (Spectrumorganics.com)
Fleischmann Unsalted Margarine, contains whey
Natural Shortening Sticks (earthbalancenatural.com)
Organic Shortening (Spectrumorganics.com)
Smart Balance Buttery Spread, contains whey (smartbalance.com)
Vegan Buttery Sticks (earthbalancenatural.com)
Vegetable oil (reduce total fat by 2 tablespoons)

To replace sour cream use an equal amount of

We Can't Say It's Sour Cream (wayfarefoods.com)
Follow Your Heart Sour Cream Alternative (followyourheart.com)
Coconut yogurt
Rice milk yogurt
Cow's milk yogurt

To replace cream cheese use an equal amount of

Puréed silken tofu
Tofutti Soy Cream Cheese (tofutti.com)
Follow Your Heart Cream Cheese Alternative (followyourheart.com)

To replace sweetened condensed milk use an equal amount of

Cream of Coconut (cocolopez.com)

Try this easy dairy-free makeover for sweetened condensed milk

For one (14 oz) can condensed milk: Combine 3 cups vanilla soy, coconut, or rice milk, and ½ cup sugar. Simmer to reduce to 1½ cups. Thicken with 1 tablespoon cornstarch or arrowroot mixed with 2 tablespoons additional milk or water. Cool and use in all recipes that call for sweetened condensed milk.

To replace cheese use an equal amount of

Cheddar style, Mozzarella style, and Pepperjack style (daiyafoods.com)
Individually wrapped rice milk cheese slices (galaxyfoods.com)
Rice Cheese (galaxyfoods.com)
Soy Cheese (galaxyfoods.com and tofutti.com)
Vegan Cheese (galaxyfoods.com)
Vegan Gourmet Cheese in Blocks (followyourheart.com)
Vegan Parmesan Sprinkles (galaxyfoods.com)

Corn

Corn is often found in three key ingredients in gluten-free baking: baking powder, confectioners' sugar, and xanthan gum (produced from the fermentation of corn sugar).

To replace xanthan gum use an equal amount of

Guar gum
Carrageenan
Carob (locust bean) gum
Gelatin (use in powdered form)

To replace commercial baking powder use an equal amount of

Featherweight Baking Powder (hainpurefoods.com)
KinnActive Baking Powder (kinnikinnick.com)

Try this easy makeover for corn-free baking powder

Blend together ⅓ cup baking soda, ⅔ cup cream of tartar, and ⅔ cup arrowroot starch. Store in an airtight container for all your baking needs.

To replace commercial confectioners' sugar use an equal amount of

Corn-Free Confectioners' Sugar (allergygrocer.com)

Try this easy makeover for corn-free confectioners' sugar

Combine 1½ tablespoons tapioca starch/flour or potato starch and enough granulated sugar to make 1 cup. Process the mixture in a blender or food processor on high speed for 45 seconds or until powdered. Store in an airtight container.

Eggs

Eggs can be replaced in many recipes. The result might be a little denser, but using the following will help to hold baked goods together and make them less crumbly. For best results, replace no more than 3 eggs. Recipes like cream puffs, crêpes, and angel food cakes that are dependent on eggs for most of the lift and texture will be very difficult to convert.

To replace 1 large egg (¼ cup)

Use an equal amount of one of the following plus ½ teaspoon baking powder per egg replaced: ¼ cup puréed soft tofu, ¼ cup soy or other yogurt, or ¼ cup applesauce
Egg Replacer (ener-g.com), follow package instructions

Try this easy makeover for eggs using flax meal and water

For each large egg, replace with 1 tablespoon flax meal (bobsredmill.com) combined with 3 tablespoons hot water. Stir and let sit 10 minutes or until the mixture has thickened. Do not strain before using.

To replace egg yolks

Separate white and yolk and use 2 whites for each large egg.
People who have a non-life-threatening allergy to eggs can try substituting duck eggs. Beat and measure into ¼ cup increments. (Be sure to check with your health professional before trying duck eggs.)

Nuts

To replace nuts use an equal amount of

Crispy rice cereal

Crushed cornflakes

Pumpkin seeds

Perky's Crunchy Rice or Flax (www.enjoylifefoods.com)

Toasted coconut

   or

Sunflower seeds (use ⅓ less)

2 to 3 tablespoons toasted sesame seeds

Oats

Some people cannot tolerate oats, even gluten-free oats.

To replace oats use an equal amount of

Quinoa flakes

Coarsely chopped almonds

Chocolate

Most chocolate contains some dairy. The higher the cocoa content (60% or more), the lower the dairy content. Bittersweet chocolate contains the least and milk chocolate contains the highest amount. Some bittersweet chocolate, especially imported brands, are dairy-free. In addition, soy lecithin can be a problem although many who cannot have soy can still tolerate soy lecithin. (Ask your health professional.)

For dairy-free options, replace with an equal amount of

Dairy-free chocolate chips and squares

Dairy-Free, Soy-Free Semi-Sweet Chocolate Chips (enjoylifefoods.com)

Chocolate Dream Dairy-Free Semi-Sweet Baking Chips
   (glutenfreechoices.com)

Baker's Semi-Sweet Baking Chocolate Squares
Baker's Unsweetened Baking Chocolate Squares

Unsweetened cocoa powder and unsweetened baking chocolate do not contain dairy. Replace 1 square unsweetened chocolate with 3 tablespoons unsweetened cocoa powder plus 1 tablespoon vegetable oil.

Try this easy makeover for replacing 1-ounce square semi-sweet chocolate with a dairy-free and soy-free option. Mix 1 tablespoon plus 1¾ teaspoon unsweetened cocoa powder with ¼ cup hot water. Add 3½ teaspoons granulated sugar and stir to dissolve. Add 1½ teaspoons vegetable oil and stir until well incorporated. Cool slightly before using.

Gums

Xanthan and Guar gum are binding agents used to replace the "stretchy" quality of gluten, add texture, and reduce crumble factor in gluten-free baked goods. Use these sparingly as too much gum will impart an unpleasant chewiness to recipes. (Some cooks find they need to add an additional ½ to 1 teaspoon when using guar instead of xanthan gum. If the texture of baked goods is too crumbly for your liking, add additional gum next time.)

Follow this rule of thumb about using gums:

- Use ½ teaspoon xanthan or guar gum per 1 cup gluten-free flour blend in cakes, cookies, bars, muffins, and quick breads.
- Use 1 teaspoon xanthan or guar gum per 1 cup for yeast breads, pizza, and other yeast recipes.

Pantry

COMMERCIAL PRODUCTS

My pantry is full of safe commercial products that I use in my recipes and every day cooking. Here are some that I mention in the recipes in this book. I list the company websites for further information but most of these products are available in grocery or natural food stores or at one of the many gluten-free mail order company websites.

Ingredients can change so please double-check labels and call the manufacturer with any questions or concerns. Not all products from every company are safe for every dietary need so check carefully before using.

Mail Order Companies

These companies carry a wide range of gluten-free flours, mixes, other baking ingredients, and baked goods.

allergygrocer.com
bobsredmill.com
food4celiacs.com
glutenfree.com
glutenfreemall.com
kingarthurflour.com/glutenfree/
kinnikinnick.com

Cold Cuts

Applegate Farms (applegatefarms.com)
Boars Head (boarshead.com)

Dietz & Watson (dietzandwatson.com)
Hormel—not all (hormelfoods.com)

Blue Cheese

Boar's Head (boarshead.com)
Rosenborg (rosenborgusa.com)

Cream-Style Corn

Del Monte Golden Corn, Cream-Style (delmonte.com)

Crumbs:
Cracker-, Cookie-, and Graham-Style

Bread Crumbs

Aleias Gluten Free Plain and Italian Bread Crumbs (aleias.com)
Gillians Bread Crumbs and Italian Crumbs (Gilliansfoods.com)
Glutino Bread Crumbs (glutenfree.com)
Kinnikinnick Panko Crumbs (kinnikinnick.com)
Orgran All-Purpose Rice Crumbs (orgran.com)
Schar Bread Crumbs (schar.com/us/)

Cookie Crumbs

Kinnikinnick Chocolate Cookie Crumbs (kinnikinnick.com)

Cookies (to make cookie crumbs)

Glutino (glutino.com or glutenfree.com)
Jo-Sef (josefsglutenfree.com)
Kinnikinnick (kinnikinnick.com)
Pamela's Products (pamelasproducts.com)

Crackers (to make cracker crumbs)

Glutino (glutino.com)
Kinnikinnick (kinnikinnick.com)

Orgran (orgran.com)

Schar (schar.com/us/)

Graham Cracker Crumbs

Graham-Style Cookie Crumbs (kinnikinnick.com)

Flours

All-Purpose Gluten-Free Flour Blends and Baking Mixes

Authentic Foods (authenticfoods.com)

Betty Crocker (bettycrocker.com/products/gluten-free-baking-mixes)

Bobs Red Mill (bobsredmill.com)

Breads from Anna (breadsfromanna.com)

Gluten-Free Pantry (glutenfree.com)

King Arthur (kingarthurflour.com/glutenfree)

Kinnikinnick (kinnikinnick.com)

Namaste Foods (namastefoods.com)

Pamela's Products (pamelasproducts.com)

Amaranth Flour

Dakota Prairie Organic Flour (dakota-prairie.com)

NuWorld Amaranth (nuworldfoods.com)

Assorted Flours

Authentic Foods (authenticfoods.com)

Bob's Red Mill (bobsredmill.com)

Dakota Prairie Organic Flour (dakota-prairie.com)

Gifts of Nature (giftsofnature.net)

Cornmeal, Corn Flour, and Polenta

Bob's Red Mill (bobsredmill.com)

Expandex

Gifts of Nature (giftsofnature.net)

Montina

Amazing Grains (amazinggrains.com)

Oats, Oat Flour, and Oat Groats

Bobs Red Mill (bobsredmill.com)
Château Cream Hill Estates (creamhillestates.com)
Gifts of Nature (giftsofnature.net)
Gluten-Free Oats (glutenfreeoats.com)

Quinoa and Quinoa Flour

Ancient Harvest Brand (quinoa.net)

Timtana Flour

Montana Gluten Free (montanaglutenfree.com)

Granola and Cereal

Bakery on Main Granola (bakeryonmain.com)
Enjoy Life Granola (enjoylifefoods.com)
Enjoy Life Perky's Crunchy Rice or Crunchy Flax (enjoylifefoods.com)

Marshmallows

Campfire Marshmallows (campfiremarshmallows.com)
Kraft Jet-Puffed Marshmallows (kraftfoods.com)
Sweet & Sara Vegan Marshmallows (sweetandsara.com)

Natural Food Dyes

seelecttea.com
indiatree.com
naturesflavors.com

Pasta

Asian Rice Noodles

A Taste of Thai Rice Noodles (atasteofthai.com)
Thai Kitchen thin rice noodles and stir-fry rice noodles (thaikitchen.com)

Gluten-Free Pasta

Ancient Harvest: a blend of quinoa and corn flour (quinoa.net)
Bionaturae: made from rice, potato, and soy flour (bionaturae.com/gluten-free-pasta)
Deboles: made with rice and corn flour (deboles.com)
Farmo: made from corn, rice, or a blend of corn and rice (farmo.com)
Jovial: brown rice (jovialfoods.com)
Le Veneziene: made from corn meal flour (quattrobimbi.com)
Lundberg: brown rice (lundberg.com)
Schar: made from either multigrain (corn, rice, and buckwheat flours) or corn and rice flours (schar.com/us/)
Tinkyada: brown rice (tinkyada.com)

Powdered Dry Milk

Bob's Red Mill (bobsredmill.com)
King Arthur (kingarthurflour.com)

Sauces

Egg-Free Mayonnaise

Follow Your Heart (followyourheart.com)
Spectrum Organics (spectrumorganics.com)

Enchilada Sauce

Hatch Red Enchilada Sauces—avoid green (hatchchilies.com)
La Victoria Enchilada Sauce (hormelfoods.com)
McCormick Enchilada Sauce Mix (mccormick.com)

Fish Sauce

Taste of Thai (atasteofthai.com)

Thai Kitchen (thaikitchen.com)

Hoisin

Premier Japan Hoisin Sauce (edwardandsons.com)

Marinara and Spaghetti Sauce

Classico (classico.com)

Prego (prego.com)

Sclafani (sclafanifoods.com)

Soy and Tamari

Kari-Out Soy Sauce in pouches (kariout.com)

Kikkoman Gluten-Free Soy Sauce (kikkomanusa.com)

San-J Organic Tamari Soy Sauce and Travel Pouches (San-J.com)

San-J Asian Cooking Sauces (San-J.com)

Spicy Chili Sauce

San-J Szechuan Sauce (San-J.com)

Huy Fong Foods Sriracha Sauce (huyfong.com)

Thai Kitchen Thai Chili Sauce (thaikitchen.com)

Teriyaki Sauce

Premier Japan Teriyaki Sauce (edwardandsons.com)

San-J Teriyaki Sauce (San-J.com)

Toasted (Dark) Sesame Oil

House of Tsang Pure Sesame Seed Oil (hormelfoods.com)

House of Tsang Hot Chili Sesame Oil (hormelfoods.com)

Kadoya Pure Sesame Oil (http://www.amazon.com/Kadoya-Pure-Sesame
-Oil-5-5/dp/B0002YB21A)

Shortcut Products

Dorot Trays—frozen puréed cubes of garlic, ginger, basil, parsley, cilantro, and chili (www.mydorot.com)

Perdue Short Cuts Carved Chicken Breast (perdue.com)

Soups

Imagine Creamy Portobello Mushroom Soup—most Imagine Soups are gluten-free and dairy free (imaginefoods.com)

Pacific Broths, Creamy Soups (pacificfoods.com)

Progresso Chicken and Beef Broth (progressobroth.com)

Shelton's Chicken Broth (sheltons.com)

Spices and Seasonings

McCormick Spices—most are gluten-free (mccormick.com)

Penzey Spices—most are gluten-free (penzeys.com)

Wraps and Pizza Shells

Corn Tortillas

Misson Brand (missionfoods.com)

Pizza Shells (Frozen)

Dad's Gluten-Free Pizza Crust (glutenfreepizza.com)

Glutino (Glutino.com)

Kinnikinnick (kinnikinnick.com)

Udi's Gluten Free Foods (udisglutenfree.com)

Wraps

Brown Rice Tortillas (Foodforlife.com)

Ivory Teff Wraps (latortillafactory.com)

—— METRIC CONVERSION CHART ——

- The recipes in this book have not been tested with metric measurements, so some variations might occur.
- Remember that the weight of dry ingredients varies according to the volume or density factor: 1 cup of flour weighs far less than 1 cup of sugar, and 1 tablespoon doesn't necessarily hold 3 teaspoons.

General Formulas for Metric Conversion

Ounces to grams	→ ounces × 28.35 = grams
Grams to ounces	→ grams × 0.035 = ounces
Pounds to grams	→ pounds × 453.5 = grams
Pounds to kilograms	→ pounds × 0.45 = kilograms
Cups to liters	→ cups × 0.24 = liters
Fahrenheit to Celsius	→ (°F − 32) × 5 ÷ 9 = °C
Celsius to Fahrenheit	→ (°C × 9) ÷ 5 + 32 = °F

Linear Measurements

½ inch = 1½ cm
1 inch = 2½ cm
6 inches = 15 cm
8 inches = 20 cm
10 inches = 25 cm
12 inches = 30 cm
20 inches = 50 cm

Volume (Dry) Measurements

¼ teaspoon = 1 milliliter
½ teaspoon = 2 milliliters
¾ teaspoon = 4 milliliters
1 teaspoon = 5 milliliters
1 tablespoon = 15 milliliters
¼ cup = 59 milliliters
⅓ cup = 79 milliliters
½ cup = 118 milliliters
⅔ cup = 158 milliliters
¾ cup = 177 milliliters
1 cup = 225 milliliters
4 cups or 1 quart = 1 liter
½ gallon = 2 liters
1 gallon = 4 liters

Volume (Liquid) Measurements

1 teaspoon = ⅙ fluid ounce = 5 milliliters
1 tablespoon = ½ fluid ounce = 15 milliliters
2 tablespoons = 1 fluid ounce = 30 milliliters
¼ cup = 2 fluid ounces = 60 milliliters
⅓ cup = 2⅔ fluid ounces = 79 milliliters
½ cup = 4 fluid ounces = 118 milliliters
1 cup or ½ pint = 8 fluid ounces = 250 milliliters
2 cups or 1 pint = 16 fluid ounces = 500 milliliters
4 cups or 1 quart = 32 fluid ounces = 1,000 milliliters
1 gallon = 4 liters

Oven Temperature Equivalents, Fahrenheit (F) and Celsius (C)

100°F = 38°C
200°F = 95°C
250°F = 120°C
300°F = 150°C
350°F = 180°C
400°F = 205°C
450°F = 230°C

Weight (Mass) Measurements

1 ounce = 30 grams
2 ounces = 55 grams
3 ounces = 85 grams
4 ounces = ¼ pound = 125 grams
8 ounces = ½ pound = 240 grams
12 ounces = ¾ pound = 375 grams
16 ounces = 1 pound = 454 grams

Resources on Celiac Disease

Celiac Disease Center at
Columbia University
http://www.celiacdiseasecenter
.columbia.edu/CF-HOME.htm

The University of Maryland
Center for Celiac Research
http://www.celiaccenter.org/

The University of Chicago
Celiac Disease Center
http://www.celiacdisease.net/

American Celiac Disease Alliance
www.americanceliac.org

Celiac Disease Foundation
www.celiac.org

Celiac Sprue Association
www.csaceliacs.org

Gluten Intolerance Group of
North America
www.gluten.net

National Digestive Diseases
Information Clearinghouse (NDDIC)
http://digestive.niddk.nih.gov/ddiseases
/pubs/celiac/

National Foundation for
Celiac Awareness
www.celiaccentral.org

National Institutes of Health
Celiac Disease Awareness Campaign
www.celiac.nih.gov

Shelley Case, R.D.
Gluten-Free Diet:
A Comprehensive Resource Guide
http://www.glutenfreediet.ca/

Tricia Thompson, M.S. R.D.
Gluten-Free Dietitian
http://glutenfreedietitian.com/

Index